Banking and Finance Series

QUESTIONS AND ANSWERS ON

Finance of International Trade

Banking and Finance Series

QUESTIONS AND ANSWERS ON Finance of International Trade

by

Leonard Waxman

Senior Lecturer in Banking and Business Studies
City of London Polytechnic

Graham & Trotman

First published in 1985 by

Graham & Trotman Limited
Sterling House
66 Wilton Road
London SW1V 1DE

Graham & Trotman Inc.
13 Park Avenue
Gaithersburg
MD 20877, USA

ISBN-13: 978-0-86010-586-2 e-ISBN-13: 978-94-009-4966-9
DOI: 10.1007/978-94-009-4966-9

British Library Cataloguing in Publication Data

Waxman, Leonard
Questions and answers on finance of international trade.—(Banking and finance series)
1. Commerce—Problems, exercises, etc.
2. Finance—Problems, exercises, etc.
I. Title II. Series
382 HF1008

Typeset in Great Britain by The Castlefield Press, Moulton, Northants

Contents

Series Forward

The *Banking and Finance Series* has been written for students who are preparing for the Associateship of the Institute of Bankers. The structure of the series follows the syllabus closely. Although the emphasis is on the Institute of Bankers' examinations the series is also relevant to students for the kinds of other professional examinations such as the different Accountancy Bodies, Chartered Secretaries, Diploma in Public Administration, undergraduate business courses, BTEC, BEC, HND, DMS, Stock Exchange courses, Association of Corporate Treasurers, Institute of Freight Forwarders, Institute of Export.

August 1985

Brian Kettell
Series Editor

Preface

This revision guide is intended to serve as a complement to the textbook. Its aim is essentially to provide past examination questions set by the Institute of Bankers and the examiners' own answers together with past questions set at the City of London Polytechnic and other questions, with their answers. This gives the reader a wider range of topics which reflects the contents of the textbook, and permits of selectivity to meet need.

It is suggested that as each textbook chapter is read, the relevant section in the Revision Guide should be attempted in order to test knowledge and understanding, thereby further enhancing the learning process.

To facilitate this, the guide is set out section by section, to match the chapters in the textbook. Several sections are prefaced by introductions to bridge the gap between textbook and questions. In addition, questions are presented in succeeding order of difficulty so that readers can move from the less to the more complex at their own speed.

November 1985 *L. Waxman*

Passing the Examination

The Banking Diploma Stage 2 Examination
Finance of International Trade.

The Institute of Bankers Diploma examinations take place twice yearly, in April and September. Prospective candidates who wish to prepare themselves as thoroughly as possible and who are using the associated textbook to this revision guide will find the question and answers which it contains an indispensable means of preparation for the examination paper "Finance of International Trade".

This section offers advice on the following:

(a) preparation methods;
(b) the examination paper;
(c) examination techniques.

(a) Preparing for the Examination

Candidates making preparation for the examination may have some pratical knowledge of parts of the syllabus and others may have none or very little. Some will have English as their mother tongue, others will not. With proper preparation a good understanding of the subject should be obtainable by all. Those who have practical experience will find that a study of the subject can give them a further insight into the basic principles underlying bank practice as well as widening their knowledge in many areas.

Making Preparation

Reading. Each chapter in the textbook sets out to deal with a particular topic or set of topics in an orderly manner, and is mirrored by the sectional structure in this revision guide. However, readers are urged to follow whatever structure they prefer and apart from certain items each chapter and section stands on its own. Exceptions to this might be a reading of documents *before* looking at letters of credit.

Having read a chapter the reader should *at once* refer to the appropriate section of this guide and tackle the question *in the order in which they are presented.* This is necessary as the questions are laid out in order of increasing difficulty. Some are past Institute questions, others are those of the author. Proceed as far as possible with the questions, referring to the answers after each one. Then re-read the relevant parts of the textbook to reinforce understanding.

Try to space your work over time; perhaps reading one chapter per week. As the examination approaches re-read the questions and attempt further answers. If at all possible check your work against that of other students. It is always useful to discuss topics with others; often ideas can present themselves that may not be apparent at first sight.

Importance of the Chapters

Each chapter in the textbook should be read with the possible exceptions of Chapters 2 and 3. These contain useful background material but are not essential for the IOB paper. Chapter 12 also contains background material encompassing parts of the Monetary Economics syllabus which are particularly appropriate to International Finance. An appreciation of much of Chapter 12 is necessary for the "Trade" paper.

(b) The Examination Paper

The paper is divided into three parts.

Section A. This contains three questions of which question 1 is *compulsory*. One other question *must* be attempted.

Section A is devoted to the problems of the UK exporter and can contain the following topics:

Question 1 (compulsory)

Spot and forward transactions
Fixed and option contracts
Close-outs and extensions
Covered interest arbitrage
Matching currency receipts and payments
Currency accounts.

Question 2 and 3 (*one* of these must be attempted)

Letters of credit
Collections
Financial and commercial documents
Other bank and non-bank finance
ECGD and other institutional facilities.

Section B. This also contains three questions of which question 4 is *compulsory*. One other question *must* also be attempted.

Section B is devoted to the problems of the UK importer and can contain the following topics:

Letters of credit
Import finance
Import documentation
Bank bonds and standby credit
Import procedures.

Note Both sections A and B can (and often does) contain references to both export and import functions. This is especially so when a customer is a merchant trader both buying and selling.

Section C. This section also contains three questions of which one *must* be attempted. However, there are no compulsory questions in this section.

Section C can contain some of the following topics:

British overseas trade board
ECGD facilities
Travel finance
Nostro/Vostro accounting
ECUs and SDRs
Transmitting funds
The euro-currency markets.

These lists are *not* exhaustive and any one question can (and often does) draw on more than one item or topic.

The paper allows for a 3-hour writing period with a preliminary 15 minutes reading period. Silent calculators are permitted (but calculations should be shown).

Each question carries 20 marks with sub-sections carrying parts of the total, e.g. in question 6 (say) there are 3 sub-questions carrying the following marks: (a) 4; (b) 5; (c) 11. Total 20.

(c) Examination Techniques

This section may best be read nearer to the examination date.

Having made full preparation for the examination and having understood the examination requirements, it now remains to consider the best methods of writing the paper. A few basic principles should be adhered to, namely:

(i) Legibility

Nothing can contribute more to a disappointing result than a paper which is almost impossible to decipher. Ensure that you use a pen to suit your handwriting (different colours to highlight certain points). You must write so that the examiner can read *easily.* To this end strike out any sentences that offend and rewrite them.

Spelling is important and good grammar is essential. Keep sentences short and easily comprehensible. If there is any doubt as to your meaning repeat the sentence using a different structure. Remember, *ambiguity can be fatal.*

(ii) Paragraphs, Headings, Numberings

Each item should have its own paragraph with a heading or number. In this way you can order your answer in a logical manner which facilitates its reading.

(iii) Data Presentation

When presenting figures set them out in an easy to read form, e.g.

Exporters account

Transaction	*Exchange rate*	*Date*	*Sterling*		*Currency*		*Balance*	
			D	*C*	*D*	*C*	*D£*	*C£*
Funds received, Delivered forward	 1.4035	1/7/86 1/7/86						
Close-out at spot, Delivered forward	1.4000 1.4035	1/7/86 1/7/86						
Further funds received, Delivered to extension	 1.4210	1/9/86 1/9/86						
						Net £		

Enter transactions in date order as and when they will be entered into the customer's account. Remember that forward contracts will not appear as entries until they *mature*.

Covered Interest Arbitrage

When dealing with a question concerning the choice of a currency to borrow you can be sure that it is a covered interest arbitrage question. Isolate the *4 variables* — spot, forward, and two sets of interest rates. After presenting your answer in arithmetical form, reconcile with a formula presentation.

I.e. $\text{IRD} = \frac{r^d - r^o}{t}$

$$\text{CFC}\ \frac{S - F}{F} \times 100$$

(See topic in textbook).

Any discrepancies between the two answers imply an error in one or both! Try it again!

Remember, that this topic can apply to exporters, importers and investors.

E.g. *Exporters* who will want to bring currency receipts from the future into the present. Should they borrow local or overseas currency?

Importers who pay on credit terms but may be offered a discount for immediate payment. Should they borrow local or overseas currency?

Investors who wish to invest overseas. Which overseas currency is best?

(iv) Selection of Forward Rates

Buy-sell spreads — remember that customers of the market (including banks) will be offered the *least advantageous* rate from the spread.

I.e. Customers who buy will receive the *minimum* currency (bank sell) and customers who sell must pay the *maximum* currency (bank buy).

Premiums and discounts. Premiums are deducted and discounts added to spot. These terms refer *only* to the currency shown in *spread form*.

Option Contracts

Whenever the text in the question indicates that there is no specific date on which currency receipts and/or payments are to be made you can be sure that an option is required.

Close-Outs

These may be called for when a customer cannot meet his forward obligations. He will be quoted the (then) currency spot rate. Remember that close-outs are no longer mandatory. Forward contracts can now be met by *borrowing* currency to deliver it forward or *depositing* currency received forward.

Extensions. These rates are more advantageous to a customer than those for a new forward contract. They are selected by a process which *starts* from the close-out rate and moves to the forward premium or discount *on the other side* of the bank sell/buy spread.

Currency Accounts

Often a question will require an operation of a currency account into which receipts can be deposited and from which payment can be made. Set out the items to be entered as for the table shown in the preceeding section (iii) on data presentation.

Whenever possible try to match receipts and payments in any one currency. You may be called upon to deal with balances as follows:

(a) net balances to be sold (bought) forward
(b) net balances to be sold (bought) spot
(c) net balances of one currency to be sold in exchange for another currency in a cross-rate deal with the currency purchased to be put against its balance in (a) or (b).

Always follow the instructions in the question.

Other Questions

Many of the other types of questions can be dealt with by use of a flow diagram to represent the parties' functions and relationships to each other. Often you will be told that "you" must advise "your customer". A basic response is *always* to offer your customer the most appropriate and cost efficient facility or advice.

E.g. where an option costs us more than a fixed forward contract, advise him to take the option.

An example of a flow diagram.

Overseas Supplier — Your Customer — Overseas Buyer

The Bank ("You")

This format can be adapted to meet almost all the circumstances you are likely to find in the examination paper. Include all the parties mentioned and indicate their functions and relationships by using arrows and terms (see the textbook). All kinds of letters of credit, collections, bonds, standby credits can be illustrated using this format.

Final Points

In the 15 minutes available for reading you may write notes on the examination paper itself. Make these notes very short, i.e. transferable credit; nostro/vostro; currency account, etc.

Once you have started writing your answers you may like to adopt the following approach:

Short notes (these may be struck through)
Flow chart
Complete answers.

Good luck!

Section 1

The Real Versus the Nominal Protective Effect of an *Ad Valorem* Tariff

OBJECTIVES FOR A TARIFF

There are two major but conflicting objectives for raising a tariff on imported good:

(1) To raise revenue;
(2) To protect a domestic industry.

(1) THE REVENUE TARIFF

A good example is the UK excise duty on tobacco which is largely a SPECIFIC duty; i.e. it is imposed on the weight of the tobacco leaf (as opposed to an *AD VALOREM* duty which is levied on the *value* of the product).

As there is no UK tobacco growing sector to protect, the object of the excise duty is to raise revenue for central government. Because the demand for tobacco products is relatively price *inelastic*; i.e. a given change in price gives a less than proportionate change in volume demanded, the authorities can calculate with some degree of accuracy the revenue receipt of a given excise duty.

The characteristics of price inelasticity of demand coupled with the SPECIFIC duty combine to achieve the objective of a calculable, steady flow of central government revenue.

(2) THE PROTECTIVE TARIFF

Clearly, a tariff raised for revenue purposes will have a less than maximum protective effect. If the tariff raises revenue, then the goods are being imported and there is little protection. On the other hand, if the tariff is intended to be protective then the object is to limit the importation of the product and, if successful, the level of revenue raised will be affected, especially where there is some price elasticity of demand.

In a sense, we can view these two objectives of a tariff as components of a spectrum with revenue at one end, protection at the other, and varying degrees of both in the centre. This is shown in Diagram 1.1.

Diagram 1.1
The Spectrum of a Protective and Revenue Tariff

No import restriction	Part restrictive	Imports prohibited
Fully revenue raising	Part revenue and part protective	Fully protective

PROTECTION

If we now consider only the protective duty we have to ask "to what degree is a tariff protective"? The obvious answer is "a tariff is 100% protective when it completely shuts out the import of a certain product". But this extreme position is not typical if only because of international agreements under the General Agreement on Tariffs and Trade (GATT).

To adequately deal with the question of the *degree* of protection we need to understand that the purpose of a protective tariff is to protect Domestic Added Value (DAV) which can be defined as "that value which has been added to it as a result of activities of *domestic* companies and persons".

Now many so-called domestic products are not 100% domestic in the sense that there may be imported raw materials or components making up parts of their value (Imported Added Value or IAV).

Thus, the degree to which a tariff protects a domestic industry depends not only on the *level* of the tariff but also on the proportion of the domestic product supplied by DAV.

Let us take a simple example. Suppose we have a domestic product which costs £100 to produce and an imported (almost identical) product which is imported for £90. To afford protection the authorities raise an *ad valorem* tariff of 12%, raising the import price to £100.80. How much protection has this given the domestic industry?

Answer, £10.80 worth of protection, which equals 10.8% of the £100 value of the domestic product.

NOMINAL VERSUS EFFECTIVE PROTECTION

However, the foregoing result is only the NOMINAL protection afforded. If (as is likely) the domestic product contains some imported items, say, to the value of £30, then the DAV is only £70.

Basing the tariff of £10.80 on the DAV of £70 we get a REAL or EFFECTIVE protection of 15.4%; $\left(\frac{10.80}{70} \times 100\right)$.

Thus, the EFFECTIVE protection of a tariff can be said to be always greater than the NOMINAL protection when the DAV of the domestic good is less than 100%.

Or to put it another way, the greater the import content of the domestic good seeking protection, the greater the EFFECTIVE protection. This can be summarised in Table 1.1.

Table 1.1
Nominal versus Effective Protection

Import good		*Home good*	
		DAV	£ 70.00
		IAV	£ 30.00
		Total	£100.00
Value	£ 90.00		
Tariff	£ 10.80		
Total	£100.80		

Nominal protection = £10.80 as a percentage of £100 = 10.8%
Effective protection = £10.80 as a percentage of DAV of £70 = 15.4%

TARIFF ON THE IMPORT CONTENT OF THE DOMESTIC PRODUCT

A further point is that the domestic good may have to bear a tariff duty *on its import content.*

Let us suppose that of the £30 of Import Added Value (IAV), £25 represents the actual cost of the imports and £5 a tariff levied on importation.

This import duty on import content is a burden on the domestic product and should be viewed as a NEGATIVE protection. It must, therefore, be *deducted* from the actual tariff value. E.g. £10.80 *less* £5 = £5.80 worth of protection.

Applying £5.80 to our DAV we have $\frac{5.80}{70}$ x 100 = 8.28% of EFFECTIVE protection.

All these factors can be put into a formula:

$$e = \frac{n - Mi}{V}$$

Where e = Effective tariff
n = Nominal tariff
M = tariff duty levied on import content of domestic good
i = import content of domestic good
V = Domestic Added Value (DAV)

Using the preceding values we have:

$$e = \frac{10.8\% - 0.2(25\%)}{70\%} = 8.28\%$$

We can now make the following observations:

(a) When the domestic good contains 100% DAV then the NOMINAL duty is the same as the EFFECTIVE duty, e.g.

$$e = \frac{38\% - 0(0)}{100} = 38\%$$

(b) When the domestic good contains a low DAV, then the EFFECTIVE duty is much greater than the NOMINAL duty, e.g.

$$e = \frac{38\% - 0(50\%)}{50\%} = 76\%$$

(c) When the domestic good contains import content which is, itself, attracting a tariff, then the EFFECTIVE protection will be reduced, e.g.

$$e = \frac{38\% - 0.1(50\%)}{50\%} = 66\%$$

Two other points can be made:

(i) The higher the NOMINAL rate the higher the EFFECTIVE rate.
(ii) The higher the rate on import content the less EFFECTIVE the protective tariff will be.

QUESTIONS

Question 1.1

Calculate the effective tariff rate where an imported good carries a 10% duty raising its price from £100 to £110 and where the competing domestically-produced good has a price of £103 which contains an import content of £60 on which a tariff of 5% is levied.

Question 1.2

A UK manufacturer of waterproof raincoats faces strong competition from imports of an almost identical quality product selling in the UK market at £50 which includes an *ad valorem* tariff of 25%. The UK product sells for £58, but this price includes costs of £17.50 to purchase imported made-up trimmings (zips, buttons, etc.) and another £10 on imported fabrics (such as canvas and linens, etc.). These latter items carry no import tariffs but the former items carry an *ad valorem* import tariff of 25% within the overall cost of £17.50.

(a) Calculate the real effective tariff protection afforded to the UK finished raincoat and compare this to the nominal tariff rate. Show your answer in both arithmetic and algebraic forms. Calculations to two decimal places. Ignore VAT.
(b) Advise the UK garment industry's Trade Association as to what tariff changes they should press for that would help to restore this member's international competitiveness in raincoats. Note that the 25% tariff on imported raincoats is subject to an International Agreement and cannot be altered unilaterally. How would your advice, if taken, affect the UK raincoat's selling price, assuming that all other costs remain constant?
(c) How would your recommended change affect the UK garment accessories industry?

[City of London Polytechnic, June 1982]

Question 1.3

Consider the outcome on the effective tariff of:

(a) a high nominal tariff rate,
(b) a low (but not zero) domestic added value for the relevant protected domestic good,

(c) a zero tariff duty on the imported content of the relevant protected domestic good.

[City of London Polytechnic, June 1981]

Question 1.4

Consider some of the more important effects of an *ad valorem* tariff. To what extent may some of them be mutually exclusive?

[City of London Polytechnic, June 1983]

Question 1.5

Why has there been an expansion in counter-trade in recent years? What functions can a UK bank play in assisting a UK exporter involved in such trade?

Section 2
Trade Data Analysis

Table 2.1
Changes in UK Trade 1981–1982

		1981	*1982*
UK Exports (FOB)		$102.2b	$97.0b
UK Imports (FOB)		$ 96.2b	$93.3b
Exchange rate per US$1	=	£0.4990	£0.5723
Consumer price indices 1980 = 100 (measured in sterling)	=	111.9	121.5
Price indices (1980 = 100)			
Exports } measured in sterling		109	117
Imports } measured in sterling		108	117
Exports } measured in dollars		93	86
Imports } measured in dollars		95	89
Population		56 m	56 m
GDP measured in sterling		£247.65b	£270.42b
World exports (FOB)		$1837.0b	$1694.5b
World imports (FOB)		$1837.0b	$1694.5b

PROBLEM

How to find the real (volume) changes using sterling values.

METHOD

First convert the dollar values into sterling values. Thus,

	1981	*1982*
UK Exports (FOB)	\$102.2b	\$97.0b
	× 0.4990	× 0.5723
	= £51.0b	= £55.5b.
UK Imports (FOB)	\$96.2b	\$93.3b
	× 0.4990	× 0.5723
	= £48.0b	= £53.4b.

SUMMARY OF RESULTS

	1981	*1982*
UK Exports (FOB)	£51.0b.	£55.5b.
UK Imports	£48.0b.	£53.4b.

These are unadjusted value figures. To find real (or volume) changes they must be adjusted by the changes in the export and import price indices.

STERLING INDICES

UK Exports	109	117
UK Imports	108	117

Percentage increase in export index $= 117 - 109$

$$= 8 \times \frac{100}{109} = 7.3\%$$

Percentage increase in import index $= 117 - 108$

$$= 9 \times \frac{100}{108} = 8.3\%$$

"Inflate" 1981 data by these percentages. Thus, UK Exports (1981)

£51.0b
+ 7.3% = £3.723b
= £54.723bb.

UK Imports (1981)

£48.0b
+ 8.3% = £3.984b
= £51.984b.

Now we can compare 1981 with 1982.

E.g. Exports 1981 = £54.723b
1982 = £55.5b = 1.42% real rise

E.g. Imports 1981 = £51.984b
1982 = £53.4b = 2.72% real rise

Using this adjusted data now let us find trade per capita and as a percentage of Gross Domestic Product.

UK TRADE PER CAPITA

	1981	*1982*
Exports	£54.723b	£55.5b
Population	56 m	56 m
Per capita	$\frac{54{,}723}{56} = £977.$	$\frac{55{,}500}{56} = £991.$
Imports	£51.984b	£53.4b
Population	56 m	56 m
Per capita	$\frac{51{,}984}{56} = £928.$	$\frac{53{,}400}{56} = £954.$

UK TRADE AS A PERCENTAGE OF GDP

Exports	£54.723b	£55.5b
GDP (unadjusted)	£247.65b	£270.42b

"Inflate" 1981 GDP by the Consumer Price Index change, i.e.

$$\begin{array}{r} 121.5 \\ -\ 111.9 \\ \hline \end{array}$$

$$= \quad 9.6 \times \frac{100}{111.9} = 8.6\% \text{ rise}$$

1981 GDP £247.65b + 8.6% (= £21.3b) = £268.95b.

		1981		1982
Thus, adjusted GDP	=	£268.95b		£270.42b
Exports as a percentage of GDP	=	$\frac{£54.723b \times 100}{268.95}$		$\frac{£55.5b \times 100}{270.42}$
	=	20.3%	=	20.5%
Imports as a percentage of GDP		$\frac{£51.984b \times 100}{268.95}$		$\frac{£53.4b \times 100}{270.42}$
	=	19.3%	=	19.7%.

NOW LET US FIND UK TRADE AS A PERCENTAGE OF WORLD TRADE

		1981		*1982*
UK Exports		\$ 102.2b		\$ 97.0b
World Exports		\$1837.0b		\$1694.0b
UK exports as a percentage	=	$\frac{\$102.2b \times 100}{1837}$		$\frac{\$97.0b \times 100}{1694}$
	=	5.56%	=	5.7%.
UK Imports		\$ 96.2b		\$ 93.3b
World Imports		\$1837.0b		\$1694.0b
UK imports as a percentage		$\frac{\$96.2b \times 100}{1837}$		$\frac{93.3b \times 100}{1694}$
	=	5.2%	=	5.5%

CALCULATING THE UK TERMS OF TRADE

Sterling measured $\frac{109 \times 100}{108}$ $\frac{117 \times 100}{117}$

= 100.9. 100.0.

Dollar measured $\frac{93 \times 100}{95}$ $\frac{86 \times 100}{89}$

= 97.9. = 96.6.

SUMMARY OF RESULTS

	1981	*1982*	*Change*
Adjusted UK Exports	£54.723b	£55.5b	+ 1.42%
Adjusted UK Imports	£51.984b	£53.4b	+ 2.72%
Adjusted Exports per capita	£977	£991	+ 1.43%
Adjusted Imports per capita	£928	£954	+ 2.80%
Adjusted Exports per adjusted GDP	20.3%	20.5%	+ 0.99%
Adjusted Imports per adjusted GDP	19.3%	19.7%	+ 2.07%
UK trade as a percentage of World Trade.			
Exports	5.56%	5.7%	+ 2.52%
Imports	5.20%	5.5%	+ 5.76%
UK Terms of Trade (£s)	100.9	100.0	− 0.89%
UK Terms of Trade ($s)	97.9	96.6	− 1.33%

COMMENTS

(1) Real imports rose faster than real exports
(2) Real imports per capita rose faster than real exports per capita.
(3) Real imports per GDP rose faster than real exports per GDP.
(4) Both UK exports and UK imports rose as a percentage of world exports and imports but imports rose more quickly.
(5) UK sterling terms of trade deteriorated slightly due to a rather faster rise in import prices than in export prices. However, measured in US dollars there was a sharper deterioration due to export prices falling more quickly than import prices.
(6) The percentage increase in UK consumer prices match the percentage increases in export prices (8.5% and 7.5%).
(7) Sterling's depreciation helped to worsen the terms of trade.

QUESTIONS

Question 2.1

Using data provided in the textbook for Brazil and Malaysia for 1972 and 1981 (dollar values) and adjusting the 1972 data by the percentage changes in trade prices (dollar based):

(a) find the real percentage changes in exports and imports;

(b) compare the adjusted and unadjusted percentage changes;
(c) give reasons for the differences.

Question 2.2

Assess the major changes that have taken place in the volume, distribution and pricing of world trade over the past ten years. In your answer, consider the part played by the UK, especially in the light of exports per capita.

[City of London Polytechnic, June 1983]

Section 3

Comparative Cost Advantages and Changes in Costs

COMPARATIVE COST ADVANTAGE

Jane Smith and John Brown can both make model cars and bake loaves of bread. If they are each given 8 hours and the identical equipment Jane can produce 60 model cars while John can turn out 80 model cars. Alternatively, and again with identical equipment, Jane can bake 50 loaves of bread while John can produce 56 loaves of bread. Jane's cars are identical to John's cars and John's bread is exactly the same as Jane's bread. They both divide their time equally between bread making and model car producing.

QUESTIONS

(1) Who has the Absolute Cost Advantage?
(2) Who has the Comparative Cost Advantage in bread?
(3) If 30 model cars are traded between Jane and John, how many loaves of bread could be involved?
(4) Are Jane and John better off if they traded with specialisation?

Show your answers in tabular and diagram form.

We can show John and Jane's output as:

	Model cars		*Loaves of Bread*
John	80	or	56
Jane	60	or	50

(1) John can produce more model cars *and* and more loaves of bread than Jane: he has an absolute cost advantage in both products.

However, his advantage in model cars is *greater* than his advantage in loaves of bread, i.e.

$\frac{80}{60} = 1.33$ and $\frac{56}{50}$ 1.12

(2) So, John has the *comparative* cost advantage in model cars giving Jane the *least comparative disadvantage* (greatest comparative cost advantage) in bread.

John will sell cars to Jane in return for her bread.

(3) If John sells 30 model cars he will want in return more than *his bread value of 30 cars*! That is, more than $\frac{30}{80} \times 56 = $ *21 loaves of bread*.

Put another way, we can say that for John, 30 model cars has the same value as 21 loaves of bread.

If Jane buys 30 model cars she will want to give in return *something less than her bread value of 30 cars.* That is, less than, $\frac{30}{60} \times 50 = $ *25 loaves of bread*.

Put another way, we can say that for Jane, 30 model cars has the same value as 25 loaves of bread.

To summarise then, we have:

John willing to trade 30 cars for > 21 bread.
Jane willing to trade 30 cars for < 25 bread.

Thus, any number of loaves between 22 and 24 is possible.

(4) Let us suppose they trade 30 cars for 23 bread.

John produces 80 cars and sells 30 leaving 50. He obtains 23 bread from Jane. His post-trade consumption is,

50 cars
+ 23 bread

This compares with his *pre-trade* output of:

40 cars
+ 28 bread

Is he better off with trade?

Well, he "consumes" 10 more model cars at a cost of 5 fewer loaves of bread; but what would it have cost him to produce 10 more cars by himself?

Answer: $\frac{10}{80} \times 56 = $ *7 loaves of bread*.

Thus, if he wants more model cars he can have them more cheaply by trading with Jane.

What about Jane? Her output is 50 bread of which 23 is sold to John leaving her with 27. She obtains in return 30 cars giving her post-trade consumption as:

30 cars
+ 27 bread

This compares with her *pre-trade* output of

30 cars
+ 25 bread. A net gain of 2 bread.

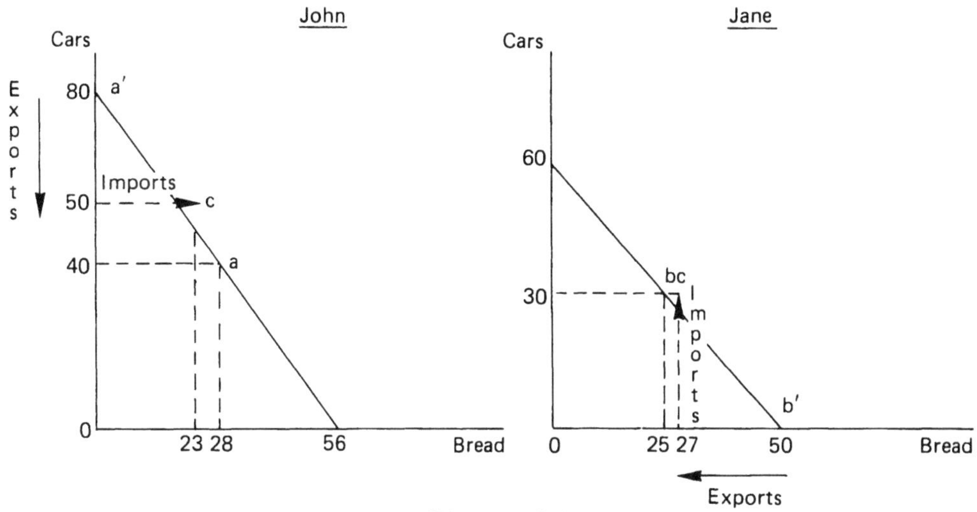

Diagram 3.1

a and b are pre-trade output and consumption points.
a' and b' are points of output specialisation.
c are points of post-trade outputs.

Note: constant cost production frontiers are assumed.

CHANGES IN COSTS

(all values to nearest decimal point)

THE SAGA OF JOHN AND JANE — CONTINUED

(the volume of traded cars is 30)

(a) John decides to make an extreme effort and is finally able to produce not 56 loaves of bread but 67 instead. His ability to produce model cars is unaltered and Jane continues to be able to produce bread and model cars as before. Has this production increase altered the trading possibilities between them?

(b) John tries even harder and with a lot of sweat and tears is able to bring off the magnificient output of 72 loaves of bread instead of 56. All the other outputs remaining the same. Will this change have any effect on trade?

(c) John happens to live in the UK and he prices his cars at 20 new pence each. Jane on the other hand lives in the USA and her price for loaves of bread is 69 cents.

With the latest production outputs as given above, what are the money prices of the two goods in their respective countries?

What is the dollar value of the pound sterling?
What is the cent price of John's goods?
What is the pence price of Jane's goods?

(a) The output schedules are now:

	Cars		*Bread*
John	80	or	67
Jane	60	or	50

As the ratio $\frac{80}{60}$ is almost the same as $\frac{67}{50}$ there is virtually no difference between the advantage John has in cars and his advantage in bread.

Although he still retains an *absolute* cost advantage in *both* products he has no *comparative* advantage in either.

This can be shown by reference to trade between them. I.e. if John sells 30 cars he will want more than $\frac{30}{80}$ x 67 = *25.125 bread*

If Jane buys 30 cars she will want to give less than $\frac{30}{60}$ x 50 = *25 bread*

Thus, John wants more bread than Jane is prepare to offer! There can be no profitable trade between them.

(b) The new schedules are:

	Cars		*Bread*
John	80	or	72
Jane	60	or	50

As a result of the improved output of bread by John he now has a comparative advantage in bread instead of cars. I.e.

$\frac{72}{50}$ = *1.44* and $\frac{80}{60}$ = *1.33*

John will export bread and Jane will export cars.

(c) John produces either 80 cars @ 20 pence each = £16, or he produces 72 bread with an equal value of £16, giving each loaf a value of 22.2 pence.

Jane produces either 50 loaves @ 69 cents each = $34.50, or she produces 60 cars with an equal value of $34.50, giving each car a value of 57½ cents.

If Jane sells 30 cars she will want in return more than $\frac{30}{60}$ x 50 = *25 bread*

If John buys 30 cars he will want to give less than $\frac{30}{80}$ x 72 = *27 bread*.

So the exchange is 30 cars for 26 bread.

John values his 26 bread exports at 22.2p = £5.772.
Jane values her 30 car exports at 57½ cents = $17.25.

Thus the exchange rate is $\frac{\$17.25}{5.772}$ = £1 = $2.9885.

The cent prices of John's goods are:

cars: = 20 pence @ £1 = $2.9885 = $\frac{2.9885}{100}$ x 20 = *59 cents*.

bread: = 22.2 pence @ £1 = $2.9885 = $\frac{2.9885}{100}$ x 22.2 = *66 cents*.

The sterling prices of Jane's goods are:

cars: $= 57.5$ cents @ £1 = \$2.9885 $= \frac{1}{2.9885} \times 0.575 = \textit{19.2 pence}$.

bread: $= 69$ cents @ £1 = \$2.9885 $= \frac{1}{2.9885} \times 0.69 = \textit{23 pence}$.

QUESTIONS

Question 3.1

A developing country (X) can, with certain inputs of economic resources, produce either 10,000 rolls of grade A kitchen-paper or, with the same value of resources, 1,000 best quality bath towels. This compares with an average output ratio for all other countries (Y) of 30,000 rolls of grade A kitchen-paper or 2,000 best quality bath towels using the same value inputs of economic resources.

Clearly the developing country (X) is less efficient in both items compared with overseas production (Y). Does this mean that there is no possibility for it to specialise in one of these products and export it profitably?

Assume that increasing marginal opportunity costs prevail everywhere and that exchange rates are allowed to find their own levels. Capital movements and all other international transactions have a zero impact on exchange rates. There are no subsidies, tariffs or other government restrictions on trade.

All consumers wish to consume some of both products, but consumers in (Y) have a distinct preference for bath towels relative to consumers in (X).

Illustrate your answer by means of production frontiers and indifference maps.

[City of London Polytechnic, June 1982]

Question 3.2

An East Anglian tomato grower has purchased a German straw-burner to replace his oil-fired burner. Straw costs £18 per ton as against £150 for the oil equivalent. In addition the waste products of burning straw contains silica which can be sold to tile manufacturers.

(a) How does the use of straw affect the comparative cost advantage of the UK tomato grower?
(b) How will it affect the UK Balance of Trade?
(c) If the changes are significant, what impact is likely on the exchange rate for sterling?
(d) What is likely to happen to straw prices, oil prices, tile prices?

Question 3.3

A study completed in 1983 indicated that it costs the USSR 3.3 tonnes of oil to produce 1 tonne of wheat and also that the USSR can buy USA wheat at a cost of 0.625 tonnes of oil. What implications do these figures have for the theory of comparative cost advantage?

Question 3.4

Examine the proposition that a country's ability to compete effectively in world markets is a function of its comparative rather than its absolute costs.

[City of London Polytechnic, June 1981]

Question 3.5

Two countries (A and B) are both industralised and both possess small but efficient agricultural sectors. They each produce steel products and medium-sized tractors and their marginal opportunity costs are:

Nation A — 100,000 tons steel per 50,000 tractors.
Nation B — 72,000 tons steel per 45,000 tractors.

Making the assumptions below:

(a) comment on the likely flow of trade in these products between A and B
(b) indicate to what extent they are both likely to specialise in these products
(c) indicate the factors that would help to determine the terms of trade in these products
(d) say why any gains from trade are unlikely to be equally divided between A and B.

Assumptions

(i) Each product is much the same in quality and type in A and B.
(ii) Both A and B can adjust their outputs and enjoy decreasing marginal opportunity costs in so doing.
(iii) There is free trade in both products and no possibility of government subsidisation or interference.
(iv) Exchange rates exactly reflect the above opportunity costs.

[City of London Polytechnic, June 1983]

Question 3.6

What is meant by the proposition that "restrictions on the free flow of goods and services between countries can only lead to net economic losses for all concerned"? What qualifications are there to this proposition?

[City of London Polytechnic, June 1984]

Section 4

Trade Intermediaries

Question 4.1

Advise a prospective UK exporter of low unit value consumer goods with a likely total annual turnover of £1 million which of the available trade intermediaries he should turn to for help in finding and expanding overseas markets.

Question 4.2

The O.K. Company Limited, which has been trading for some five years, is well managed, but is short of working capital. The managing director, who is also responsible for financial matters, comes to see you to discuss various methods of obtaining finance to cover new export contracts (goods are sold on 90 day bill terms). The company has recently taken out an ECGD Comprehensive Policy.

As a manager of your bank, you do not wish to extend the company's facilities any further without a completly reliable guarantee from an independent body. You explain the bank's position and outline a source of finance which might be available through the bank, as well as other sources of non-bank finance which might be available and which should satisfy your customer's needs.

Required

Brief notes on each of the schemes discussed showing their salient features.

[IOB, September 1982]

Question 4.3

One of your customers, Plant Propagations Limited, makes arrangements for a director, A. Grafton, to call to see you to discuss an enquiry which the company has had from one of the Arabian Gulf States. The proposal is that your customer should supply a range of plants which will be used to landscape a new hotel, office and shopping arcade complex in the Gulf. The enquiry emanates from the main contractor, a resident company in the Middle Eastern country in question. Your customer does not necessarily need finance.

Required:

Brief notes showing the help, other than financial, which is available to the customer from yourself and other interested agencies.

[IOB, April 1985]

Section 5

International Trade Documents

Question 5.1

Explain the following terms:

Bills of Lading which are:

(a) "on board"
(b) made out to order and blank endorsed
(c) claused
(d) freight paid
(e) common short form
(f) negotiable
(g) combined transport
(h) liner
(i) charter party

Question 5.2

How does a sea waybill differ from a marine bill of lading?

Question 5.3

Bright Sparks Limited are buyers and sellers of electrical goods and components. They have successfully competed for a contract to sell goods to an American electronics company based in Atlanta. Many of the goods will be manufactured in the UK but, because of the complexity of the contract, a number of components will have to be imported from Germany and Norway for processing in the UK.

As the company have not imported goods before, they need to know the meaning of the following terms quoted to them:

Germany Terms CIF UK Airport

Payment in Deutsche Marks by SWIFT to a nominated bank in Dusseldorf 10 days after the shipment of goods from Germany to the UK.

Norway Terms FOB Oslo Airport

Payment in Sterling by TT to a named bank in Oslo within five days of the shipment of goods from Oslo airport to the UK.

Required

A brief explanation of:

(a) the terms of shipment mentioned above and the respective responsibilities of buyer and seller;
(b) the terms 'SWIFT' and 'TT' and how these methods of payment operate.

[IOB, September 1983]

Question 5.4

Your customers, Home Fires Ltd., have been successful in selling a wide range of consumer products in the UK for a number of years, but they are now seeking markets overseas. They have been asked by a potential overseas buyer to quote prices based on the following terms:

(i) FOB
(ii) C and F
(iii) CIF
(iv) CIF Liner Terms.

Required

An explanation of these terms for your customer indicating the precise meaning and the contractual relationship which will exist between buyer and seller arising out of those terms.

[IOB, April 1984]

Section 6

Bank Collections

Question 6.1

Examine the advantages and disadvantages for a UK importer of the use of a documentary bank collections facility.

[City of London Polytechnic, June 1982]

Question 6.2

Differentiate the costs to a drawer of a bill of exchange which is (a) negotiated, or (b) discounted by a bank.

[City of London Polytechnic, June 1984]

Question 6.3

(a) Is a bill of exchange always used in open account trading?
(b) Does a bill of exchange always give the holder title to the goods?
(c) Is a holder of a bill of exchange always also the payee?
(d) Is an advance against a bill of exchange the same as discounting it?
(e) Does an acceptor of a bill of exchange have the same liability as a discounter?
(f) Is a bill of exchange always used in a bank collection?
(g) Is a drawer of a bill of exchange always liable on it in the event of a drawee's default?
(h) Is a bank bill of exchange the same as a trade bill?

Question 6.4

You have received in your branch direct from an Indonesian bank a documentary collection for £100,000. The bill of exchange accompanying the documents is drawn at 90 days' sight on International Traders (Fluid Sea) Limited, who are good customers of yours.

Among other things the collection order states:

(i) "Subject to Uniform Rules for Collections" (ICC Publication No. 322).
(ii) Release documents against acceptance.

(iii) Protest if unpaid.
(iv) In case of need refer to Indonesian Agents (UK) Ltd.

Required

(a) A brief explanation of the significance of the statement contained in (i) above.
(b) A statement of the action you would take if the transaction developed as follows:

> The bill of exchange is accepted by your customers but at maturity they refuse to pay the bill on the grounds that the goods are substandard and not in accordance with the commercial contract. They further state that they are in the process of negotiating new terms and that they will pay only £50,000 on account.

[IOB, April 1982]

Question 6.5

As the manager of your branch you call to see a new customer, International Importers Limited, to discuss with their financial director the various aspects of their importing business and how the branch can help. The financial director advises you that, apart from a few letters of credit, the majority of imports will be covered on a 60 day sight bill D/A basis or on "cash against document" terms. All presentations are apparently routed through banks.

Required

Brief notes on:

(a) any international regulations you may have to be aware of when handling documents in the manner mentioned above;
(b) any instructions you would expect to receive from remitting banks;
(c) any aspects you can foresee which might cause problems between yourself and your new customer, and your responsibilities to the parties involved in overcoming the difficulties.

[IOB, September 1982]

Question 6.6

Your branch has received in the morning post a "Notice of Arrival" from an airline company based at the local airport. The notice indicates that three packing cases of fancy goods have been consigned to the bank for account of Far Eastern Imports Ltd., customers of your branch.

(a) What is your position under current international rules?
(b) What immediate steps would you take to protect the interests of your customers?
(c) If your customers are unable to pay for the goods immediately, you are willing to rely on the goods as your ultimate security. Pending a buyer being found for the goods, what immediate steps must you take to protect the bank's position?

[IOB, April 1983]

Question 6.7

Your customer, Import Anything Limited, purchases goods from the Far East. On 30 September you receive, for presentation to your customer, a 90 days sight documentary bill of exchange dated 1 September, together with a collection order indicating the following:

(i) Subject to Uniform Rules for Collections (ICC Publication No. 322).

(ii) Release documents against acceptance.
(iii) Protest if unpaid.
(iv) In case of need contact Far Eastern agents.
(v) Collect interest at 10 per cent from date of bill to the due date.

The customer accepts the bill of exchange but at maturity declines to pay, and offers 50 per cent down, stating that the drawer has agreed to reduce the bill amount because of faulty goods. The customer also claims that in any event interest is *not* payable on the bill and he must therefore refuse to pay any.

Required

(a) A brief explanation of the meaning of (i) above.
(b) Your advice to the customer concerning their offer.

[IOB, September 1983]

Question 6.8

Sellers International Limited sell a variety of goods to Western Europe, the USA and Canada in a number of currencies on open account and DP terms. In settlement they receive a large number of small cheques or bank drafts expressed in foreign currency or occasionally in sterling. All these have been payable overseas and have been collected on their behalf by your bank. Cash flow considerations have now caused the company's new finance director to call to see you to discuss the means by which the company could improve its immediate cash position.

Required

(a) A brief note of the explanation you would give to the finance director, indicating a specific *bank arrangement*, which would immediately improve the customer's cash flow.
(b) What are the advantages and disadvantages of such a scheme and the significant effect on the company's cash flow of receiving small items payable overseas expressed in sterling as opposed to foreign currency?
(c) If sterling cheques/drafts continue to be used, how can the disadvantages to the customer be minimised?

[IOB, April 1984]

Question 6.9

Tall Tale Limited wholesale booksellers, wish to import expensive rare books and have come to you for help and advice. They have been given to understand that payment will have to be made to their main suppliers of these books by means of either an irrevocable letter of credit calling for bills of exchange drawn at 90 days sight or a documentary collection through the bank on sight D/P terms.

Required

(a) a description of each method of payment;
(b) the advantages and disadvantages of each method.

[IOB, April 1984]

Question 6.10

Mr Weinberg, a very good customer of yours, occasionally buys wine whilst on holiday. At your request, he calls to discuss a consignment of five cases of wine which have arrived at your counters addressed to the bank but clearly indicating the ultimate consignee as your customer. You examine and discuss with Mr Weinberg the terms of the documents which accompanied the wine and which included a draft at 30 days' sight. Mr Weinberg's arrangements with the sellers are that he is to receive credit provided that the goods are handled through your office. The shipment of five cases which you received was delivered free to your office and you know that it is the first of a number of consignments Mr Weinberg has ordered during his continental holiday.

Required:

(a) Set out what you would tell your customer about consigning goods to the bank and the generally accepted rules which might govern this transaction.

(b) Assuming that you would continue to allow your customer to make such arrangements, what must he do to satisfy you so that you are able to fulfil your duties to the sellers of the produce?

(c) The accompanying documents reveal a letter addressed to you by the seller's bankers. What would you expect to find by way of instructions in such a letter?

[IOB, April 1985]

Section 7

Letters of Credit*

Question 7.1

What are the principal factors that determine whether a documentary letter of credit is with or without recourse to the beneficiary?

[City of London Polytechnic, June 1981]

Question 7.2

A bank in West Germany has opened an irrevocable documents letter of credit calling for a London bank's confirmation, in favour of a UK exporter who is to draw a bill of exchange on the confirming bank with a tenor of one month from presentation of documents. The credit is for DM100,000 dated 1 January and calls for shipment of 40,000 lbs of tin CIF Hamburg not later than 1 February.

The UK exporter ask their confirming bank to issue a second credit in favour of a Malaysian supplier for shipment CIF Hamburg of 40,000 lbs of tin; payment to be against documents including a sight draft bill of exchange drawn on the second issuing bank and to be negotiated by a confirming bank in Malaysia.

Required

(a) Illustrate these transactions by means of a flow chart;
(b) Explain the meaning of each transaction;
(c) Outline the benefits of these procedures to the UK exporter.

[City of London Polytechnic, June 1984]

Question 7.3

Advise an exporter who seeks ways of obtaining pre-shipment finance.

Question 7.4

Answer the following questions with reference to Specimen Documents A and B shown on pages 28 and 29.

* (Section 7 deals only with documentary credits. Credits with foreign exchange contents are dealt with in Section 9.)

DOCUMENT A

BARCLAYS International

Barclays Bank International Limited
168 Fenchurch Street, London, EC3P 3HP.

date 20th July 19..

DOCUMENTARY CREDITS DEPARTMENT

SPECIMEN

IRREVOCABLE CREDIT No:- FDC/2/6789
To be quoted on all drafts and correspondence.

Beneficiary(ies)	Advised through
Speirs and Wadley Limited, Adderley Road, Hackney, London E.8.	

Accreditor	To be completed only if applicable
Woldal Incorporated, Broadway, New York, U.S.A.	Our cable of Advised through Refers

Dear Sir(s)

In accordance with instructions received from The Downtown Bank & Trust Co.
we hereby issue in your favour a Documentary Credit for £4108
(say) Four thousand, one hundred and eight pounds sterling available by your drafts
drawn on us
at sight
for the 100% c.i.f. invoice value, accompanied by the following documents:–

1. Invoice in triplicate, signed and marked Licence No. LHDL 22 19..
2. Certificate of Origin issued by a Chamber of Commerce.
3. Full set of clean on board Shipping Company's Bills of Lading made out to order and blank endorsed, marked "Freight Paid" and "Notify Woldal Inc., Broadway, New York."
4. Insurance Policy or Certificate in duplicate, covering Marine and War Risks up to buyer's warehouse, for invoice value of the goods plus 10%.

Covering the following goods:-

400 Electric Power Drills

To be shipped from London to New York
not later than 10th August 19..
Partshipment not permitted Transhipment not permitted
The credit is available for presentation to us until 31st August 19..

Subject to Uniform Customs and Practice for Documentary Credits (1974 Revision,) I.C.C. Publication No. 290

Drafts drawn hereunder must be marked "Drawn under Barclays Bank International Limited 168 Fenchurch Street London branch, Credit number FDC/2/6789".
We undertake that drafts and documents drawn under and in strict conformity with the terms of this credit will be honoured upon presentation.

Yours faithfully,

Co-signed (Signature No. 9847) Signed (Signature No. 10247)

CRE 202 (replacing CRE 83, 606 series) PLEASE SEE REVERSE

DOCUMENT B

BARCLAYS International SPECIMEN Barclays Bank International Limited

DOCUMENTARY CREDITS DEPARTMENT

168 Fenchurch Street Branch

Speirs and Wadley Limited
Adderley Road
Hackney
London E.8.

Date 20th July 19..

Our Reference No. FDC/2/7698
to be quoted in all correspondence

Dear Sir,

IRREVOCABLE CREDIT No. 6889

OF Barclays Bank of California, San Francisco

We are to-day informed by cable ~~post~~ from Barclays Bank of California, San Francisco that they have established an Irrevocable Credit in your favour for account of Philmen Int., Longtown, California to the extent of £ U.S. $7394.40

(Say Seven thousand three hundred and ninety-four U.S.$ forty cents)

available for your drafts on Barclays Bank of California, San Francisco

at sight to be accompanied by the following documents:

1. Invoice in triplicate, signed and marked Licence No. LHDL 22 19..
2. Certificate of Origin issued by a Chamber of Commerce.
3. Full set of clean on board Shipping Company's Bills of Lading made out to order and blank endorsed, marked "Freight Paid" and "Notify Philmen Int., Longtown, California".
4. Insurance Policy or Certificate in duplicate, covering Marine and War Risks up to buyer's warehouse, for invoice value of the goods plus 10%.

Covering: 400 Electric Power Drills
To be shipped from London to New York c.i.f. not later than 10th August, 19..
Partial shipment not permitted.
Transhipment not permitted.

The expiry date of this credit is 31st August 19.. which is the latest date for negotiation in London.

Kindly note that all drafts drawn under this Credit must be marked "Drawn under Irrevocable Credit of Barclays Bank of California, San Francisco No. 6889 dated 20th July 19.. "

Barclays Bank of California, San Francisco undertake that all drafts drawn under and in conformity with the terms of this Credit will meet with due honour provided that they are marked as being so drawn.

We have no authority from our principals to confirm this credit and therefore this letter is solely an advice of it and conveys no engagement by us. Any drafts negotiated by us under the credit will be subject to recourse to yourselves.

Subject to Uniform Customs and Practice for Documentary Credits (1974 Revision) I.C.C. Publication No. 290.

Yours faithfully,

Accountant. *Manager.*

CRE 209 (replacing CRE 78)

		ANSWERS	
QUESTIONS		SPECIMEN A	SPECIMEN B
1	Who is the Drawee?		
2	Who is the Importer?		
3	Is Barclays International acting in a confirming or advising capacity?		
4	Who is the issuing bank?		
5	Does the credit allow for recourse to the Drawer?		
6	Does the credit give the importer time to pay?		
7	Is it a Payments, Acceptance or Negotiations Credit?		
8	Could the reference to the bills of lading read "Freight Forward"?		
9	Which Credit is more advantageous for the Importer?		

Question 7.5

	QUESTIONS	ANSWERS	ARTICLE NO.
1	When instructions sent to an overseas bank are ignored is the Issuing bank liable to the Applicant?		
2	Under what conditions is it not possible for a Transferable Credit to be allocated to more than one 2nd beneficiary?		
3	What action to recover can an Advising bank take when a Revocable credit is cancelled after payment has been made against a sight draft drawn upon itself?		
4	Must a documentary presentation always include an Insurance document?		
5	When an irrevocable credit is subject to agreed amendments and it is followed by a second credit calling on the bank to confirm on the same terms as in the first credit, is the second credit to incorporate the amendments?		
6	If no last date for presentation of documents is stipulated in the credit, when will banks refuse to accept transport documents?		
7	Will banks accept claused transport documents		

Question 7.6

	QUESTIONS	ANSWERS
	If a Documentary Letter of Credit:	
1	Does not indicate whether it is revocable or not — is it revocable?	
2	Is confirmed; is this by way of (a) request, or (b) authorisation by the Issuing Bank?	
3	Allows for presentation of documents including transport documents stating that goods *may* be carried on deck — will Banks refuse to accept such a presentation?	
4	Fails to specify whether partial shipments are permitted — are they permitted?	
5	Is issued by *cable* to the Advising Bank, does there need to be a mail confirmation?	
6	"Deals in Documents and not Goods" — specify the Article setting this out.	
7	Involves the presentation of documents which includes a Forwarding Agent's transport documents — will the Banks accept such a presentation?	
8	Must call for *two* documents in which the description of the goods are the same — which two documents are they?	

Question 7.7

Your customer, International Traders (Electronic Suppliers) Limited, has received a letter of credit in its favour covering the supply and shipment of goods to Australia. The sources of supply will be partly the company's own manufacturing capacity and partly goods obtained from West Germany.

The German supplier requires a secure method of payment, and you have been asked to arrange this by opening a documentary credit in favour of the German supplier using the Australian letter of credit as security.

(a) What features would you require in the Australian letter of credit?
(b) What are the dangers (if any) to the bank and its customer in the proposed arrangements?
(c) Still using a documentary credit, suggest an alternative method which would help to overcome any problems you have identified under (b) above.

[IOB, April 1982]

Question 7.8

Your customers, Junk Galore Limited, are negotiating to purchase goods from overseas for the first time. They advise you that they wish to purchase electronic calculators and that their suppliers have asked for an irrevocable letter of credit to be established in their favour. Under the terms of the letter of credit, the bills of exchange will be drawn on a United Kingdom bank in sterling at 90 days sight. You are also advised that shipment will be effected by sea and that the price basis is CIF UK port. Junk Galore Limited have a contract to supply a buyer in the south of England within one month of the goods being received in the United Kingdom. Your customers' facilities are fully extended but you would like to assist them in financing this import.

Required

Brief notes listing:

(a) the points you must consider from the bank's point of view when establishing a letter of credit on behalf of your customer and the protection which may be available in the transaction itself;
(b) the practical steps necessary to ensure that at all stages the bank is fully protected.

[IOB, September 1982]

Question 7.9

Your customers, Northern Trading Company, are finding it difficult to obtain adequate sources of supply of raw materials for their operation in the UK. They have identified an Australian manufacturer who can meet their needs against secure methods of payment. You have been asked to establish an irrevocable letter of credit in favour of the Australian suppliers but the customers advise you that they do not understand the implications for the company.

They would like to know:

(a) What is an irrevocable letter of credit.
(b) The basic documents they should call for and the details which they would expect to find in those documents if the bank agreed to establish a letter of credit.
(c) Any precautions that the buyers can take to ensure that they receive the goods they have contracted to buy, whilst at the same time satisfying the seller's needs.

State briefly, in note form, what you would tell your customer.

[IOB, April 1983]

Question 7.10

Antipodes Limited, a customer of yours of many years' standing, has a thriving business. As manager of your branch you have been able to offer facilities which have been utilised to your complete satisfaction as well as to the benefit of the company. Imports include many products from the antipodes and the company has set up a chain of trusted buying agents to act on their behalf. The agents in the past have been able to offer to the company 90 days D/A terms.

The agents are suffering from cash-flow problems and have asked Antipodes Limited to finance them on a temporary basis. You have been called in by your customer to discuss the methods which might be available to provide the agents with post-shipment finance and, possibly, pre-shipment finance.

Required

(a) *Brief notes* describing a basic instrument which would arrange for post- and pre-shipment finance, together with a note of the particular document which, if post-shipment finance is arranged, would afford your customers some degree of protection.

(b) *Brief notes* showing the explanation you would give to Antipodes Limited on how the instrument would work and its benefit or otherwise to them and their agents.

[IOB, September 1983]

Question 7.11

As manager of your branch, you have arranged an appointment with Mr. Dealer, managing director of Counter-Trade Limited. The account of Counter-Trade Limited, has been with you since incorporation some two years ago and during that time, has worked in credit to your satisfaction. There is little, if any, strength in either the company's balance sheet or the latest set of managment accounts which Mr. Dealer places before you. He asks you to provide a facility to cover an irrevocable letter of credit for £100,000 in favour of a South American company selling coffee — for which he can demonstrate a firm purchase contract from France — Counter-Trade Limited's profit margin for this transaction would be 25% gross if the deal goes through.

Required

(a) Your response to Mr. Dealer concerning this *specific* proposal, indicating the means by which your bank could help this company to finalize *this* transaction without involving the bank in hazardous liabilities.

(b) State briefly the method by which your proposal would operate.

[IOB, April 1984]

Question 7.12

At a recent meeting of an Export Club you took part as a member of a banking panel to answer questions from the floor. One of the questions asked by a member of the audience was:

> "Banks have in the past been able to advise letters of credit with impunity. They have had little regard for the well-being of the beneficiaries when passing on letters of credit without responsibility. It is now understood that this has changed and the panel are asked to comment on this and other changes in international practice which have recently taken place and which affect the responsibility of the banks as parties to letters of credit".

Required:

(a) What does the questioner mean by "international practice" in this context?

(b) What is meant by the statement that banks "passed on letters of credit without responsibility"?

(c) Indicate eight other changes which have occurred in this "international practice".

[IOB, April 1985]

Section 8

Other Trade Finance

Question 8.1

A UK manufacturer of heavy engineering machinery has a potential buyer abroad who insists on terms of payment over at least five years. Discuss and compare the local facilities open to the UK manufacturer to permit him to meet such terms.

[City of London Polytechnic, June 1982]

Question 8.2

Consider the advantages of export factoring to UK traders seeking a medium-term financial facility. What other facilities may offer them similar advantages?

[City of London Polytechnic, June 1983]

Question 8.3

At a recent meeting, sponsored by the British Overseas Trade Board, the virtues of foreign banks in providing export finance for customers were highlighted. One of the speakers discussed in glowing terms one such facility which is made available by banks on the continent of Europe and which is effected without liability (recourse) being incurred by the exporter.

Required

Your brief explanation of this facility covering the *salient points*, and giving the advantages and disadvantages to the exporter.

[IOB, April 1983]

Question 8.4

Your customer, Sell The Lot Limited, manufactures and exports to a number of countries in Eastern Europe and the third world a range of capital goods and related spare parts. They are finding it increasingly difficult to obtain traditional export finance and their managing director calls to see you to discuss developments which have taken place over the last few years. He has heard that various forms of finance, other than normal bank finance, are available to companies such as his, and asks you to outline them briefly.

Required

Brief notes on the points you would make concerning three of the methods of finance available to the company.

[IOB, September 1983]

Question 8.5

A Soviet trade buying agency contracts to purchase 100,000 word-processor units from a UK supplier at $900 each unit.

It will pay 10% on shipment and the balance to be financed by way of Promissory Notes as follows:

(a) at regular intervals over 6 years with each Note maturing after 12 months;
(b) the 1st Note to be for 5% of the balance and each subsequent Note to be for an additional 5% points of the original balance, with the final note being for the residual;
(c) interest to be paid by the obligor is 9.5% per annum on each outstanding balance;
(d) forfaitor to receive 10% interest per annum;
(e) the beneficiary receives sterling at the rates £1 = US$1.4710 – 1.4730;
(f) the Promissory Notes are to be given a guarantee by the Soviet Export/Import Department.

Questions

(1) What is the total sterling receipt of the beneficiary?
(2) What is the total dollar cost to be obligor?

Show you answer by completing the columns in the table on page 37.

Question 8.6

Your customers, Armchair Sales Limited, have built up a successful business, but have always been short of working capital. Their sales are solely in the UK and recently there has been a shortage of home demand.

At a recent trade fair they received enquiries from a number of overseas companies who have now placed firm orders. You have ascertained that the only way your customers could obtain the business would be to offer similar terms to those applicable to the existing UK business, namely open account. A number of European currencies will be involved.

The company's finance director seeks your advice asking for details of a scheme which would help them to obtain immediate cash against the export receivables and at the same time give some measure of foreign exchange cover.

Required

Your brief explanation, outlining a *single* scheme which would assist your customer.

[IOB, April 1984]

Question 8.7

General Import Limited buy and sell many foreign products. A. Grummet, their financial director, calls to discuss payment for supplies of rope washers from the Far East. To date, the company have tended to take extended credit, settling accounts only when called upon. However, you have confidence in their management ability. The suppliers of

COLUMN A	COLUMN B	COLUMN C	COLUMN D	COLUMN E	COLUMN F	COLUMN G	
Notes due in (no. of months)	Principal sum of each note US$	Balance outstanding US$	Interest per annum on each balance outstanding US$	Principal plus interest (B + D) US$	Forfaitor's straight discount percentage on notes (E) US$	Net receipt by Exporter (E − F) US$	

rope washers have now called upon the company to accept 90 days sight sterling bills of exchange which have to be "guaranteed". Mr Grummet tells you that, to assist the company's cash flow position, he would like the bank to guarantee these sterling 90 days sight of bills of exchange, thus enabling the company to sell the goods prior to payment.

Required:

(a) An explanation of what is meant by the bank agreeing to "guarantee" such a bill of exchange.
(b) A statement, with reasons, as to whether, as a UK bank, you would or would not undertake to guarantee such a bill of exchange.
(c) A compromise you could suggest which would satisfy the seller, General Import Limited, and the bank.

[IOB, April 1985]

Question 8.8

Your customers, Woodwork Limited, are timber merchants and act either on their own behalf or as agents for timber stockists. They buy hardwood from various parts of the world for on-selling in Western Europe. Inward and outward payments have normally been made by cable transfer (Express International Money Transfer) upon shipment but occasionally by letters of credit.

A recent re-organisation in the company has taken place because of their deteriorating trading position. The new finance director, Mr Oakbeam, calls to see you to discuss a new general strategy for the company, and one particular transaction which he is trying to arrange involving a Malaysian supplier and a West German buyer. Payment will be by sight letter of credit and the terms of shipment CIF Hamburg. The German buyer has no objection to arranging an irrevocable letter of credit in favour of your customers, who have ascertained that the Malaysian supplier requires to be paid by the same method. The letter of credit is to be issued by a West German bank and will be advised through you. Mr Oakbeam says that when the company has used irrevocable letters in the past there had usually been dificulty with CIF contracts because it had never been able to get its documentation right. Following the recent banking changes, however, he is hoping to arrange for an irrevocable letter of credit to be established in the company's favour which will cater for the needs of Woodwork Limited as well as those of the Malaysian supplier.

Required:

Brief notes covering the following:

(a) A description of the basic instrument which will satisfy the needs of all parties and an indication of why it will be satisfactory:
(b) To what is Mr Oakbeam referring as "recent banking changes" and how will these changes help in this particular transaction?

[IOB, April 1985]

Section 9

Foreign Exchange

Question 9.1

(a) Convert the following to and from indirect/direct rates:

£1 = Y 361½ − 362½
£1 = SF 3.12¾ − 3.13¾
DM1 = £0.26368 − 0.26438
K.D1 = £2.4361 − 2.4369.

(b) Find the cross rates for DK/PE and SK/C$, where:

(i) £1 = DK 13.90½ − 13.92½ and £1 = PE 194.00 − 195.00.
(ii) £1 = SK 11.17 − 11.19 and C$1 = £0.5576 − 0.5579.

Specify which of your answers are bank buying rates and bank selling rates.

(c) (i) If £1 = $1.3025 what is $210 worth?
(ii) If $1 = £0.76787 what is £157 worth?

(d) *Simple arbitrage*

In London £1 = $1.3025 − 1.3035
In New York $1 = FF 8.9305 − 8.9315
In Paris $1 = FF 8.9400 − 8.9410

Calculate a profitable simple arbitrage set of transactions, starting with £100,000 and returning to sterling at the end. Ignore bank charges.

Question 9.2

(a) Given the following exchange rates calculate the various currency values for one Special Drawing Right.

$1 = DM 2.4315	SDR1 = $0.54 + DM 0.46
= Y 237.10	+ Y 34 + FF 0.74
= FF 6.8925	+ £0.071
= £0.6638	

(b) If a UK exporter wishes to charge an overseas buyer £10,000 or its equivalent, how many dollars and SDRs must he charge if he wants to invoice either in dollars or SDRs?

Use the above rates.

(c) How much sterling will the exporter receive if he sells the above dollar or SDR receipts spot at the following rates:

SDR1 = $1.08850 – 1.08860
£1 = SDR 1.3822 – 1.3832

Question 9.3

On 1 December a UK exporter expects to receive $400,000 some time in February and covers forward against the exchange risk.

On 10 February he receives $300,000 and is advised by his buyer that the remainder will not be paid until some time in April. On 1 March he is closed-out and enters into a new forward contract. Assuming no currency borrowing, calculate his net sterling receipts.

1 December	Spot £1 = $1.3180 – $1.3190	
	1 month forward	0.05c pm – 0.05c dis
	2 months forward	Par – 0.10c dis
	3 months forward	0.05c dis – 0.15c dis
1 March	Spot £1 = $1.3185 – $1.3195	
	1 month forward	0.10c pm – 0.05c pm
	2 months forward	0.15c pm – 0.10c pm
	3 months forward	0.20c pm – 0.15c pm

Question 9.4

Repeat question 9.3 substituting a UK importer who expects to pay $400,000 some time in February but who delays payment of $100,000 until some time in April. Assume no holding of foreign currency. Calculate his total net cost in sterling.

Question 9.5

On 1 April a customer wishes to buy forward US $100,000 option 3 months. The bank's quotations are as follows:

1 April	1.3810 – 1.3820
1 month forward	1.33 – 1.23c pm
2 months forward	2.40 – 2.30c pm
3 months forward	3.48 – 3.38c pm

On 1 July the customer asks the bank to extend the contract for a further option period until 1 September — the rates are as follows:

1 July	1.3790 – 1.3800
1 month forward	1.10 – 1.00c pm
2 months forward	2.10 – 2.00c pm
3 months forward	3.10 – 3.00c pm

Show:

(a) the original forward rate, and the amount of sterling the customer contracts to pay;

(b) the rate for closing out and the amount actually debited to the customer's account (allowing for close out);
(c) the extension and the amount finally debited to the customer's account.

Question 9.6

Your customer is purchasing three pieces of machinery costing Dutch guilders 10,000 each. Part shipments are to be made. The first item will definitely arrive during April, the second possibly during April, but may be delayed until May, whereas the third piece will definitely not arrive until sometime in June.

On 1 April your customer asks you to make the agreed initial payment of 10% of the total price. The balance is due to be paid on arrival of each item in this country and you are requested to sell your customer the necessary forward currency, the rates are as follows:

1 April	DG 4.26½ – 4.27½
1 month forward	1 – 2c discount
2 months forward	2 – 3c discount
3 months forward	3 – 4c discount

The first two pieces arrive safely on 16 April and 28 May respectively and payment is made. The third piece is found to be unsatisfactory and the buyer refuses to pay. The bank closes out the unutilised balance on 1 July when the spot rates were DG 4.22 – 4.23.

Assuming there is no extension or further forward contract what is the customer's total sterling outlay?

Question 9.7

On 11 January your customer High Tech PLC booked a Forward Option Contract for three months in respect of the proceeds of an Outward Bill for collection they were anticipating from Sweden. The amount involved is SK 500,000 and the booked rate was 11.32.

Unfortunately these proceeds have not yet been received and they require a further option for another two months. The proceeds arrive on 3 June.

Outline the procedure for extending the Contract by showing the amounts debited and credited to your customer's account, and state the rate of exchange for the extension.

11 April	SK 11.17 – 11.19
1 month forward	0.05 – 0.08 ore discount
2 months forward	0.09 – 0.12 ore discount
3 months forward	0.10 – 0.13 ore discount

Question 9.8

On 1 April a customer enquires as to the rates 1, 2, 3 and 6 months forward.

Spot	$1.3832 – 1.3850
1 month forward	1.15 – 1.06c pm
2 months forward	2.20 – 2.10c pm
3 months forward	3.55 – 3.40c pm
6 months forward	6.34 – 5.30c pm

At what rates would you sell him forward $ for 1, 2, 3 and 6 months; do you think he is an importer or exporter, give reasons for your answer.

Question 9.9

During January you advise your customer that an irrevocable credit expiring *30 April* has been opened in his favour to sell 1,000 tonnes of nickel to Italy at LIT 11 million per tonne CIF. On 1 February he requests you to open a credit expiring *31 March* in New York in favour of a seller in the USA to purchase the nickel at US $6,300 per tonne CIF. The terms of both credits state that shipment is to be on or after 1 March.

At the same time your customer asks you to cover him by forward contract for the US dollar and Italian lire transactions. Your quotations for these currencies are as follows:

	US Dollars	*Italian lire (LIT)*
Spot	1.3950 – 1.3960	2338½ – 2340½
1 month forward	1.15 – 1.05c pm	11 – 13 dis
2 months forward	1.30 – 1.20c pm	20 – 22 dis
3 months forward	1.90 – 1.82c pm	32 – 34 dis

Shipment is actually made on 14 March and the documents reach London on 19 March. These being in order, your customer's invoices are immediately substituted and the documents are forwarded to the Italian buyer.

What are the ultimate sterling amounts to be debited and credited to your customer's account?

Question 9.10

Your customers, Buy and Sell PLC, have contracted to buy machine tools from the USA at a cost of US $60,000. Half the goods are eventually sold to a German buyer for DM 125,000 and half to a French buyer for FF 250,000.

The contract to buy is arranged on 1 July, payment to be made on 30 September.

The contracts to sell are arranged as follows:

With Germany on 1 August, payment to be made on 31 October.
With France on 1 September, payment to be made on 30 September.

Buy and Sell cover all the foreign currency payments on the days the contracts are arranged: in the case of the French and USA contracts on an option basis: in the case of the DM contract on a fixed basis.

On the assumption that all payments are made and received on the right days and using the rates of exchange shown below, what are the sterling equivalents of the payments and receipts of Buy and Sell PLC?

	US$	*DM*	*FF*
1 July			
Spot	1.3235 – 1.3225	3.87 – 3.88	12.02 – 12.03
1 month forward	1.30 – 1.20c pm	4½ – 3½pf pm	10 – 15c dis
3 months forward	2.95 – 2.85c pm	10½ – 9½pf pm	17 – 22c dis
1 August			
Spot	1.3050 – 1.3070	3.80 – 3.81	12.00 – 12.01
1 month forward	1.50 – 1.40c.pm	5½ – 4½pf.pm	10 – 15c.dis
3 months forward	3.10 – 3.00c.pm	12 – 11pf.pm	17 – 22c.dis

1 September

Spot	1.3345 – 1.3365	3.90 – 3.91	11.99 – 12.00
1 month forward	1.10 – 1.00c pm	4½ – 3½pf pm	9 – 14c dis
3 months forward	2.60 – 2.50c pm	10 – 9pf pm	16 – 21c dis

Question 9.11

On 15 March a British merchant orders two machines from a West German factory at cif UK port prices of DM 105,000 and DM 104,466 respectively, for shipment within one month, on "30 days (from bill of lading date) open account" terms (i.e. shipping documents are sent to the British merchant, for him to remit thirty days after bill of lading date).

The British merchant at once covers the exchange forward.

The machine costing DM 105,000 is shipped on a bill of lading dated 12 April, but the UK merchant is advised that because of a fire at the West German factory shipment of the second machine will be between two weeks and a month later than arranged. On the maturity date of the forward exchange contract the UK merchant therefore arranges the appropriate extension of the unused balance, at the rates then ruling.

The second machine is eventually shipped on a bill of lading dated 16 May. No currency holdings permitted.

On the basis of exchange rates as under, calculate the total cost of the machines.

Rates	*15 March*	*15 May*
Spot	3.82½ – 3.83	3.83 – 3.83½
1 month forward (premium)	¾ – ½ pfg	½ – ¼ pfg
2 months forward (premium)	1½ – 1¼ pfg	1 – ¾ pfg
3 months forward (premium)	3 – 2¾ pfg	2¼ – 2 pfg

[IOB, April 1967 (amended)]

Question 9.12

On 1 January a London Merchant contracts to sell, for payment one month after shipment, 600 tons of rice to an importer in Holland at D.Fls. 360 per ton cif Rotterdam. Shipments are to be made as follows:

200 tons during January
400 tons during February.

The merchant immediately asks his bank to cover the exchange.

The first shipment is made on 14 January and the payment duly received. However the buyer complains that the quality of the rice shipped on 3 February is sub-standard and he refuses to pay the original price. After inspecting the goods, the London merchant quotes a reduced price of DFls 180 per ton cif Rotterdam, which the buyer accepts. Final payment is received on 25 March, when the balance of the forward contract is also "closed-out".

On the basis of the rates quoted below calculate the total sterling amount received by the London merchant.

1 January	4.65½ – 4.66
1 month forward	3 – 2½ cents premium

2 months forward	5½	– 5 cents premium
3 months forward	8½	– 8 cents premium
25 March	4.62	– 4.62½

[IOB, April 1969 (amended)]

Question 9.13

A British importer contracts to purchase from a French manufacturer 50 dozen pairs of ladies' fashion boots at a cost of Fr 1195.20 per dozen. Despatch is to be by air-freight in two separate consignments of 25 dozen pairs (one in January and one in February) and payment is to be made immediately upon receipt of telex advice of despatch. On 1 January, the importer requests his bank to cover him forward for these transactions.

Whilst the first consignment arrives safely and is paid for on 25 January, the second is delayed by industrial action, with the result that delivery cannot take place until some time in March. The importer arranges for his bank to extend the contract, and the goods are eventually despatched on 20 March. No currency holdings allowed.

On the basis of the rates quoted below calculate the total sterling amount paid by the importer.

	1 January	*1 March*
Spot	11.34½ – 11.35	11.35½ – 11.36
1 month	4½ – 3¾c prem	5 – 4¼c prem
2 months	6½ – 5¾c prem	7 – 6¼c prem
3 months	8½ – 7¾c prem	9 – 8¼c prem

[IOB, September 1971 (amended)]

Question 9.14

Your customer, Sandals Limited, has contracted to buy 500 dozen pairs of sandals from Brazil at a price of US $40 per dozen cif London Airport.

Payment is to be made on a cash against documents basis and deliveries are to be made in two lots of 250 dozen during October and November.

On 1 September Sandals Limited ask you to cover them forward for the relative payments. The documents for the first consignment are received and settlement made on 15 October. The documents for the second consignment are received and settlement made on 28 November.

As the goods are selling well and the customer wishes to catch the Christmas trade he arranges an urgent consignment of another 100 dozen for which the documents arrive on 3 December when Sandals Limited ask you to sell them the currency spot.

Using the rates below calculate the total sterling cost to the customer.

	US $	
1 September spot	1.3000	– 1.3010
1 month forward	0.50	– 0.40c.pm.
2 months forward	0.95	– 0.85c.pm.
3 months forward	1.47	– 1.37c.pm.
3 December spot	1.3190	– 1.3200

[IOB, September 1975 (amended)]

Question 9.15

On 1 November a UK exporter sells $300,000 worth of goods to a US buyer for delivery after two months but not later than three months. Payment is to be in dollars and on delivery. This turns out to be not earlier than the end of three months by which time the UK exporter discovers that his US buyer has gone out of business and will not pay. He then immediately finds a new US buyer who is to pay $250,000 but who wishes delivery at the end of two months with payment on delivery.

Calculate the UK exporter's net sterling receipts after allowing for forward contracts to cover all currency positions including an extension and a close-out.

1 November spot £1	= $1.3320	– 1.3330
1 month	Par	– 0.10c dis
2 months	0.10c dis	– 0.20c dis
3 months	0.20c pm	– 0.10c pm
1 February spot £1	= $1.3230	– 1.3240
1 month	0.40c pm	– 0.30c pm
2 months	Par	– 0.10c dis
3 months	0.20c.pm	– 0.10c pm

Question 9.16

A UK importer buys $200,000 worth of goods from a US supplier for delivery after one month but not later than three months. Payment is to be on delivery in dollars. At the end of three months he discovers that his US supplier has gone out of business and cannot supply. He then immediately obtains a new US source of supply for delivery within two months at $250,000 also for payment on delivery in dollars which he covers with a new forward contract. Assuming that he covers forward for the initial deal and is not prepared to hold currency, calculate his net sterling costs.

Initial rates £1	= $1.3418	– 1.3428
1 month	Par	– 0.10c dis
2 months	0.02c dis	– Par
3 months	0.05c	– 0.10c dis
Subsequent rates £1	= $1.3721	– 1.3731
1 month	0.27c	– 0.37c.dis.
2 months	0.61c	– 0.71c.dis.
3 months	0.97c	– 1.07c.dis.

Question 9.17

On 1 December 1983 a UK importer buys two months forward $100,000 to pay for goods to be supplied on 31 January, on which day he hears that his supplier is unable to honour the contract on time and he therefore cancels the commercial order.

As exchange control regulations no longer apply in the UK he now considers the possibility of holding the $100,000 for one month on deposit with a bank, as an alternative to closing-out.

He is constantly in an overdraft position on his sterling account and pays 3% over Base rate.

Given the rates below advise him whether it would be in his interest to hold his purchased dollars for one month bearing in mind that at no time is he prepared to run an exchange risk.

1 December spot £1	= 1.3170	– 1.3180
1 month	Par	– 0.10c dis
2 months	0.10c pm	– 0.08c pm
3 months	0.12c pm	– 0.02c pm
UK Base rate	= 11% per an. (365 day year)	
Euro-dollar rates	= 16½% per an. (360 day year).	
31 January spot £1	= 1.4230	– 1.4240
1 month	0.30c	– 0.40c dis

Question 9.18

Your customer expects to receive French francs 200,000 sometime in June and approaches you on 1 April as to the best method of bringing his expected receipts forward in time to the present. He wishes to know whether it would be better to borrow in the currency of his receipts or in the sterling equivalent, without taking a currency exposure.

Advise him, using the rates below.

Spot £1	= FF 11.76¾ – 11.77¾
1 month	3¼ – 4¼c dis
2 months	6 – 7c dis
3 months	12¼ – 13¼c dis

Interest rates — Sterling 12% per an. (365 day year)
Euro-francs 18% per an. (360 day year)

Question 9.19

The management of your bank has lent one million pounds to a local authority for one month fixed at 14% per annum and has requested the foreign exchange dealer to replace this money by borrowing the necessary foreign exchange for one month and selling it for sterling with forward cover.

Assuming one month is exactly one-twelfth of a year and disregarding all expenses, with the following rates which currency borrowing will yield the greater profit?

Spot rates	*One month forward*	*Interest rates*
$ 1.3255 – 1.3265	0.07 – 0.03c pm	12%
DM 3.8202 – 3.8302	2¼ pf – 2pf pm	5%
DG 4.305 – 4.315	2¼ – 1⅞c pm	6%

Calculate all interest at one-twelfth of the respective annual rates.

Question 9.20

A UK company's net profit position has improved significantely this year allowing it to repay its bank overdraft and leaving it with £100,000 net bank deposits on which it earns 6% per an. net of tax. This is likely to remain on deposit for up to the next three months, but there is some uncertainty about this because a new piece of machinery could arrive at any time which would mean that a large payment would have to be made.

The managing director, in discussions with his bank manager learns that 9% net of tax is available on US dollar deposits. Bearing in mind that he would only be prepared to switch half of his cash balance and only for up to three months, and using the rates below, advise him as to his best course of action.

Make the following assumptions:

(1) interest rates apply throughout any selected period;
(2) ignore bank charges;
(3) take one month to be one-twelfth of a year;
(4) deposits are withdrawable on demand;
(5) the company refuses to take a currency position.

Spot £1	= $1.4170	– 1.4180
1 month	Par	– 0.10c dis
2 months	0.06c	– 0.08c dis
3 months	0.12c	– 1.20c dis

Question 9.21

The Treasurer of a large UK multinational company is increasingly aware that with the suspension of exchange control regulations in the UK there are no longer any legal limits to the amount of foreign currency deposits his company may hold abroad.

As a result, on 1 November he scans the foreign exchange and money market columns of the Financial Times for data which he finds are as follows:

Spot	= US$2.4170	– 2.4190
1 month forward	Par	– 0.10c dis
2 months forward	0.05c.pm	– 0.05c dis
3 months forward	0.25c.pm	– 0.02c pm

Euro-currency interest rates

	£s	$s
For one month	16⅝ – 16½%	17 – 17¼
For two months	16½ – 16¾	17 – 17¼
For three months	16⅝ – 16⅞	16¹⁵⁄₁₆ – 17³⁄₁₆%

At the moment he finds that his company's US subsidiary is holding constant working balances of $2m while in the UK the parent company's working balances are £4m and stable over time. Both deposits attract the above interest rates.

The Treasurer is prepared to move one half of these working balances out of dollars and into sterling or vice versa and seeks your advice as to the likely profitability of so doing. Under no circumstances however, is he prepared to take any foreign exchange risks.

Ignore bank charges.

Calculate monthly interest rates at one-twelfth of annual rates.

Show your answers in both money values and in percentage terms relating to the cost of forward cover.

Question 9.22

Inter-Foods is an expanding UK food wholesaler who has suffered a decline in sales to domestic retail outlets and is considering the possibility of entering the West European markets for the first time.

Their managing director is in the process of completing negotiations to purchase a privately-owned wholesaling company in Milan for LIT 1,000 million. Completion is expected at the end of three months. The cost is to be met by running down existing sterling deposits which attract the rates below.

To pay for their purchase should Inter-Foods:

(a) Wait for three months and then buy spot lira?
(b) Buy spot lira now and hold for three months, selling the interest forward?
(c) Buy forward lira?

Quantify your answers by reference to the following rates:

Spot £1	= LIT 2305 – 2307
1 month	14½– 17½ lira dis.
2 months	26 – 29 lira dis.
3 months	44½– 47½ lira dis.

Three months interest rates:	Sterling	13$\frac{15}{16}$ – 14$\frac{7}{16}$% per an.
	Lira	20¾ – 21⅜% per an.

Ignore bank charges.

[City of London Polytechnic, June 1983]

Question 9.23

Inter-Food's first shipment is for £10,000 worth of goods on three months credit terms invoiced in lira and sold forward at the appropriate rate. The Milan subsidiary on-sells the goods to a Swiss buyer for LIT 30 million for cash against documents.

The Italian subsidiary holds a two month lira deposit account into which is put the receipts from Switzerland prior to remitting funds to the parent company. This attracts the rates shown below. Assume that as a result of the time it takes to ship the goods and to receive payment from Switzerland the end of the two month lira interest period coincides with the end of the three month Bill of Exchange. One half of the resulting interest yield on the Swiss payment, and one half of the subsidiary's gross trading profit are attributable to the UK parent.

Using the rates below calculate the lira invoice value of the goods shipped to Milan and the lira trading and interest profits accrued by the UK parent.

			Interest rates (per an.)	
Spot £1	= LIT 2056 – 2057	*Sterling*	1 month	16½ – 16¾%
1 month	8¾ – 10¾ dis		2 months	16 – 16¼%
2 months	16 – 19 dis		3 months	15¾ – 16%
3 months	42 – 45 dis	*Lira*	1 month	22½ – 24%
			2 months	23 – 24%
			3 months	24½ – 25½%

[City of London Polytechnic, June 1983]

Question 9.24

Bearing in mind the information in questions 9.22 and 9.23 and using the data in 9.23, when the remittance to the UK parent falls due, advise their managing director:

(a) whether they should allow the invoice value of the goods plus the interest and trading profit to be remitted as planned (the latter two being sold spot); or

(b) whether they should consider retaining their lire receipts for an additional one month and cover forward.

[City of London Polytechnic, June 1983]

Question 9.25

Calculate the net sterling receipts of a UK company that enters into foreign exchange transactions to avoid any exchange risks resulting from the following expected receipts and payments. At no time is it prepared to hold currency. Ignore all interest charges and bank commission.

Payments (debits)
(a) $200,000 on 1 September.
(b) FF 1,200,000 in two equal lots; the first on 1 September and the second three months later.
(c) $400,000 in two equal lots; the first on 1 October and the second five months later.

Receipts (credits)
(a) $300,000 on 1 September.
(b) $400,000 on 1 December.
(c) $250,000 on 1 March.

Rates on 1 September

Spot	£1 = $1.4625	– 1.4635	Spot $1 = FF8.2050	– 8.2110
1 month forward	0.08	– 0.13c dis	1.70	– 1.85c dis
3 months forward	0.20	– 0.25c dis	6.20	– 6.60c dis
6 months forward	0.42	– 0.47c dis	8.25	– 8.85c dis

[City of London Polytechnic, June 1984]

Question 9.26

Consider the special financial data a UK investor would need to take into account for a profitable, non-speculative short-term investment overseas.

[City of London Polytechnic, June 1984]

Question 9.27

What steps can a UK importer take when faced with a situation where the payment date may be anywhere between three and six months after taking delivery of his goods and where he is unwilling to accept the foreign exchange risk? Payment is in currency.

[City of London Polytechnic, June 1983]

Question 9.28

Consider the factors that an importer would have to take into account when faced with a choice between paying for his imports on delivery with a price discount, or paying three months after delivery without a price discount. Note that his bank account is in constant overdraft.

[City of London Polytechnic, June 1982]

Question 9.29

Outline the major factors affecting forward exchange rates.

[City of London Polytechnic, September 1983]

Question 9.30

Differentiate between covered interest arbitrage and speculation in the spot and forward foreign exchange markets. Illustrate your answer with reference to both traders and investors.

[City of London Polytechnic, June 1981]

Question 9.31

The suspension of exchange control regulations in the UK has increased the options open to contractors in the forward markets in the event that they face a close-out position. Specify clearly what these options are and examine the principles employed in determining their selection.

[City of London Polytechnic, June 1983]

Question 9.32

Examine the impact on short-term interest rates and forward rates for currencies of the activities of covered interest arbitrageurs. Are such activities the only factors that determine forward rates?

[City of London Polytechnic, September 1982]

Question 9.33

Interest rate parity theory holds that interest rate differentials will tend to be offset by the cost of forward cover. Outline the major principles of this theory and suggest why it may not apply in practice.

[City of London Polytechnic, June 1984]

Question 9.34

Your customers, Ancient Mariners Limited, are sterling based and are negotiating with a major UK contracting company to transport building equipment and materials to a remote island in the Indian ocean. Payment is secure and will be made in US dollars, the contract being worth US$900,000. To complete the deal successfully, they will need to charter the following vessels:

(a) one roll-on/roll-off vessel from the USA;
(b) one tug and landing barge, complete with derrick, from Holland;
(c) one general cargo vessel, of about 5,000 tons cargo weight from Singapore.

You know your customers will require bank finance and the directors call to see you to discuss the matter. Your enquiries reveal that Ancient Mariners Limited will obtain the contract subject to their agreeing to the following financial arrangements:

(i) Payment in respect of (a) above is to be $100,000 in all and is to be payable *to the US owners* upon the sailing of the vessel from the USA (the charter will be for one month from the date of the contract and sailing will take place immediately upon signing of the contract).
(ii) Payment in respect of (b) above is for a total of DM 300,000 payable *to the Dutch owners* in two equal lots. The first is to be made upon the sailing of the vessel, which will take place immediately the contract is signed, and the balance is to be paid three months later. (The total charter time will be exactly six months.)
(iii) Payment in respect of (c) above is for a total price of US dollars 500,000, payable *to*

the Singapore owners in two equal lots. The first payment is to be made one month after the signing of the contract and the second exactly six months after signing the contract.

(iv) Payment *from the main contractor* will be in three instalments as follows:

US$200,000 immediately upon signing the contract;
US$500,000 three months after signing the contract;
US$200,000 six months after signing the contract.

(a) Assume that the contract is awarded and signed on 1 June and the bank is willing to support the customer;
(b) Ignore commercial risks, such as chartering risks, weather and penalty clauses which might be included in the commercial contract;
(c) Ignore any charges or interest payable in connection with any overdrawings;
(d) Assume that the vessels sail on the same day as the contract is awarded, i.e. 1 June.

The rates applying on 1 June are as follows:

	£/US$	*US$/DM*
Spot	1.6100 – 1.6180	2.4096 – 2.4145
1 month	0.21 – 0.16c.pm	8.33 – 8.30pf.pm
2 months	0.38 – 0.33c.pm	8.55 – 8.25pf.pm
3 months	0.51 – 0.46c.pm	9.00 – 8.83pf.pm
6 months	0.66 – 0.61c.pm	13.03 – 12.95pf.pm

(1) What is the commercial business of your customer?

Answer . . . .

(2) Complete the following table concerning their use of other companies' property:

Type of property			
Country of origin			
Period of use (show dates)			
Non-£ cost			
Date of payment			

(3) Complete the following table concerning their receipts and payments, showing dates and values:

	Date	*Dollar value*	*Date*	*DM value*
Receipts due on				
Payments due on				

(4) Specify the forward exchange contracts called for in order to avoid the exchange risks, and calculate the net sterling receipts. Do this in date order.

(5) Complete the following table:

Date of Forward Contract	*Date of Contract Maturity*	*Contract Currency Value*	*Customer Buying or Selling*	*Exchange rate. Show whether $s or DMs*	*Sterling receipts or payments*
				Net £ receipts →	£

[Based on IOB question, September 1983]
(See question 9.39)

Question 9.35

Under an agreement with an associated company abroad, Byen and Cellin receive rough diamonds which are polished and then returned. The UK company initially pays for the goods, but at the same time receives an accepted bill due three months later in repayment which includes the cost of processing. The gross profit from the transaction is converted into sterling.

Your bank has agreed either to provide currency finance by way of a loan, or support for sterling finance for the period involved. The latter is made available by means of an acceptance credit, whereby a term currency bill for the amount due to the associated company is accepted by the bank, converted at the spot rate into sterling, and placed on the discount market. The sterling funds thus obtained are utilised towards the necessary purchase of the currency actually required to make the payment to the associated company. Discount charges are debited to the company's currency account, which is normally overdrawn.

Required

(a) Explain briefly what you understand by an acceptance credit in this context. What is its purpose?

(b) On the basis of the details set out below, show by calculations whether it would have been better for your customers to have obtained finance in currency or in sterling for a purchase amounting to $255,000 on 6 August. The amount of the bill received from their associated company is $290,000. Wherever possible exchange risks would be covered.

	Spot	*One month forward*	*Three months forward*
6 August	US$2.3545 – 2.3555	1.60 – 1.50c pm	3.57 – 3.47c pm
6 November	US$2.3425 – 2.3435	1.50 – 1.40c pm	3.45 – 3.35c pm

Interest rates on 6 August

Bank's US$ loan rate to customer for three months	12% pa
Bank's Sterling overdraft rate for the three months	18% pa

London Money Rates for Eligible Bank Bills on 6 August

One month	$16\frac{7}{16} - 16\frac{1}{2}$% per annum
Two months	$16\frac{1}{8} - 16\frac{3}{16}$ per annum
Three months	$15\frac{1}{2}$% per annum

Bank's acceptance commission 1% pa (debited on maturity of bill).

NB: for simplicity, in all cases calculations should be made on the basis that three months = one quarter of a year.

[IOB, April 1981]

Question 9.36

Your customers, Middletrust and Company, act as buying agents for a Government purchasing authority abroad and enter into various CIF contracts on their behalf.

One such transaction was as follows:

8 April

They receive an irrevocable, transferable documentary credit issued at the request of their principals in the following terms:

Amount: [Not to exceed US$1,699,500]

Goods: *3,000 tons* of Indian long grain rice maximum 10% brokens, packed in new strong single jute bags of 50 kgs net weight each, at *US$550* per ton CIF Utopia.

Shipment: *Middle of June*

Validity: For payment at the counters of your bank until 11 July with TT reimbursement to your nominated correspondent.

11 April

You are requested to transfer the credit as follows:

(A) To Letap and Company, Bombay *2,000* tons @ *US$500* per ton [not exceeding US$1,030,000].

(B) To Hahs and Company, Calcutta *1,000* tons @ *US$510* per ton [not exceeding US$25,300].

You subsequently receive the following advice on the dates stated:

30 June

(1) Documents in order have been presented in respect of 1,990 tons under transferred credit (A), for which your customer has already provided you with the necessary substitute invoices etc.

(2) The original credit has been extended to *30 August* to provide for shipment of *1,000 tons* at the *beginning of August*. (You are requested on the same day similarly to extend transferred credit (B)).

25 August

Documents in order have been presented in respect of 1,020 tons under transferred credit (B). Once again, the necessary substitute invoices, etc., have already been provided.

On the basis that payment in each case is made on the day that you are advised that documents are in order, (i.e. 30 June and 25 August respectively), calculate from the following information the gross profit in sterling to your customers, who habitually cover their exchange risks through the forward market in the most prudent way, i.e. initially on *11 April* they arranged two forward contracts to cover their estimated profit in respect of the *2,000* and *1,000* tons respectively.

	Spot	*One month*	*Two months*	*Three months*
11 April	2.3980 – 2.3990	1.10 – 1.20c dis	1.70 – 1.80 dis	2.15 – 2.25 dis
30 June	2.3330 – 2.3340	1.38 – 1.28c pm	2.40 – 2.30c pm	3.45 – 3.55c pm
25 August	2.3400 – 2.3410	45 – 55c dis	1.40 – 1.50 dis	2.30 – 2.40c dis

Notes

(i) Ignore all commissions and charges.
(ii) The items which require to be considered in answering this question have been printed in italic.

[IOB, September 1981]

Question 9.37

XYZ Limited, an export company customer of your bank, has sold goods to a buyer in the USA for $100,000, to be paid in exactly three months' time against an accepted bill of exchange. The finance director of the company wishes to know which of the following methods of financing the transaction would be the more profitable for the company (which normally operates on overdraft):

(a) borrow $100,000 now, convert the dollars immediately into sterling to provide working capital, and repay the borrowing from the dollar proceeds of the bill of exchange when it falls due;
(b) borrow sterling through the company's ECGD Bills and Notes Scheme and repay from the proceeds of the bill of exchange (due in three months' time) which is covered forward (fixed).

Required

Using the additional information given below, show by calculation which would be the more profitable method for your customer.

		Spot	*Three months' forward*
(i)	US dollar rates	$1.8950 – 1.9150	2.47 – 2.54c disc

(ii) US dollar three months' LIBOR rate is 17⅛% and for this important customer you would apply a margin of ¾%.
(iii) UK base rate is 12% for the whole period.
(iv) Three months can be regarded as exactly one quarter of a year.
(v) Interest in (a) is to be converted at the middle rate today of 1.905 (the correct rate would not be known at the time when the transaction was discussed with the customer, and this "middle" rate is used to give the customer an indication of the amount of interest to be charged when effecting transactions of this nature).

[IOB, April 1982]

Question 9.38

In early July, as the new manager of a branch, you call to see one of your corporate customers for the first time. He complains that he has received little help or advice from your predecessor concerning his payments and receipts in foreign currency. His business in this section is increasing, and you are asked for practical advice in connection with the following payments and receipts, including information on the protection available. The company normally has reasonable sterling credit balances but does swing into occasional overdraft.

Payments

1. US$100,000 by 30 September to Alnite Entertainments, Las Vegas.
2. Aus, $75,000 accepted bill in favour of Cobbers Pty Limited, Brisbane, due 15 November.
3. Swiss Francs 50,000 to Deutsche Suppliers GMBH, Hamburg re goods sent to Holland, due during July.

Receivables

4. US$250,000 due 15 July from Pigalle Shows SA, Paris.
5. Bank acceptance under a letter of credit for Aus. $55,000 for goods shipped to Irish Ashes Limited, Cork, due end of October.
6. Equivalent in Deutsche Marks of Swiss Francs 50,000, due end of June from Swiss Rolls Limited.

Required

(a) What immediate advice can you give your customer in connection with these payments/receipts?

(b) As the foreign business will grow, what further help/advice would you suggest that the bank should give?

[IOB, April 1982]

Question 9.39

Your customers, Ancient Mariners Limited, are sterling based and are negotiating with a major UK contracting company to transport building equipment and materials to a remote island in the Indian Ocean. Payment is secure and will be made in US dollars, the contract being worth US$900,000. To complete the deal successfully, they will need to charter the following vessels:

(a) one roll-on/roll-off vessel from the USA;
(b) one tug and landing barge, complete with derrick, from Holland;
(c) one general cargo vessel, of about 5,000 tons cargo weight from Singapore.

You know your customers will require bank finance and the directors call to see you to discuss the matter. Your enquiries reveal that Ancient Mariners Limited will obtain the contract subject to their agreeing to the following financial arrangements:

(i) Payment in respect of (a) above is to be $100,000 in all and is to be payable *to the US owners* upon the sailing of the vessel from the USA (the charter will be for one month from the date of the contract and sailing will take place immediately upon signing of the contract).
(ii) Payment in respect of (b) above is for a total of DM 300,000 payable *to the Dutch owners* in two equal lots. The first is to be made upon the sailing of the vessel, which will take place immediately the contract is signed, and the balance is to be paid three months later. (The total charter time will be exactly six months.)
(iii) Payment in respect of (c) above is for a total price of US dollars 500,000, payable *to the Singapore owners* in two equal lots. The first payment is to be made one month after the signing of the contract and the second exactly six months after signing the contract.
(iv) Payment *from the main contractor* will be in three instalments as follows:

US$200,000 immediately upon signing the contract;
US$500,000 three months after signing the contract;
US$200,000 six months after signing the contract.

(a) Assume that the contract is awarded and signed on 1 June and the bank is willing to support the customer;
(b) Ignore commercial risks, such as chartering risks, weather and penalty clauses which might be included in the commercial contract.
(c) Ignore any charges or interest payable in connection with any overdrawings.
(d) Assume that the vessels sail on the same day as the contract is awarded, i.e. 1 June.

The rates applying on 1 June are as follows:

	£/US$	*US$/DM*
Spot	1.6100 – 1.6180	2.4096 – 2.4145
1 month	0.21 – 0.16c.pm	8.33 – 8.30pf.pm
2 months	0.38 – 0.33c.pm	8.55 – 8.25pf.pm
3 months	0.51 – 0.46c.pm	9.00 – 8.83pf.pm
6 months	0.66 – 0.61c.pm	13.03 – 12.95pf.pm

Required

Your advice to the company covering the following points:

(a) the risks that the company will have to face in accepting and arranging the contract described above;
(b) how the bank can help to *minimise* those risks, indicating quite clearly the technical description of the risks;
(c) a statement of the currency account and a calculation of the total sterling receipts the company will have at the end of the contract period, assuming that they will sell forward any surplus dollars to the bank.

Notes

It was unfortunate that the examination paper contained a printing error in that the final rate quoted as part of the additional information should have been shown as a 6 months rate, whereas the question paper showed a 4 months rate. Comment will be made by the Chief Examiner in his Examiner's Report, but for the purpose of this answer it is taken as read that the correct figure was shown, namely that the final set of rates were in respect of a 6 months margin.

[IOB, September 1983]
(See also question 9.34)

Question 9.40

You agree to finance your customer who has just sold goods to the USA for $100,000 against a bill of exchange for that amount, payable in exactly three months' time. Calculate which of the following is the more profitable way of financing the transaction from the customer's point of view:

(a) to borrow US$100,000 at an interest rate of 5 per cent per annum with repayment from the proceeds of the bill of exchange. The borrowing is to be converted into sterling immediately at the current spot rate of exchange for US dollars and the interest will be debited to the customer's account in sterling when the loan is repaid;
(b) to borrow the sterling equivalent (at the middle rate of exchange) of US$100,000 under an ECGD bills and notes guarantee; repayment is to be made from the proceeds of the bill of exchange covered forward three months fixed.

The spot rates of exchange are	$2.4290 – 2.4360
3 months forward	1.90 – 1.80c pm

Base rate for the full period is 7 per cent.

Three months, for interest purposes, may be regarded as exactly one quarter of a year.

Assume that interest will be converted into sterling at a rate of $2.42. Collection and exchange commissions may be ignored as they are the same in both cases.

[IOB, April 1973]

Question 9.41

In early May you are asked to confirm an irrevocable letter of credit on behalf of a Japanese correspondent bank. The terms are briefly as follows:

In favour of:	Associated Noxious Distributors, London.
For account of:	Nippon Oriental Traders, Yokahama.
Expiring:	15 November 1982 in London.

Amount:	About Japanese Yen 43,000,000 (forty three million).
Covering:	About 1,000 metric tons of chemicals to be shipped in two approximately equal instalments, one during the first half of July and one during the first half of August.
Price:	Yen 43,000 per metric ton CIF Yokahama, shipment from UK port.

Drawings will be made as follows:

95 per cent of the value of a provisional invoice upon presentation of documents strictly in order.

The remaining 5 per cent will be available against final invoice accompanied by an independent weight and analysis certificate showing the final weight and chemical analysis.

On 25 May the beneficiary asks you to cover the forward receivables in the foreign exchange market, as follows:

(i) Arrange forward contracts immediately in respect of the value of each 500 metric ton shipment.
(ii) Upon presentation of documents close out any differences between the forward contract amounts and the actual values claimed.
(iii) Ignore forward cover for the balance to be claimed in October.

The documents were presented in order on the following dates:

15 July	Documents showing a shipment of exactly 490 metric tons.
10 August	Documents showing a shipment of exactly 526.316 metric tons.
31 October	Final invoice claiming an agreed figure of Japanese Yen 43,550.

Required

Using the following rates of exchange calculate the sterling sums your customer will receive on the appropriate presentation dates.

25 May	Spot	430.50	434.50
	1 month forward	2.50 prem.	2.00 prem.
	2 months forward	3.90 prem.	3.10 prem.
	3 months forward	6.75 prem.	6.25 prem.
	6 months forward	12.40 prem.	11.65 prem.
15 July	Spot	429.00	433.50
10 August	Spot	433.50	438.00
31 October	Spot	432.00	434.40

Notes

1. For the purpose of this question, the bank and the beneficiary assume that shipment and presentation of documents will be made on the same day.
2. Ignore letter of credit charges as these are for the buyer's account.
3. Ignore any close out figures of less than 100 Yen.

[IOB, September 1982]

Question 9.42

Your customers, Scrap Metals Limited, are scrap metal dealers exploiting the flourishing merchanting trade between the United States and the Far East. They buy scrap metal from the USA and sell it to buyers in the Republic of Korea, Republic of China (Taiwan) and Japan.

The American suppliers generally require secure methods of payment, and your customers have been able to arrange for the buyers in the Far East to establish in their favour (i.e. the first beneficiary — your customers) an irrevocable letter of credit, transferable in whole or in part, some of the terms of which are as follows:

Amount: *about* US$1,000,000.
Expiry: 10 July in London (i.e. at your counters).
Covering: a shipment of non-ferrous metal scrap to be effected in one lot between 1 May and 30 June inclusive.
Shipment: from San Francisco to Kaohsiung.

On 1 April, you, as the advising bank, are asked to transfer 75% of the value of the letter of credit in favour of a second beneficiary — the US Scrap Company Incorporated, San Francisco. On the same day your customers ask you to cover their potential earnings of US$250,000 forward, based upon the following rates:

1 April	Spot $1.7755	$1.7775
1 month forward	0.36 cents discount	0.41 cents discount
2 months forward	1.18 cents discount	1.23 cents discount
3 months forward	2.40 cents discount	2.45 cents discount
15 May	Spot 1.7950	1.8000

The documents are presented in order at your counters on 15 May. The documents cover a shipment valued at US$760,000 exactly. On that day your customers substitute their invoices to allow claims for the full value of the scrap metal shipped. In effect, they are increasing the value of their invoices by one-third of the value of the invoices presented by the second beneficiary. This claim brings it into line with the amount available under the letter of credit.

NB: For the purposes of this question, assume that the entries will be passed on the day that the documents are presented, namely, 15 May. Ignore the proceeds which will be made available to the second beneficiary in the USA and any commissions which might be claimed in connection with documents presented under the credit.

Required

(a) Your calculations showing the rates which would be applied, and a final figure of the sterling proceeds which will be credited to your customer's account.
(b) BRIEF notes indicating any specific international rules which apply to *this particular* transaction.

[IOB, April 1983]

Question 9.43

Your customers, South Sea Traders Limited, have exported their products to the South Seas and the Pacific coast of the United States for many years. Recently, they reached an agreement with their buyers in the United States which enables them to draw bills so that they fall due for payment 120 days after the shipment date. The documents are collected through your office. Because of restricted profit margins over the past few months and shortage of working capital, the customers call to see you on 30 March to seek your advice on how best they can *protect* their profit margins on immediate transaction and for future transactions. The bill amount specifically discussed is 100,000 US dollars, accepted by the buyer and falling due on 30 June. Past experience indicates that the buyer effects payment on the due date of the bills and so South Sea Traders do not have to worry about being out of funds for any length of time.

Additional information available on 30 March is as follows:

(i) US $ rates

Spot	$1.5180 – 1.5260	
1 month forward	Par	– 0.03c dis
2 months forward	0.05c	– 0.08c dis
3 months forward	0.09c	– 0.12c dis
4 months forward	0.20c	– 0.24c dis

(ii) UK base rate = 9.5%.
(iii) US three month LIBOR rate = 10.25%.
(iv) The customers are borrowing sterling from your office at 2% over the bank's rate and you have agreed with them that, in the event of their requesting foreign currency, you would charge them at the rate of 1½% over the US LIBOR rate.
(v) Your customers do not purchase goods for which they have to pay in foreign currency.

Required

(a) By what methods can your customers be protected from foreign exchange risks whilst preserving their profit margins?
(b) Outline any contractual obligation in respect of foreign exchange that your customers would have to undertake.
(c) Show by calculation the costs of each method proposed in answer to (a) above, and the sterling proceeds which each method would produce.
(d) Set out a formula which your customers would use to compare sterling and foreign currency borrowing costs, taking into account, where appropriate, the advantages or disadvantages of forward cover.

Notes

(i) Ignore all bank charges in respect of commission etc.
(ii) Base your calculation on a thirty day month and a 360 day year.

[IOB, April 1984]

Question 9.44

Tiger Moth Limited, customers of your bank, are a sterling-based aircraft charter company operating mainly in the UK, Western Europe and the Caribbean. They have been awarded a contract to provide freight and passenger services for a number of remote islands in the mid-Atlantic and the Caribbean.

The contract, which is guaranteed by the governments of the various territories, is to be signed on 1 June 1985. The value of the contract to the customer is US$1.5 million, and it will be necessary for Tiger Moth Ltd to charter three aircraft at a total cost of US$900,000. Payment and receipt terms are as follows:

Payments by Tiger Moth

(i) One third upon signing the contract.
(ii) One third six months after signing the contract.
(iii) One third twelve months after signing the contract.

Receipts by Tiger Moth

(i) One third ($500,000) three months after signing the contract (guaranteed).
(ii) One third ($500,000) six months after signing the contract (guaranteed).

(iii) A third payment of up to $500,000 (one third of the contract value) 12 months after signing the contract. (According to the contract this payment may be reduced if Tiger Moth generate extra business on their own account).

You customers ask you to make the best possible financial arrangements to obviate any risks to them.

US dollar rates on 1 June 1985 are as follows:

Spot	1.3195	1.3210
Three months	0.16c disc	0.21c disc
Six months	0.44c disc	0.72c disc
Twelve months	0.85c disc	1.05c disc
Spot 1 June 1986	1.4610	1.4670

Additional information and assumptions

1. The *full* expected *net* receipts are sold forward on 1 June, 1985 for delivery on 1 June, 1986.
2. For the purpose of this question, ignore the possibility of any other forward contracts which might be arranged.
3. The contract is performed in its entirety except that, when the third payment falls due on 1 June 1986, it is calculated that Tiger Moth Ltd has generated extra business on its own account which requires a reduction in the contract payment from US$500,000 to US$250,000. (The "extra earnings" should be ignore for the purpose of the calculations required in (c) below).
4. All commercial risks, such as chartering risks, credit risks etc. which may be included in the commercial contract, may be ignored.
5. Any charges or interest payable in connection with any overdraft or transfers may be ignored.

Required

The advice you would give to the company covering the following:

(a) The risk that the company has to face in accepting the contract which is awarded to them.
(b) The method that you would recommend to Tiger Moth Limited in order to minimise the risk mentioned in (a).
(c) A statement of the currency account you would operate on behalf of the customer, including a calculation at the end of the period showing the total sterling proceeds which would be credited to the customer's sterling account.

[IOB, April 1985]

Question 9.45

Wavy Navy is a British company producing high quality work boats which take approximately six months to build from date of order. In the past, the company has had a positive cash-flow and has not demanded payment for the vessels until the time of delivery. Sales have been confined to the United Kingdom and to the Federal Republic of Germany. Payment for the goods sold to Germany has been effected in Deutsche marks. Wavy Navy has produced some components in its own yard and purchased the balance from UK sources. Up to now, it has sold any surplus Deutsche marks for sterling.

Recently, a buyer of undoubted standing has made a positive enquiry for a number of vessels indicating that it would pay for them in sterling on delivery. However, this potential buyer is insisting that the engines, which would have to be fitted at a very early stage in construction, should be supplied from Scandinavia. The Scandinavian engine manufacturer requires payment in Deutsche marks but would grant Wavy Navy 90 days' credit terms.

Required

(a) Brief notes indicating the areas in which Wavy Navy is at risk if it agrees to deliver vessels to the potential buyer.
(b) Advice, in note form, on how these specific risks can be reduced.

Note

Ignore normal payment risks and concentrate on the specific risks mentioned in the question.

[IOB, April 1985]

Section 10

ECGD

Question 10.1

On 1 April a UK exporter ships £100,000 (FOB) worth of goods to a Swedish buyer against a 91 day Bill of Exchange payable in Swedish Krone which is covered forward to yield the necessary sterling; the krone price being agreed beforehand.

The UK exporter is insured with an ECGD Comprehensive (Shipments) policy which includes a Foreign Currency Contracts Endorsement. He also takes out a Bills and Notes Financial Guarantee which he uses to obtain shipment finance from his bank. His sterling bank account is in constant overdraft.

Questions

(a) Using the rates below, calculate his expected receipts in Krone if all goes well.
(b) If the Swedish importer fails to pay by the following 1 January;

  (i) What happens to the forward contract?
  (ii) When will the exporter be able to claim against his ECGD policy?
  (iii) What proportion of loss will ECGD indemnify and what additional loss will it cover?

(c) Calculate the exporter's net loss in sterling after costs and indemnification including interest charges on £100,000 for the period outside ECGD cover.

1 April	Spot £1 = Swedish Krone 8.96 – 8.97
	3 months forward 9 ore – 11 ore discount
1 July	Spot £1 = 9.04 – 9.05

Base rate at 1 April = 12%. Interest rates for periods outside ECGD cover is base rate + 4%. 3 months to be taken as ¼ of a year.

Bank charges are £40.

Comprehensive policy costs 40p per £100.

Bills and Notes guarantee costs 15p per £100.

Note: the exporter requires, and the bank agrees, for his advance to be rolled-over pending final ECGD payment.

[City of London Polytechnic 1981]

Question 10.2

A UK exporter who is currently financing most of his overseas sales by way of confirmed letters of credit is informed by his bank that future credits are unlikely to be confirmed by them. Explain the significance of this information and offer an analysis of the comparable alternative that ECGD may be prepared to provide.

[City of London Polytechnic, June 1984]

Question 10.3

A UK exporter is in receipt of an Unconfirmed Irrevocable Negotiations Documentary Letter of Credit for French francs 500,000 calling for a 3 month term draft Bill of Exchange to be drawn on a buyer in Gabon. Negotiation is to be in sterling at the appropriate forward rate on presentation of documents. The exporter has an ECGD Comprehensive (Shipments) policy covering all his export business, but no ECGD Bills and Notes Guarantee.

The goods were shipped and documents presented on 1 June and the negotiation was effected. However, on 30 August the exporter learns that due to Balance of Payments problems in Gabon the authorities there have issued a general moratorium on all external debit with immediate effect and on the next day the Advising Bank receives a telex message from the Issuing Bank regretting its inability to transmit funds on the due date. The moratorium is eventually lifted on 26 January and funds remitted on 1 February and converted at spot.

Questions

(a) Is the exporter assured of a non-recourse finance under the terms of the Credit? Substantiate your answer.
(b) Will there be a need to utilize the ECGD policy?
(c) Does the exporter have a valid claim on ECGD?
(d) If so, when is the claim to be met and what is its value?
(e) Assuming that the Advising Bank agrees to a bridging overdraft facility which is for the full value of the expected sterling receipts and is withdrawn as and when all or, most of the value is received, calculate the exporter's net sterling receipts.

Ignore bank charges and ECGD premiums.

Bank interest is to be debited at 18% per annum.

One month to be taken as 1/12 of a year.

1 June	*1 February*	*1 September*
Spot £1 = FF 11.02 – 11.03 3 months forward 6 – 8c dis	Spot £1 = FF 10.98 – 10.99	Spot £1 = FF 10.97 – 10.98

Question 10.4

A UK exporter asks his bank to supply him with details of their Small Exporter's Credit Insurance Scheme which are as follows:

(i) Maximum export turnover £500,000 per annum.

(ii) Maximum individual export transaction £30,000.
(iii) No existing ECGD cover.
(iv) Exporter's credit rating to be vetted.
(v) Exporter must present either bills of exchange or promissory notes.
(vi) Maximum of 6 months credit for buyer.
(vii) Exporter must complete his export contract satisfactorily.
(viii) Details of buyer required by the bank.
(ix) On shipment, bills or notes are presented and the bank pays 90% of face value, less interest and charges.
(x) The remaining 10% is paid on maturity of the bill or note.
(xi) Interest is at 1½% over bank base rate and is for the period of the credit plus 20 days for transmission delays. Base Rate is 14% per annum.
(xii) A charge of 1% (minimum £10) of the value of the bill or note is made to cover the bank's own ECGD premiums and handling charges.
(xiii) Sight or unaccepted term bills are *with recourse* until they have been paid. Promissory notes are *without recourse*.

The UK exporter's average turnover for the past 3 years have been about £300,000 per annum and no individual transaction has been for more than £15,000. He has no existing ECGD cover.

To help him decide whether to take advantage of their scheme or, alternatively, to take out ECGD cover direct, the exporter attempts to calculate his costs and benefits with reference to the following single transaction:

A 60 day draft bill of exchange for FF120,000 drawn on an overseas French buyer with the expected proceeds sold forward.

Required

(a) calculation to show the costs to the exporter of the Small Exporter's Credit Insurance Scheme and the equivalent costs of direct ECGD cover using data supplied above and also below,
(b) a comparison of the benefits each method provides.

Rates Spot £1 = FF 11.66½ – 11.67½
2 months ½ pm – ¾ dis.

ECGD Insurance premiums

Comprehensive Cover @ 40p per £100.
Bills and Notes Guarantee @ 30p per £100.

Question 10.5

Plant and Machinery who are exporters of capital goods to all countries in Europe, and who up till now have not been required to grant more than 18 months credit, are now being requested to offer extended terms of up to 5 years without any support from the buyer's bank.

Required

Summarise the ECGD scheme under which your bank might provide finance to the exporter. In doing so, explain the position of the relative parties, i.e. exporter, ECGD, the bank.

[IOB, April 1981]

Question 10.6

Your customers, E.X. Porter Ltd. sell their light industrial products outside Europe through the agency of associated companies abroad who look after their interests entirely in the countries concerned. Each consignment is for a relatively large amount. Their terms are either 30 days net receipt of goods, or 45 days sight D/A bills, the credit period in the latter case approximating to the estimated time for the goods to arrive at their destination.

Your bank has been asked to provide finance for these exports, in respect of which it is looking for maximum security in addition to that which can be provided directly by the customers themselves. State what support might be available in such circumstances, how it is obtained, and how the facility/facilities operate.

[IOB, September 1981]

Question 10.7

Your customer, International Traders Limited, is a holding company for a number of trading companies engaged in direct exports and imports and in the merchanting trade. The group, which has ECGD cover, including the bank guarantee schemes, is anxious, for balance sheet purposes, to minimise its liability exposure in connection with finance for its exports. It has been asked to quote for a number of export contracts, each valued at several million pounds and requiring medium-to long-term finance.

Explain how such finance might be arranged by the bank at special fixed interest rates to meet the group's requirements. Set out the salient features of this type of financing.

Note: Ignore non-banking sources such as confirming houses or export financing houses.

[IOB, April 1982]

Question 10.8

Following a trade mission to the south east corner of the United States, your customers, Sellers Limited, have for the first time entered into serious negotiations with a buyer in that country for a large export order. It is a buyers' market, and Sellers Limited have been advised that the following payment terms are the best that they can obtain at the present time:

Payment to be effected in US dollars against 120 days sight draft D/A — terms of shipment CIF Charleston.

Required

The financial director asks you to explain the four aspects of the terms of payment specified below. Set out *brief notes* covering the answers you would give.

(a) the meaning of the payment terms offered;
(b) the credit risk for the company in accepting this method of payment;
(c) your suggestions to lessen any or all of the credit risk;
(d) ways in which the customer can guard against exchange risk.

[IOB, September 1982]

Question 10.9

The OK Company Limited, which has been trading for some five years, is well managed, but is short of working capital. The managing director, who is also responsible for financial matters, comes to see you to discuss various methods of obtaining finance to cover new export contracts (goods are sold on 90 day bill terms). The company has recently taken out an ECGD Comprehensive Policy.

As the manager of your bank, you do not wish to extend the company's facilities any further without a completely reliable guarantee from an independent body. You explain the bank's position and outline a source of finance which might be available through the bank, as well as other sources of non-bank finance which might be available and which should satisfy your customer's needs.

Required

Brief notes on each of the schemes discussed showing their salient features.

[IOB, September 1982]

Question 10.10

Your customers, major suppliers of power generating equipment, are negotiating large contracts on near-cash terms in the USA and Middle East which will involve them in erection and commissioning on site.

(a) What support, other than direct financial support, can your bank give in connection with this type of business?
(b) Is there any UK government-backed support also available?

Tabulate your answers in brief note form.

[IOB, September 1982]

Question 10.11

Your customers, Capital Plant Limited, have been able to sell their goods without any need to resort to the facilities offered by long-term credit agencies. They have normally been paid by letter of credit within 18 months to 2 years of shipment. They have now been asked to quote for a contract which would require them to ship goods to a country which is insisting upon credit terms in excess of 2 years. It is understood that the extended terms required will not have the support of the buyer's bank. Your bank might provide finance to the exporter, providing there is backing under an appropriate ECGD scheme.

Required

A brief summary of the appropriate ECGD scheme with an explanation of the position of the relative parties, i.e. the bank, ECGD and the exporter customer.

[IOB, April 1983]

Question 10.12

Your customers, X Port Limited, have developed a large export market in various countries for their consumer goods. The terms of sale call for 120 days' credit and, owing to difficult trading conditions, the customers are in danger of becoming short of working capital. You meet the financial director to discuss the various facilities which are available to the customers to enable them to overcome their shortage of working capital.

Required

Your brief reference notes which you will make for record purposes following these discussions with your customers.

[IOB, April 1983]

Question 10.13

The finance director of your customers, Sleep Well Limited, calls to see you to discuss a developing export trade selling the company's night attire range. During your discussions you learn that the company has been successful in obtaining orders from two very large American chain stores. Payment is to be made against presentation of 30 days sight bills of exchange. The finance director has already contacted ECGD and the company has taken out an ECGD comprehensive short-term guarantee policy.

Sleep Well Limited are already operating on overdraft and the financial director asks whether, as cashflow problems may arise in the future, you would consider providing finance for the exports *against the protection of the ECGD guarantee (policy) itself.*

Required

A brief explanation of:

(a) (i) the various methods whereby this might be done;
(ii) the risks which the bank will face if it relies wholly on the security offered;
(iii) why 100 per cent advances will not be available.

(b) Any additional security which might be available to the bank which would make its assistance more likely. Outline the steps that the bank and the customers may have to take and indicate any advantages accruing to the customer.

[IOB, September 1983]

Question 10.14

Capital Products Limited are manufacturers of large capital plant and are now seeking orders in a number of overseas markets. Their business is capital intensive and they seek your guidance on the support available to them other than direct financial assistance, either from your bank or by way of government-backed assistance, that will help them to compete successfully for these contracts.

Required

Tabulate details of:

(a) the bank services which you believe would help the company to expand in the markets mentioned above;
(b) any government schemes which are complementary to those services.

[IOB, April 1984]

Question 10.15

A Shrimpton Limited have successfully traded for many years selling sea foods, both fresh and frozen, to many parts of Western Europe. Competition is fierce and they have, therefore, been forced to sell on 30 days sight D/A bills of exchange. Recently, many of these payments have been 30 to 40 days later than expected and this has had an adverse effect on the company's cash flow. Very few bad debts have occurred and reports on the buyers are encouraging. As Shrimpton's bank manager, you are asked to provide further lending to the company for whom you provide other banking facilities. You would be willing to provide further finance but would require security additional to that which is already provided by the company and the directors. You wish the bank to be fully secured.

Tom Shrimpton, the export sales director, calls to see you to discuss what facilities the bank can arrange which will help them to continue selling overseas on bills of exchange. The company have an ECGD shorter-term guarantee.

Required

Brief notes on a single package which ALL UK banks can provide which will assist A Shrimpton Limited in the circumstances described.

[IOB, April 1985]

Section 11

Traveller's Finance and Inter-Bank Settlements

Question 11.1

Outline the particular role of London in the Euro-currency system and comment on the special risks it faces in this respect.

[City of London Polytechnic, September 1982]

Question 11.2

Detail the various inter-bank transactions received when customers wish to remit funds overseas as follows:

(a) in domestic currency,
(b) in the currency of the overseas recipient,
(c) in a third currency.

Note the currency impact of these transactions on the banks concerned and specify what consequential steps, if any, they may wish to take.

[City of London Polytechnic, June 1984]

Question 11.3

Amongst Plant and Machinery's recent acquisitions is a small company whose payment terms are "cash with order". This has resulted in a large number of cheques, drawn in sterling by buyers in Europe, and in dollars from others in the USA, being paid into your bank for collection.

Required

(a) Detail the various steps taken by banks in both cases, whereby funds are eventually received for the sterling account of the company.
(b) The parent company has expressed concern as to the cost and delay involved in obtaining these funds and seeks your advice. It is understood that whilst it might be possible to persuade customers in Europe to adopt other methods, any attempt to

make a complete change in the USA would seriously affect the business. Their buyers in the USA insist on sending the actual payments in dollars with orders and in a few cases would not be prepared for any alteration whatsoever.

What advice would you give the parent company regarding payments by customers, with a view to reducing cost and delay in the availability of funds:

(i) in Europe;
(ii) in the USA?

State any possible disadvantages for your customers which your suggestions in relation to (ii) might involve.

[IOB, April 1981]

Question 11.4

Using FOUR main headings, describe briefly the role played by banks in the field of international trade. Under each heading show concisely the relevant services normally provided by UK banks giving examples where necessary. Lengthy explanations and detailed examples are not required.

[IOB, April 1981]

Question 11.5

(a) Explain what is to be understood by the T.T. reimbursement referred to in the general introduction to question 9.36.
(b) Without mentioning any actual passing of entries, outline the three basic actions which would be taken by your bank on receipt of advice that documents had been negotiated abroad whereby arrangements would be made for appropriate payment to be received both by the overseas negotiating bank and your own customer in repect of transferred credit (A) mentioned in the general introduction:

i.e. \$995,000 to the Indian bank
\$ 99,500 to your customer.

Note: the three banks involved — the issuing bank, the negotiating bank in India, and yourselves — all hold accounts in New York, each with a different bank.

(c) Explain briefly what you understand by Nostro and Vostro accounts. Which of these two types of accounts would you be using for your records of the transaction described in the general introduction. Detail the entries which would appear over such an account in your own books and those of your correspondent bank as regards transferred credit (A).

[IOB, September 1981]

Question 11.6

"Today, as more and more people travel outside their own countries, there is much to be said for payment services which remove the need for travellers to carry large amounts of local currency."

Describe the four major facilities now available in Europe and state, very briefly, how they operate.

[IOB, September 1981]

Question 11.7

State what advice you would give or, where appropriate, what action you would take to help your bank's customers in the following circumstances:

(a) Customer A wishes to send a birthday gift of £20 to his nephew who lives abroad and will be staying somewhere in Zurich during the next month. Unfortunately, the only means of reaching the nephew is through a forwarding address in France. [No reference to use of accounts is required.]

i(b) Customer B has received a payment of £50,000 which he does not need to utilise until he must himself make payment of US$110.250 — in three months' time.

Note: Give two alternative proposals.

(c) You have been advised of the arrival at London Airport of goods consigned to yourselves for the account of a valued customer. No instructions have so far been received from abroad, but your customer, who produces a pro-forma invoice, requests immediate release of the goods to avoid high demurrage charges.

(d) Your customer's buyer in France is readily accepting bills drawn on him at 90 days sight, but payment is usually not made until some time after the due date. Although he could insist on a documentary credit being opened, your customer does not wish to do this, and asks if there is some additional condition which might be introduced into the present acceptance arrangement to provide a guarantee for payment on the due date.

[IOB, September 1981]

Question 11.8

As manager of the local branch of your bank you have been invited to speak at a combined meeting of the Small Business Club and the Export Club. Your subject is: "What advice and practical help can a bank give to the small business which is seeking new export markets or endeavouring to enter the export field for the first time?"

Prepare brief notes covering the points you would make.

[IOB, April 1982]

Question 11.9

Mr. & Mrs. Snowy White, who are very good customers of yours, call to see you as a matter of urgency. They ask what support, advice and action you can provide in the circumstances described below:

(1) Their daughter, who is abroad on holiday in Greece, requires funds immediately.

(2) Within the next few weeks Mr. & Mrs. White plan to fly to the Canary Islands on holiday and, whilst they are there, to look for a suitable second home. They wish to know:

   (a) the travel facilities you can arrange to cover their expenses whilst in the Canary Island;

   (b) what help and advice you can give in connection with finding and purchasing suitable property.

Required

Set out in brief note form the action you would recommend in both cases and include the office procedures and accounting entries which would be involved under (1).

[IOB, April 1982]

Question 11.10

Your customers, European Consortium Limited, wish to establish a manufacturing and trading enterprise in Holland to service their EEC and Scandinavian needs. During a visit to their office you discuss with their finance director various methods of raising short-medium and long-term finance for their operations in Holland.

Required

Brief notes explaining the various methods of obtaining finance, other than sterling, which will satisfy your customers' needs.

[IOB, September 1982]

Question 11.11

Your customers, XYZ plc, who have only a sterling account with you, have to pay US$50,000 to the Italian Transport Company in Genoa. They seek your assistance.

Required

Brief notes describing;

(a) instructions you will need to receive from the customer;
(b) the methods by which a remittance may be made and also the accounting procedures necessary for each method described.

[IOB, September 1982]

Question 11.12

Your customer, James Jones, has been sent by his company, an international oil corporation, to work in Stavanger for six months on a special assignment. His salary will continue to be paid in the United Kingdom in sterling and he asks for your advice as to the best way of drawing money in Stavanger to meet his living expenses in Norway.

Required

(a) A list of suggestions *appropriate to his needs.*
(b) Brief notes on the advantages and disadvantages of each method.

[IOB, September 1982]

Question 11.13

You call to see I.M.A. Bowler, a keen cricket fan and an esteemed personal customer. He is going to the West Indies for a two month tour to watch the forthcoming Test series and wishes to know what facilities you can arrange for him so that he will have ready access to funds, appropriate to his needs, for his expenses in the West Indies.

Required

Brief notes setting out your recommendations.

[IOB, April 1983]

Question 11.14

Runway Renovators Limited, customers of yours, have recently been awarded a contract to repair and rebuild runways at Hong Kong International Airport. This is the first international contract they have been awarded and you are advised that payment is to be made to them in sterling. Although local subcontractors will be employed, your customers will have to send out a team of qualified people to supervise and control the operation, which is likely to take some 18 months to complete.

You are approached by the company to discuss all the financial aspects of the contract. Arising out of the discussions, the company ask you the various methods by which they could pay, in local currency, part of the salaries of the expatriate staff in Hong Kong during their stay in the colony. In addition to the salary arrangments, the company will have to make available, to its senior representatives in Hong Kong, funds to cover company expenses.

Required

Your recommendations regarding:

(a) the provision of appropriate travel facilities for the company representatives at the start of the project;
(b) the payment in local currency of part of salaries of expatriate staff during their stay in Hong Kong;
(c) the provision of adequate day-to-day funds for the company's senior representatives for expenses/disbursements during the 18 months, indicating any disadvantages that there may be to the company in your suggestion.

[IOB, September 1983]

Question 11.15

Ice Cream Components Limited are a small manufacturing company which has developed a good business locally. Owing to stiff competition in the United Kingdom, they are seeking new markets overseas and their aim is to obtain substantial export sales. Their preliminary market research has shown that they might be successful in setting up a marketing enterprise in Iceland. The costs are estimated to be in the region of £250,000.

The company have asked you to visit them and, during your visit, you are asked to outline the various methods of non-bank finance which might be available to ICC Limited, to enable them to break into their new overseas market.

Required

Brief details of the scheme available to small and medium-size companies in the circumstances described above.

[IOB, September 1983]

Question 11.16

Bright Sparks Limited are buyers and sellers of electrical goods and components. They have successfully competed for a contract to sell goods to an American electronics company based in Atlanta. Many of the goods will be manufactured in the UK but because of the complexity of the contract, a number of components will have to be imported from Germany and Norway for processing in the UK.

As the company have not imported goods before, they need to know the meaning of the following terms quoted to them:

Germany Terms CIF UK Airport.

Payment in Deutsche Marks by SWIFT to a nominated bank in Dusseldorf

10 days after the shipment of goods from Germany to the United Kingdom.

Norway — Terms FOB Oslo Airport.

Payment in Sterling by TT to a named bank in Oslo within five days of the shipment of goods from Oslo airport to the United Kingdom.

Required

A brief explanation of:

(a) the terms of shipment mentioned above and the respective responsibilities of buyer and seller;
(b) the terms "SWIFT" and "TT" and how these methods of payment operate.

[IOB, September 1983]

Question 11.17

Your customers, By-Overseas Limited, have traded for a number of years with suppliers in many parts of the western world and the far east. They have always paid for their imports by means of sterling drafts issued by your bank. The company's competitors in the UK appear to be offering quicker payment terms to the overseas suppliers and your customers now seek your advice as to how they can arrange quicker methods of payment. The only concern of the suppliers in the various countries is the delay they experience in clearing the sterling drafts which have been sent to them.

Required

A brief statement of the alternative methods of settlement which are available and which would satisfy the overseas suppliers. Outline the salient features of these methods, including the accounting procedures involved.

If the new methods were adopted, what difference would it make to your customers if foreign currency were used instead of sterling?

[IOB, April 1984]

Question 11.18

Every year Arthur Rose, a gardener of some standing, organises party visits to many gardens throughout the world. This years he is organising a number of visits to gardens in the United States and, as in the past, each member of the party will pay for his hotel and travelling costs through Mr Rose's company, Hybrid Tea Limited. Mr Rose now approaches you to make a series of payments in US dollars to various beneficiaries in the USA. In addition, Mr Rose wishes to discuss the provision of suitable funds during his forthcoming visit.

Required

(a) A brief description of the following:
    (i) The system by which you would arrange to remit funds to the US.
    (ii) The appropriate accounting procedures employed.
(b) Giving reasons, tabulate the travel facilities that you would recommend that Mr Rose take with him on this tour to cover his expenses, limiting your answer to the facilities which are *appropriate to his needs*.

[IOB, April 1985]

Section 12

Monetary and Financial Background

Question 12.1

What factors would a bank specify in answer to a customer's query concerning the pros and cons of invoicing and being invoiced in currency?

[City of London Polytechnic, June 1984]

Question 112.2

Given the rates below, and after making the necessary cross-rate calculations, calculate the expected and actual receipts of a UK exporter and the corresponding payments of a German importer of the sale of £10m worth of goods by the former to the latter in the following cases:

(i) where the UK exporter invoices in sterling,
(ii) where the UK exporter invoices in D. Marks at the current spot rate,
(iii) where the UK exporter invoices in US dollars at the current spot rate,
(iv) where the UK exporter invoices in SDRs at the current spot rate but where payment is to be in the D. Mark equivalent of the SDRs.

Current spot rates	*Rates when payment falls due*
SDR1 = $1.22834	SDR1 = $1.05670
= £0.61005	= £0.73433
= DM 2.6245	= DM 2.7955

Note: all *expected* receipts and payments are to be calculated at the current spot rates and all *actual* receipts and payments at the rates shown as "rates when payment falls due".

Also, comment on the actual compared to the expected receipts and payments, saying why they differ.

Question 12.3

Consider the developments that have led to the use of Special Drawing Rights (SDRs) as a denominator of commercial bank deposits. What problems still remain?

[City of London Polytechnic, June 1984]

Question 12.4

At various times there have been suggestions that the UK should join the European Monetary Systems (EMS). However, the British government so far has been content to allow sterling to float.

Explain what you understand by:

(i) the EMS, outlining its salient features;
(ii) allowing sterling to float.

[IOB, April 1981]

Question 12.5

What is the relationship between an appreciation of a European Community member's currency against other members' currencies and the payment of Monetary Compensation Amounts in connection with the "green" rates of the Communities Common Agricultural Policy?

[City of London Polytechnic, June 1981]

Question 12.6

Calculate the D. Mark value of ECU1 derived from the following cross-rates and using the basket currency amounts (shown in the text book).

D. Mark 1	= French francs	3.07253
D. Mark 1	= Sterling	0.26330
D. Mark 1	= Dutch guilders	1.12950
D. Mark 1	= Italian lire	615.1700
D. Mark 1	= Belgian francs	20.2570
D. Mark 1	= Danish krone	3.65610
D. Mark 1	= Irish punts	0.32530
D. Mark 1	= Luxembourg francs	20.2570

Question 12.7

"The IMF does not enter into contractual engagements with banks on any form of conjoint or parallel financing, does not participate in tripartite negotiations with a member and banks, and does not make representations to banks in connection with their lending." Sir Joseph Gold, senior consultant to the IMF.

In the light of this statement consider what use, if any, commercial banks can make of IMF facilities, to limit risk in connection with their loans to IMF members.

[City of London Polytechnic, June 1984]

Question 12.8

The International Monetary Fund (IMF) refers to its members as debtors and creditors depending on whether purchases or repurchases are made. In what sense can a purchasing member be said to be in debt?

[City of London Polytechnic, June 1984]

Question 12.9

Table 12.9

Total Quotas – SDR 61059.8m

IMF Drawings

Member	USA	UK	W. GERMANY	"OTHER"	INDIA	"OTHER"
Currency	Convertible	Convertible	Convertible	Convertible	Inconvertible	Inconvertible
Quota	SDR 12607.5m	SDR 4387.5m	SDR 3234.0m	SDR 20,000m	SDR 1717.5m	SDR 19113.3m
(a) Reserve currency sub. = of which:	SDR DMs.40% £s.10%	SDR $s 100%	SDR $s 100%	SDR $s 100%	SDR $s 100%	SDR $s 100%
(b) Dom currency sub. =	SDR	SDR	SDR	SDR	SDR	SDR
(c) Total IMF Holdings in =	US $s SDR	£s = SDR	DMS = SDR	"Other" Convertible = SDR	Rupees = SDR	"Other" Inconvertible = SDR
(d) Above as a % of country quota	%	%	%	%	%	%
(e) India and other inconvertible currency members draw as shown in their section	—	—	—	—	India draws: Convertible currencies to bring IMF holdings of Rupees to 200% of India's quota US $s 60% DMs 10% "Others" 30%	"Others" draw: Convertible currency drawings to bring "other" currencies held by IMF to 200% of "other" quotas US $ 65% DMs 10% £s 5% "Others" 20%
(f) Total IMF holdings of the respective currencies as a % of the quotas =	US $s %	£s %	DMs %	"Other" Convertible %	Rupees %	"Other" Inconvertible %
(g) USA now draws up to her Reserve Tranche level in "other" Convertible currencies	USA drawings are in "Other" convertible currencies					
(h) Total IMF holdings of the respective currencies as a % of the quotas	US $s %	£s %	DMs %	"Other" Convertible %	Rupees %	"Other" Inconvertible %

Question 12.9

Complete the spaces in Table 12.9 as follows:

(a) Indicate the reserve currency subscription of all the parties (measured in SDRs).
(b) Indicate the domestic currency subscriptions of all the parties (measured in SDRs).
(c) Show total IMF holdings of the various members currencies (measured in SDRs) after taking into account the currency subscriptions of members (a).
(d) Show (c) as a percentage of each party's quota.
(f) Show total IMF holdings of the members' currencies (measured in SDRs) as a percentage of their quotas after allowing for the drawings indicated in (e).
(h) Show total IMF holdings of the members' currencies (measured in SDRs) as a percentage of their quotas after allowing for the USA drawing shown in (f) in addition to the drawings shown in (e).

Question 12.10

The International Monetary Fund, the World Bank and the International Development Agency, and the Euro-market all channel finance from capital intensive to capital scarce places, yet their functions are specialized but complementary. Briefly examine their principal functions and show their degree of complementarity.

[City of London Polytechnic, June 1981]

Question 12.11

"A country's Balance of Payments deficit can only be adjusted by a currency depreciation if the price elasticities of demand are right." Comment on this statement.

[City of London Polytechnic, September 1982]

Question 12.12

Your customers, Europe Forever Limited, call to see you to discuss the renewal of their existing facilities for the coming twelve months. As a large import/export organisation, they are always interested in movements of foreign currency. Among the subjects they raised during your discussions is the rise in the use of European Currency Units (ECU). They are interested in this type of currency and also want to discuss the use of currency certificates of deposit and euro-bond issues, both of which they think might be expressed in ECUs.

Required

A brief explanation for your customers of the salient features of:

(a) an ECU and the reasons for its rise in popularity over recent years;
(b) a currency certificate of deposit; and
(c) a Eurobond.

IOB, April 1984]

Section 1

Answers

Answer 1.1

Price of imported good		£100.00
10% duty		10.00
Total price		£110.00
Price of domestic good		
D.A.V.	(V) (38.83%)	£ 40.00
Import content	(i) (58.25%)	£ 60.00
Tariff on import content @ 5%	(M) (2.92%)	3.00
Total price	(100%)	£103.00

(Note: to find money values, calculate the 5% of £60 = £3, and add this to the £60; add the residual of £40 to give £103).

Each value is then found as a percent of the total.

The NOMINAL tariff is £10; as a percentage of £103.00

$= 9.7\%. \quad \left(\frac{10}{103} \times 100\right)$

The EFFECTIVE tariff is £10 − £3 = £7 as a percentage of £40

$= 17.5\%. \quad \left(\frac{7}{40} \times 100\right)$

$$\text{or e} = \frac{9.7\% - 0.05(58.25\%)}{38.83\%} = 17.5\%.$$

(Note: some roundings make the calculated figure 17.4%)

Answer 1.2

(a)

Price of imported raincoat		£40.00
25% *ad valorem* tariff		£10.00
Total price		£50.00
Price of UK raincoat (£58.00)		
Import content		
Canvas and linens, etc	= 17.24%	£10.00
Zips, buttons, etc	= 24.14% (i)	£14.00
25% tariff on above	= 6.03% (M)	£ 3.50
D.A.V.	= 52.59% (V)	£30.00
Total price		£58.00

NOMINAL tariff = £10 as a percent of £58 = 17.24%.
EFFECTIVE tariff = £10 − £3.50 = £6.50; as a percent of £30.50 = 21.31%.

$$\text{or } e = \frac{17.24\% - 0.25(24.14\%)}{52.59\%} = 21.31\%$$

(b) Eliminate the tariff of 25% on imported zips and buttons. This would give:

$$e = \frac{17.24\% - 0(24.14\%)}{52.59\%} = 32.78\%$$

The UK raincoat's selling price is now £54.50.

(c) Such a change would reduce the competiveness of the UK's garment accessories industry.

Answer 1.3

An effective tariff is one which indicates the real level of protection afforded to a domestic product. It is found by considering the formula:-

$$e = \frac{n - Mi}{v}$$

where e = effective tariff
n = nominal tariff
M = tariff on import content of domestic good
i = import content of domestic good
V = domestic added value.

Thus, the effective tariff is found *after* allowing for any tariff on the import content of the domestic good (a *negative* protection) and basing the result only on the domestic added value of the domestic product.

Thus,
(a) a high nominal tariff rate will by itself induce a *high effective tariff*
(b) a low (but not zero) domestic added value for the domestic good will *increase the effective tariff*
(c) a zero tariff duty on the import content of the domestic good will allow for the full impact *of the tariff to be effected.*

Summary: all three items taken together will allow for a maximum effective tariff.

Answer 1.4

An *ad valorem* tariff is one based as a percentage of the value of the imported product. I.e. 15% of (say) £100. Its purpose is to afford a degree of protection to a domestic good while at the same time producing revenue for Customers and Excise. It differs from a Specific tariff which is based on the *volume* of an imported product.

To the extend that an *ad valorem* tariff is successful in restricting imports, its ability to raise central government revenue is limited. A 100% protective *ad valorem* tariff will yield zero revenue.

Other effects:

Income distribution. By switching domestic demand towards the domestic product income is switched from customers to suppliers. However, the more price elastic the demand and the more elastic the supply the less will this effect take place. Any such income switch will be at the expense of central government revenues.

Balance of trade. To the extent that the tariff is protective, it will have a positive balance of trade effect (in the short-run). This will be to the disadvantage of revenue collection.

Deadweight loss. To the extent that the tariff is protective there will be a net deadweight loss as real incomes fall. However, this may be offset in the long-term if the product protected benefits from economies of scale or is part of an "infant industry".

Answer 1.5

Counter-trade involves the exchange of goods for goods in one way or another and it has grown in recent years because of the shortages of foreign exchange experienced by many developing countries. It also assists them in the export of their own products which may be difficult to sell otherwise.

Counter-trade can take various forms. For example:

(a) in its simplest form it involves (say) a UK exporter selling goods for cash which is then used to purchase "compensation" or reciprocal goods from the importing country.
(b) *Link purchases.* In this case there is still an exchange of goods for goods but the exporter has to find another company to make the purchases from the overseas country.
(c) *Counter-purchase.* Here, the UK exporter agrees to accept payment arising from the proceeds of the sale of goods produced by the original UK exports.

Functions of a UK bank

1. Advising the UK exporter on the extra costs he is likely to meet which should be loaded into his export price.
2. The provision of finance to permit the overseas party to pay for the UK exports before the sale of their own goods.
3. The provision of Evidence and Escrow accounts to protect and assist the traders in their deals.
4. The provision of bonds to protect the overseas party against the UK trader's default in the purchase of the compensation goods.
5. Matching UK exporters with UK importers in a "Link" purchase agreement.

Section 2

Answers

Answer 2.1

Brazil and Mexico

Export and import values in billions of US dollars

	1972	1981
Brazil exports	\$4.0	\$19.7
Malaysia exports	\$1.7	\$11.2
Brazil imports	\$4.8	\$23.0
Malaysia imports	\$1.6	\$11.6
Brazil export prices (in dollars)	58	141
Brazil import prices (in dollars)	46	195
Malaysia export prices (in dollars)	50	198
Malaysia import prices (in dollars)	49	164

Find percentage changes in prices

Brazil Export prices: $\frac{141 - 58 \text{ x } 100}{58} = 143.1\%$ rise

Import prices: $\frac{195 - 46 \text{ x } 100}{46} = 323.9\%$ rise

Malaysia Export prices: $\frac{198 - 50 \text{ x } 100}{50} = 296.0\%$ rise

Import prices: $\frac{164 - 49 \text{ x } 100}{49} = 234.7\%$ rise

"Inflate" 1972 values by these percentages.

I.e. Brazil exports of \$4.0b raised by 143.1%

$$= \frac{\$4.0b \times 143.1}{100} = \$5.724b, \text{ added to } \$4.0b$$

$$= \underline{\$9.724b}$$

Brazil imports of \$4.8b raised by 323.9%

$$= \frac{4.8b \times 323.9}{100} = \$15.55b, \text{ added to } \$4.8b$$

$$= \underline{\$20.35b}$$

Malaysia exports of \$1.7b raised by 296.0%

$$= \frac{\$1.7b \times 296}{100} = \$5.032b, \text{ added to } \$1.7b$$

$$= \underline{\$6.732b}$$

Malaysia imports of \$1.6b raised by 234.7%

$$= \frac{\$1.6b \times 234.7}{100} = \$3.755b, \text{ added to } \$1.6b$$

$$= \underline{\$5.355b}$$

Summary

Adjusted trade for price changes

	1972	1981
Brazil exports	\$ 9.724b	\$19.7b
Brazil imports	\$20.35b	\$23.0b
Malaysia exports	\$ 6.732b	\$11.26b
Malaysia imports	\$ 5.355b	\$11.6b

Real percentage changes

$$\text{Brazil exports} = \frac{\$19.7b - \$9.724b \times 100}{9.724} = 102.6\% \text{ rise}$$

$$\text{Brazil imports} = \frac{\$23.0b - \$20.35b \times 100}{20.35} = 13.02\% \text{ rise}$$

$$\text{Malaysia exports} = \frac{\$11.26b - \$6.732b \times 100}{6.732} = 67.48\% \text{ rise}$$

$$\text{Malaysia imports} = \frac{\$11.6b - \$5.355 \times 100}{5.355} = 116.6\% \text{ rise}$$

Summary

	1972 ⟷ 1981
Brazil exports	+ 102.06%
Malaysia exports	+ 67.48%
Brazil imports	+ 13.02%
Malaysia imports	+ 116.06%

Result

Brazil had a much larger real increase in exports and Malaysia in real imports.

Comparison with unadjusted figures

1. The adjusted figures *reverse* the country with the largest increase in exports.

   Reason? Malaysian export value increase was due to a large degree to *export price rises* rather than a rise in the *volume* of exports. Brazil's export price rises were much more modest.

2. The adjusted figures *accentuate* the bigger increase of Malaysian imports.

   Reason? Brazil import prices rose more quickly than those for Malaysia. Thus Brazil's real imports were less in volume terms than the unadjusted figures imply.

Answer 2.2

Between 1972 and 1981 volume of trade expanded by about 4% per annum in real terms. More recently there has been a slow-down related to the international recession.

There are four major flows of trade distribution, namely,

inter-industrial
inter-Pacific
inter-EEC
inter-Soviet bloc.

The industrial nations were responsible for about two thirds of all trade and the top six nations did about one half of all world trade.

The terms of trade (export prices relative to import prices) have fluctuated markedly. The major change came with the oil price rises of 1973 and 1978. In addition domestic inflation, especially in Latin America pushed domestic currency prices very high. However, after allowing for exchange rate changes, the movements are less marked. The prices of raw materials and other commodities are dependant on demand in the industralised countries; in the slow-down of 1980–84 such prices were depressed.

The UK is one of the top six exporting and importing nations. Its exports per capita puts it in fourth position after Canada, West Germany and France.

Section 3

Answers

Answer 3.1

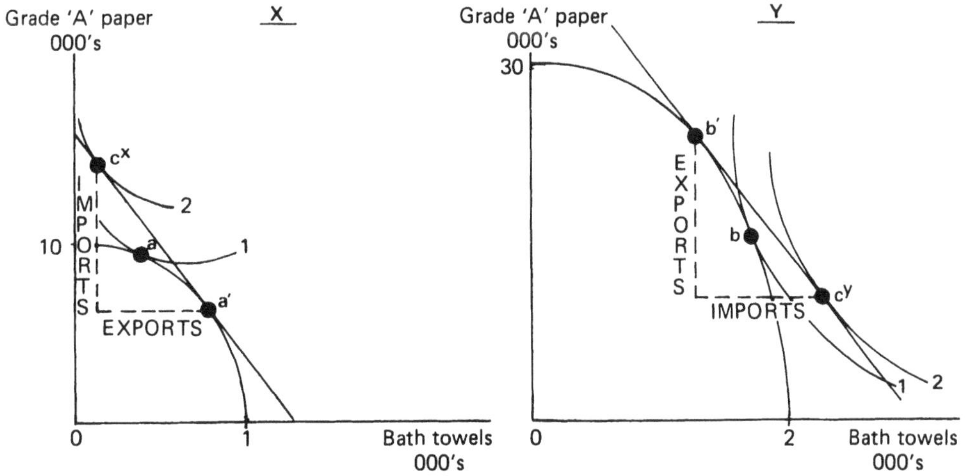

Analysis

(i) X's production frontier is nearer the origin than Y's, indicating an absolute disadvantage in the production of both products.

(ii) As Y's preference is said to be for bath towels (relative to X) then its pre-trade output and consumption point is shown at point b and X's at point a. The resulting indifference curves show a steeper map for Y than for X indicating a relative preference for bath towels in Y.

(iii) Both production frontiers are shown concave to the origins indicating increasing marginal opportunity costs for both X and Y.

(iv) At a and b the tangencies are not parallel (tangencies not shown); this indicates that X has a comparative advantage in bath towels and Y in paper.

(v) X moves output to a^1 and Y to b^1.

(vi) From a^1 and b^1 they both trade volumes indicated by the sides of the two trade triangles.
(vii) Final post-trade consumptions are at points c^x and c^y.
(viii) Both have gained from trade as consumption is now at a higher indifference curve (No 2 instead of No 1).

Answer 3.2

(a) The use of straw will reduce overseas tomato suppliers' comparative cost advantage in their sales to the UK market.
(b) This will tend to reduce tomato imports into the UK.
(c) There will be a slight effect in the appreciation of sterling but offset by the original purchase of the German burner.
(d) Straw prices are likely to rise.
Oil prices will fall slightly.
Tile prices will tend to fall as the supply of cheaper silica increases.

Answer 3.3

	Wheat	Oil
USSR	1 tonne	3.3 tonnes
USA	1 tonne	0.625 tonnes

USSR has a comparative cost advantage in oil relative to wheat over the USA. The USA has a comparative cost advantage in wheat.

If the USSR purchased more wheat from the USA she could save resources equal to 2.675 tonnes oil. However, a significant increase in USSR demand for USA wheat would tend to push up its price. Even if wheat prices rose to halfway between the USSR and USA prices — namely 1.9625 tonnes oil, there would still be considerable savings to be made by both countries. However, to the extent that increasing marginal costs of production prevails, the extent of the increase in output of wheat in the USA and oil in the USSR would not be infinite. Also, other, non-economic factors, may make such exchanges difficult.

Answer 3.4

This question refers to the concept of comparative cost advantage theory which holds that it is the comparative or relative costs between countries that determine trade, rather than whether costs are absolutely high or low within a single country.

Thus, any one nation may have higher costs in all of its output compared to the costs for the same or similar products in other countries and yet still possess a *comparative* cost advantage in some of its production.

This must be the case so long as the country's uncompetitiveness is not identical in all its outputs relative to other countries. As this is most unlikely (except for only some of its products or tradeable services) then it must be rather *less uncompetitive* in some things relative to other things.

By increasing production in those outputs where it has a least comparative disadvantage it will be able to compete with other countries who, in their turn will tend to specialize in those products in which they possess the grestest comparative advantage.

Answer 3.5

(a) B produces less steel *and* fewer tractors than A. It has an absolute cost disadvantage in both products. However, its disadvantage in tractors is less than its disadvantage in steel. I.e.:

A	B
each tractor is worth 2 tons steel.	each tractor is worth 1.6 tons steel.

Thus, tractors in B cost (or exchanges for) less steel than in A. B will export tractors to A and import steel from A.

(b) As both A and B enjoy *decreasing* marginal opportunity costs, they can both go on increasing outputs of their favoured good. However, sooner or later *increasing* costs will take over, making specialization more and more expensive. They will continue to specialize until their marginal opportunity costs become identical. Further specialization will mean that output is being incurred at costs greater than is being incurred in the other country.

(c) The terms of trade, or the prices at which tractors will exchange for steel depends on both countries' supply and demand positions. Supply is determined by the curvature of the production frontier and demand by the slope and curvature of the indifference map. If trade is on the basis of the original opportunity costs, then possible terms of trade could be one tractor for 1.8 tonnes of steel.

(d) The gains (or profits) from trade are unlikely to be equally divided because supply and demand factors are likely to be dissimilar. For example, if the demand for tractors is strong in A but the demand for steel is weak in B, then the terms of trade (and thus the gains from trade) are likely to be in B's favour.

Answer 3.6

This proposition is based on the theory of comparative cost advantage which holds that if nations took advantage of their comparative cost positions and both specialized and exported those goods and tradeable services in which they possessed the greatest cost advantage, then the maximum gains from trade would result giving income gains for all participants.

Qualifications

1. The proposition ignores the social costs of moving people from one industry to another.
2. The elasticity of supply may be low. I.e. it may be difficult to obtain (or train) further quantities of labour for the required industry.
3. Where an industry is in an "infant" stage, restrictions on imported competition may allow it to expand and become more efficient leading to gains for the country as a whole as well as other countries who can now import more cheaply.
4. There may be certain industries where consideration other than econimic may be important. I.e. food supplies may be seen as vital to protect in case of a cut-off of imported supply. Or certain "key" industries may be seen as vital to protect in order to provide for defence.

Section 4

Answers

Answer 4.1

The prospective UK exporter's situation is:

(a) he has no export experience
(b) his product is a low price consumer good
(c) his overall turnover is medium-sized.

He should start by asking his bank and also the British Overseas Trade Board for assistance (see Chapter 11 in the textbook).

The bank will be able to offer general economic reports on overseas markets and information on trade restrictions and will also be able to obtain status reports on prospective overseas buyers and also details of overseas agents.

The BOTB will give assistance for market research, overseas trade fairs and outward missions.

However, neither can offer a selling function, and as the trader is in a "start-up" situation, he might be best advised to consider the following:

(a) *The confirming/buying house*

The BOTB will give details of such organizations in the UK. They will want to see samples of the goods. Sales through them are likely to be limited to begin with but they do take the load of export administration and the risks associated with exports.

(b) *The export merchant*

If an acceptable product is offered, a merchant might be prepared to make regular purchases. Useful information about the product will also be made available to the exporter which can stand him in good stead should he wish to self-export in the future. Once again, the burden of export administration and risk is taken from him.

(c) *Overseas agents*

If he can define his overseas markets, he can contact an overseas agent to handle his product. This is more risky because failure to sell can lead to deterioration and the costs associated with storage and possible return of goods.

(d) *Piggy-back scheme*

Another possibility is to find an existing UK exporter of a complementary product and try to interest him in promoting the product along with his own, to the benefit of both parties.

Summary

Overall, it would be too risky for the trader to attempt to sell overseas by his own efforts alone. Although the use of the above intermediaries will reduce his profits, it will also reduce his risks and allow him to build up some experience and expertise to enable him to become more adventurous later on.

Answer 4.2

(a) *ECGD Bank Guarantee Scheme*

If ECGD is agreeable — which depends upon the company's balance sheets and trading position — they may issue in favour of the bank, a direct guarantee. The appropriate guarantee in this instance would be the bills and notes scheme which would allow the bank to lend without recourse to the customer immediately after acceptance of the appropriate bill of exchange. Finance is often cheaper than overdraft being at ⅝ of 1% over base rate, although the cost of the additional bank guarantee together with bank collection charges must be taken into consideration.

(b) *Confirming Houses*

Confirming Houses act as agents for the buyers and place orders on behalf of their principals. They take on responsibility for the debt and in respect of a sight bill immediate payment is effected as soon as they take the goods over for shipment. In the event of credit being allowed the bill will be accepted by the Confirming House who would normally command fine trade bill rates in the discount market. Selling through a Confirming House is equivalent of a domestic sale.

(c) *Export House/Export Agents/Export Managers*

These organisations act in a similar manner to the Confirming House, except they are acting as agents for the exporters. This means that the contractual relationship with the overseas buyer is maintained as far as the seller is concerned. Export Houses do, however, give credit to the overseas buyer and as such are responsible for effecting payment to the seller. If a sight bill is involved, immediate payment will obviously be effected whereas if acceptance is involved the name of the Export House will obviously rank higher than that of the ordinary overseas buyer.

(d) *Export Merchants*

These organisations are often confused with Export Houses or Confirming Houses but, in effect, they buy goods in their own right from suppliers and arrange to ship and sell them to their own buyers abroad. In effect this is equivalent of a domestic market sale.

(e) *Factoring Companies*

(i) Some factoring companies will arrange to handle the sales ledger of the company arranging to collect the debts on their own behalf. Payment of the invoice amount is guaranteed at maturity without recourse to the exporter.

(ii) In cases of approved buyers and countries the factoring company may agree to advance a substantial proportion of the invoice value immediately the goods are shipped to the exporter. The balance will be paid upon settlement of the invoice by the buyers but the original advance will be made without recourse to the seller.

Both systems relieve the supplier of the sales accounting and debt collection services and also bad debts are not incurred. If foreign currency is involved the factoring house will arrange to take out forward cover thus obviating any exchange risk.

(f) *International Credit Unions*

These are organisations and associations of finance houses in the buyers and sellers countries. Finance is arranged through the medium of the Credit Union for the importer to have time to pay for the goods. These Unions consist of a number of European finance houses or banks which introduce an instalment credit basis to their foreign partners on a reciprocal arrangement. The importer, having received credit, can arrange to pay the exporter without too much difficulty. The exporter does receive payment without recourse to himself.

Answer 4.3

(i) The preliminary point which should be discussed with the customer is: are they able to deliver goods ordered? In other words, have they the nursery or the growing capacity, or ability to purchase plants? Can they arrange packing, shipping and despatch? They can be given advice on these matters including an introduction to a good Forwarding Agent who can assist them.
(ii) Is the country viable? Will it allow remittance of funds out of the country? Local Exchange Control regulations, if any? Suggest the customer should first of all read an Economic Report on the country in question.
(iii) The creditworthiness of the buyer? Is he able to pay and can a good status report be obtained by the bank or the BOTB?
(iv) Investigate the normal methods of payment used in the country in question. Information on these matters can be obtained from the banks, the BOTB, a local Chamber of Commerce or probably an Export Club. Although finance is not necessarily a problem, enquires should be made and an introduction given to ECGD so that the customer can investigate whether they are able to obtain cover for credit risks.
(v) It would be wise, if the enquiry appears to be serious, to visit the country to meet the potential buyer. The bank would be willing to give a Letter of Introduction and the BOTB could also arrange for somebody from the local Port to discuss this potential business with the customer.
(vi) When visiting a foreign country, it may be possible to take advantage of a Trade Mission organised through the auspices of the BOTB or a Chamber of Commerce or a Trade Organisation who can provide help and assistance to all exporters visiting countries for specific purposes at what are usually subsidised rates.
(vii) If so far so good, specific status reports should be taken on the potential buyer and consideration should be given to the terms and conditions offered.
(viii) Payment terms should be checked by the bank to see if the method of payment suggested is acceptable (possibly a Letter of Credit or Open Account Trading). The bank should be used to collect debts until a good trading relationship is set up between the parties.
(ix) Although the company does not apparently need finance, general discussions

should take place in case the company does run into cashflow difficulties and needs the assistance of the Bank, whether supported by ECGD or otherwise. It is possible, if a large contract is involved, that Medium Term Finance may be necessary and the bank may be asked to consider entering into Bond Support for the company which may entail the need for Tender/Big Bonds, Advance Payment Bonds, Performance Bonds, Retention Money Bonds and the like.

(x) The question of bonding might be appropriate in that if the company starts to 'land' large orders. It may require payments in advance or the company may be asked to tender for contracts. The question of Bond Support by the bank and ECGD should be discussed and considered by the customer. It level will depend upon the strength of the company's balance sheet.

Section 5

Answers

Answer 5.1

(a) Indicates that the goods have been received on board a specified vessel.
(b) Allows the document to be transferred by endorsement by not consigning the goods to the buyer and by the signature of the consignee on the back.
(c) A notation by the carrier indicating some deficiency in the goods and/or the packaging.
(d) Indicates that the goods are going C and F, CIF, DCP, CIP, EXS or EXQ.
(e) It does not carry the shipping line logo and carries an incorporation clause making it subject to a uniform set of clauses.
(f) This means that the bill can be transferred to another party for a consideration by the process of endorsement and making it out "to order".
(g) Indicates that the goods are to be transported by more than one form of transportation.
(h) Indicates that the bill has been issued by a Liner shipping company with vessels plying scheduled runs between ports on pre-announced dates and times.
(i) Indicates a bill issued by a party who is not the owner of a vessel but merely the hirer, and will incorporate the terms of the hirer.

Answer 5.2

A sea waybill has much the same properties as a bill of lading, except that it is non-negotiable. Its purpose is to facilitate the handing over of goods to the consignee without the need for a negotiable copy of a bill of lading to be presented. Because it is non-negotiable, it must not be made out "to order" but to a named consignee who must provide proof of identity to obtain possession of the goods.

Because of the speed of modern transportation and the delays that can occur in processing and delivering associated paper-work, it sometimes happens that goods arrive before the paperwork. The sea waybill has the advantage that no copy of it need be available to the buyer for him to obtain the goods.

Banks may be reluctant to provide finance when a sea waybill is used because it fails to provide them with the same control of the goods as do bills of lading. For example, because title is retained by the seller until the goods are delivered, and the carrier has a contract only with the seller, the goods could be prevented from reaching the buyer by the seller.

Answer 5.3

(a) (i) *CIF UK airport — cost, insurance and freight UK Airport*

The seller is responsible for paying all charges up to the delivery at the UK airport including the cost of goods, their insurance, and the freight charges up to UK aiport. The seller is responsible for booking space on the aircraft and advising the airline and aircraft flight number to the buyer. The buyer is responsible for taking delivery of the goods or arranging to take delivery for the goods at the UK airport and to clear the goods through customs.

(ii) *FOB Oslo airport — free on board the aircraft at Oslo airport*

The seller is responsible for getting the goods up to and arranging for them being loaded up on board an aircraft at Oslo airport. The buyer is responsible for arranging for an aircraft to be available and advising the seller of the airport and the date when the shipment on board that aircraft can be effected. The price quoted by the seller covers all costs of the goods up to and including placing on board the aircraft and the buyer is responsible for all charges including freight and insurance charges after that event takes place.

(b) (i) *SWIFT — Society for Worldwide Interbank Financial Telecommunications*

Payment will be made in Deutsche Marks and remitted by the SWIFT system to a named bank in Germany 10 days after the date of despatch of the goods to a UK airport. Bright Sparks purchases the DMs from their bankers and is debited with the sterling equivalent. Deutsche Marks are remitted out to a German bank by the UK bank utilising the SWIFT computerised system. The UK bank will instruct the German bank to debit its Nostro (namely Deutsche Mark account) with that German bank who will arrange to debit the UK bank's account and pay the Deutsche Marks to the beneficiary.

(ii) *TT — Telegraphic Transfer*

The British bank will debit its customer with the sterling sum to be remitted and arrange to credit this to either an account held by the Oslo bank or place cover with another bank in the UK with whom the Oslo bank has an account. The telex or cable message will advise the Oslo bank where cover has been placed and request that bank to pay the funds to the named beneficiary. The Oslo bank will arrange to pay either the sterling to the beneficiary, if the beneficiary has a sterling account, or alternatively, will buy the sterling from the beneficiary, crediting that beneficiary with the Norwegian Kroner equivalent.

Answer 5.4

1. *FOB (Free on Board)*

The goods are placed on board a ship by the seller at the port of shipment named in the sales contract. The responsibility for the goods passes to the purchaser immediately the goods pass over the ship's rail.

Seller's responsibility

The seller must:

(i) supply goods in accordance with the sales contract agreed between the two parties;)
(ii) arrange for the packing of the goods at their own expense unless it is normal form to ship goods unpacked;
(iii) provide the appropriate documentation and pay the cost thereof in connection with any checking or measuring operations and provide customary clean documentation of proof of delivery to the vessel. The goods must be delivered on board a vessel named by the buyer at a named port, in accordance with the customs of that port and between the shipping dates indicated by the buyer. The responsibility of the seller for the goods including insurance charges, will pass to the buyer immediately the goods have passed over the ship's rail. Any customs or exportation charges will have to be borne by the seller. The seller must notify the buyer, without delay, that the goods have been loaded on board and provide the appropriate documentation.

The buyer's responsibility

The buyer must:

(i) at his own expense, charter a vessel or reserve the necessary place on board a scheduled sailing, advising the seller of the name, the loading berth and the delivery dates etc.;
(ii) pay all the costs and risks from the time that the goods pass over the ship's rail including freight insurance, customs duty etc.;
(iii) bear any additional costs due to the named vessel failing to arrive during the period that shipment should be effected. If he fails to name a vessel or a period when the shipment will take place he will have to bear any additional costs incurred by the seller because of such failure.

2. *C and F (Cost and Freight)*

This means that the seller must pay the cost and freight necessary to bring the goods to their main destination, but the risk of loss or damage to the goods, as well as any cost increases etc. is transferred to the buyer immediately they pass over the ship's rail, at the named port of shipment. In addition to most of the responsibilities indicated under FOB the additional responsibility of the seller is that he must arrange for a vessel to accept the goods advising the name of the vessel and the port of shipment etc. to the buyer so that the buyer can arrange appropriate insurance charges.

The seller's responsibility

(i) He will load the goods at his own expense, on board the vessel at an appropriate port of shipment and between the dates or periods fixed for shipment. He is responsible for notifying the buyer without delay, that the goods have been loaded on board the vessel.
(ii) He must furnish to the buyer without any delay with a clean negotiable Bill of Lading showing the port of destination. This document must be in a transferable form and indicate that the goods have been loaded on board.

NB: If the goods are sold "C and F Landed", unloading costs including the lighterage and wharfage charges must be borne by the seller.

The buyer's responsibility

(i) The buyer must accept the documents and arrange to receive the goods at the agreed port of destination and their unloading charges, with the exception of freight, and all costs and charges incurred in respect of the goods in the course of their transit by sea until their arrival at that Port.

(ii) Unloading charges including lighterage, wharfage etc. must be borne by the buyer unless the term "C and F Landed" has been applied to the shipment. The buyer therefore respectively accepts all risks the moment the goods pass over the ship's rail, and must pay any charges in obtaining the appropriate certificate of origin and consular documents as well as paying the customs duties.

(iii) If an import licence is required it is the responsibility of the buyer.

3. *CIF (Cost, Insurance and Freight)*

This term is the same as C and F but with the addition that the seller has to procure marine insurance against the risk of loss or damage to the goods during their carriage. The seller contracts with the insurer and pays the insurance premium. Unless the contract of sale indicates the specific insurance charges which have to be covered, the seller will normally be responsible only for covering insurance charges to a named Port on the Insitute of London Underwriters' Institute Cargo Clauses C Clause Arrangement (the old FPA condition).

The seller's responsibility

In addition to the responsibility the seller will have to bear under a C and F Contract, the seller is responsible for obtaining, at his own cost and in a transferable form, a marine insurance policy against the risks of carriage involved in the contract. As indicated above, the CIF price should be covered, plus 10%, but unless specific risks are included in the contract of sale, the normal responsibility would normally end with the provision of an Institute Cargo Clause C certificate or policy (which is the equivalent of the old FPA Clauses).

NB: If the goods are sold "CIF landed" then unloading costs, including lighterage and wharfage charges, are borne by the seller.

Buyer's responsibility

The buyer undertakes to accept the documents as tendered and to pay for the costs and charges incurred in obtaining the certificate of origin and any consular documents and to pay any customs duties if appropriate. If an import licence is required this is the responsibility of the buyer.

4. *CIF Liner Terms*

Liner terms apply where there are scheduled and regular sailings between either two ports or on a particular route. The shipping company issues a timetable showing the scheduled journeys and they are reserved berths at the appropriate destinations along the route until the final destination. The bills of lading issued are subject to the terms of conditions of the shipping company concerned, relating to specific routes. Freight charges tend to be cheaper when liner terms are available than if shipping space is booked on a vessel which sails on an *ad hoc* basis.

Section 6

Answers

Answer 6.1

A bank documentary collections facility operates under the "Uniform Rules for Collections" I.C.C. Publication No. 322 (1978) which sets out the rights and responsibilities of both banks and customers. The bank to whom the documents are presented for onward despatch (the Remitting bank) has a duty to follow the seller's instructions in the Collection Order. This will indicate what financial documents (if any) and commercial documents are to be presented, who is to pay for the collection charges, whether the documents are to be released to the buyer on a documents against payments or documents against acceptance basis.

In addition the Collection Order should give the bank instructions as to the steps to be taken in the event of default by the buyer.

1. Where a negotiable and blank endorsed marine bill of lading is used or where the goods are consigned to the Collecting bank (with its approval) control over the goods is witheld from the buyer until he either pays or accepts a time bill of exchange.
2. The exporter may be able to establish a financial facility from the Remitting bank (i.e. an advance or negotiations facility, discounting a bank bill).
3. Banks are more likely to spot errors and omissions in the documents.
4. The ICC rules for collections ensures that all the parties are aware of the underlying conditions that apply if the collection order is silent or ambiguous on important matters.
5. The Collecting bank may be in a better position to press the buyer for payment.
6. A collections facility is cheaper than a letter of credit.

Disadvantage to the exporter

1. Bank finance is likely to be with recourse.
2. Such finance will carry a charge.
3. Buyer's failure to take up goods will incur further costs.

Answer 6.2

(a) *Negotiating a bill of exchange*

When a bank agrees to a negotiations facility it effectively means that it is prepared to buy the rights to the proceeds of any trade draft sent for collection, but on a recourse basis.

The draft is first endorsed on the back by the exporter, thus transferring it to the bank, who will then present it in its own right. Before granting such a facility, the bank will want to pursue the usual investigations into the credit-worthiness of its customer.

The bank will impose a negotiations charge and fee for this facility. However, because the actual date of payment by the buyer is not exactly determinable (due to delays by the buyer and/or delays in the actual receipt of payment) it is not possible to accurately calculate the cost of money (interest rate) and thus the negotiations *charge*. As a result, the exporter will receive the gross (full) value of the draft bill exchange less the fee and pay the negotiations *charge* at the time that final payment is received (back-end credit).

The cost to a drawer is thus,

(i) on the negotiation of the draft — the fee.
(ii) on receipt by the bank of payment — the charge.

Assuming a 91 day draft for £10,000 with a fee of 1½% and a charge of 16% per annum we have:

$$Fee = \left(\frac{\text{Value of draft}}{\text{Proceeds}} - 1\right) \times 100$$

$$= \left(\frac{£10{,}000}{£9850} - 1\right) \times 100 = \mathit{1.523\%} \text{ cost.}$$

$$Charge = £10{,}000\ @\ 16\% = \frac{£1600}{365} \times 91 = £398.90$$

$$= £398.90 \text{ as a \% of } £10{,}000 = \mathit{3.989\%} \text{ cost}$$

Total cost = 5.512%

(b) *Discounting a bill of exchange*

To qualify for discounting a bill must be accepted and it must also be a time bill. In addition it can only be discounted in the country where it is payable.

When a bill is discounted, the discounter buys the rights to an *accepted* financial instrument. Most discounted bills are therefore accepted by the exporter's bank to permit this. As a result there are two costs; the acceptance fee and the discount charge.

These costs are known at the time of discounting because they are not dependent on the receipt of monies from the overseas buyer. They are "front-ended" costs.

Assuming an acceptance fee of 1% and a discount charge of 14% per annum we have:

$$Acceptance\ fee = \left(\frac{\text{value of bill}}{\text{proceeds}} - 1\right) \times 100$$

$$= \left(\frac{£10{,}000}{9900} - 1\right) \times 100 = \mathit{1.01\%} \text{ cost}$$

$$\textit{Discount charge} = \left(\frac{\text{value of bill}}{\text{proceeds}} - 1\right) \times 100$$

$$= \left(\frac{£10{,}000}{£9650.96} - 1\right) \times 100 = \textit{3.617\%} \text{ cost}$$

$$\textit{Total cost} = \textit{4.627\%}$$

Note that the discount charge is 2% points less than the negotiations charge because there is less risk for the discounter. However, the real total difference between negotiation costs and discount costs are somewhat mitigated by the extra "hidden" costs of discounting as a "front-ended" facility; whereas negotiations is mostly a "back-ended" facility.

Answer 6.3

(a) Not ever. Open account trading involves the despatch of goods for payment at a previously agreed later date. This requires trust between the parties but could be a suitable arrangement between (say) sister companies in a multi-national organization.
(b) Not ever. The holder (or payee) has the right to receive the value of the bill of exchange.
(c) Not always. An overseas bank may hold a bill (pending its maturity) on behalf of the exporter (payee).
(d) No. Advances are made by banks who arrange for the collection of documents. They are usually only for a part of the value to be collected and are always with recourse to the exporter. Discounting is for full value and where the bill is a bank one (which is usual) the discounter has recourse to the acceptor and not to the exporter/drawer. However, the accepting bank may call for a separate recourse agreement with the exporter/drawer.
(e) Once a bill is discounted, a discounter has no further liability. An acceptor of a bill is liable to the discounter in the event that on its maturity its value is not met by the exporter.
(f) Not always. A collection need have no financial documents at all. Banks may be prepared to negotiate commercial documents.
(g) Yes, except where it is part of a confirmed and irrevocable letter of credit.
(h) No. A bank bill is one drawn on a bank usually so that it can be accepted by that bank and then discounted at favourable interest cost. A trade bill is one that is drawn on a trader and as such is unlikely to be discounted.

Answer 6.4

(a) Uniform Rules for Collections (Publication No. 322). These came into force on 1 January 1979, and their purpose is to assist banks in the collection operations and to codify the International Rules to be applied. They are also intended to lay down the conditions governing the presentation and payment of clean and documentary collections, thus attempting to lessen the difficulties likely to be encountered by both banks and their customers when attempting to reconcile the differences in phraseology and commercial practise worldwide.

(b) (i) Accept 50% (hold on suspense pending remitting bank's approval).
(ii) Retain the bill of exchange and protest the bill for the balance, after marking the bill to the effect that 50% has been paid.
(iii) Advise the case of need (do not act on his instructions).
(iv) Advise remitting bank by cable and request further instructions.

Answer 6.5

(a) International Rules are "Uniform Rules for Collection" (Publication No. 322), which came into force on 1 January 1979. Their purpose is to assist banks in collection operations and clarify the International Rules to be applied, and to lay down the conditions given in the presentations and payment of clean and documentary collection, thus attempting to lessent the difficulties likely to be encountered by both banks and their customers when attempting to reconcile the differences in phraseology and commercial practice worldwide.

(b) *60 Day Sight Bills D/A*

(i) Name and address of the customer.
(ii) Instructions to release documents against acceptance.
(iii) Protest instructions in respect of non-acceptance/non-payment.
(iv) Instructions on how the remitting bank is to be advised in the event of non-acceptance/non-payment.
(v) Warehousing and insurance instructions.
(vi) The case of need and their powers, if any.
(vii) Who is to pay for charges, and may they be waived, etc.
(viii) Instructions on how proceeds are to be remitted, and payment.

Cash Against Documents Basis

The same instructions will be required as in (b) above except that documents should be be released against payment as acceptance would not be appropriate.

(c) (i) If the customer refuses to accept the bill of exchange or pay it at maturity, and protest instructions have been given, customers sometimes object when their own bankers follow the instructions on the remitting schedule.

(ii) As a collecting bank one is acting as agent for the remitting bank and sometimes there can be a clash of interests with one's own customer, to whom the documents or Bill of Exchange have to be presented. Nevertheless, the collecting bank must act in accordance with the instructions of its principal, but at the same time endeavour to keep its own customer happy.

Answer 6.6

(a) The international rules referred to are "Uniform Rules for Collection" (Publication No. 322, issued by the International Chamber of Commerce) which came into force on 1 January 1979. The international rule under article 6 is that goods should not be despatched direct to the address of the bank or consigned to a bank without prior agreement on the part of that bank. Therefore, the airline company can be told to refer back to the remitter/shipper at the remitter/shipper's expense. The bank need take no other action.

(b) Immediate steps which can be taken to protect the interest of the bank's *customers* are as follows:

(i) Contact the customer, the Far Eastern Imports Company Ltd, to ascertain if the goods are required.
(ii) If not, advise the airline company to refer back to the shipper/remitter as in (a) above.
(iii) If the answer is "yes", and only if the customer is undoubted, advise them that they will be liable to pay for the goods when the documents covering

the goods arrive. *The customer will be unable to refuse to pay for them.*

(iv) Take a letter of Hypothecation/Certificate of Pledge from the customer covering the particular shipment.

(v) *Only if the customer is undoubted and can pay for the goods* will the bank issue a delivery order to the airline company instructing them to deliver the goods to the customer. The delivery order must be marked that all charges are for account of the goods. A trust receipt must be taken from the customer at this stage.

(c) Where the customer is short of working capital, adequate protection of the goods must be made in order to ensure that they are available for disposal by the bank by taking the following steps:

(i) Take a Letter of Hypothecation/Certificate of Pledge from the customer.

(ii) As the goods have arrived by air, the goods will be warehoused in the bank's name at the customer's expense (using the services of a responsible local forwarding agent).

(iii) Any warehouse warrants will be issued in the bank's name, which clearly identifies the goods.

(iv) Take out or arrange for existing insurance cover to be available for the bank's protection i.e. in the bank's name, again this is done at the customer's expense.

(v) The goods are inspected when they are warehoused so that it can be seen that the regulations of the bank are clearly being met.

(vi) In the event of an advance being made to the customer against security of the goods, this must be done on a separate loan account, identifying the goods as security.

Answer 6.7

(a) "Uniform Rules for Collection" (Publication No. 322) came into force on 1 January 1979, and their purpose is to assist banks in their collection operations and to codify the international rules to be applied. They are also intended to lay down the conditions given in the presentation for payment of clean and documentary collections, thus attempting to lessen the difficulties likely to be encountered by both banks and their customers when attempting to reconcile the differences in phraseology and commercial practice worldwide. The rules are contained in general Provisions and 23 articles.

(b) (i) Unless the bill is paid in full i.e. the full face amount of the bill, the bill must be protested for non-payment.

(ii) One might accept 50 per cent now (place it on a suspense account), protest the bill for the balance and inform the principal by telex/cable as well as the case of need.

(iii) As there are no specific instructions concerning the case of need, one cannot take any instructions from them.

(iv) Interest can be refused unless the collection order clearly states that it cannot be waived. In this case the collection order does not indicate that it must not be waived and therefore the drawee has the right to refuse it (Article 21).

Answer 6.8

(a) A specific bank arrangement which would immediately improve the customer's cash flow would be to grant a negotiation facility so that the customer would get immediate credit or at least credit within a few days of presenting the cheques to the bank for negotiation.

(b) The advantages of a negotiation facility are as follows:

(i) Immediate credit is given to the customer, thus improving its cash flow whether the items are expressed in sterling or in currency.
(ii) The account is credited, where sterling is involved, with the face amount of the cheque, less interest for the number of days it is believed it will take before the item is cleared. Where currency is involved, the interest factor is taken into account in the rate itself and experience shows that the interest involved is usually much cheaper than for that shown in sterling.
(iii) Following the point (ii) above, reasonable foreign exchange rates are given where currency is involved, because the bank is able to "bulk up" a number of items received from a considerable number of sources.
(iv) It is possible to cover exchange risk forward where currency items are involved.
(v) Very few cheques are unpaid after the "liability" period is involved and this usually is between twenty and thirty days.
(vi) Perhaps another great advantage is the questions of costs, in that banks charge less for handling items on a negotiation basis where they are able to send cheques overseas in bulk expressed in the foreign currency of that country as opposed to handling each individual item on a collection basis.

Disadvantages

(i) Where sterling is involved the charges for negotiation items to which the interest charge must also be added, are the same as for collecting currency cheques.
(ii) The customer never really knows if an item is paid simply because an advice of final payment is not normally received.
(iii) Where a negotiation line has been arranged for a customer, this may mean that some other facilities are taken up and the customer is unable to borrow as much as it otherwise would. This should be offset by the immediate benefit of its cash position.

STERLING — the only advantage is that the exchange risk is not borne by the customer.

Disadvantages

(i) The cheque has to be handled on a collection basis as it is payable overseas. This means it must be processed individually, and the charges indicated above are higher than those applied to negotiation of currency cheques.
(ii) There will be no saving on any advances made as the interest factor applied will be that which applies to the customer's normal overdraft rate. The charges levied by the overseas bank tend to be higher than those charges which are applied when an item expressed in the currency of the collecting country is involved. These may include a transfer charge where the collecting bank has to arrange for the transfer of funds back to the United Kingdom.

(c) *Remedy*

If Sterling has to be used the cheques or bank drafts should be issued payable in the United Kingdom so they can be placed through the normal UK clearing system.

Answer 6.9

(a) A full description of each method of payment required a clear indication of the main features of a documentary letter of credit and a documentary collection. One of the easiest ways of describing a documentary credit is to quote, or at least summarize, Article 3 of "Uniform Customs and Practice" (ICC Publication 290, now 400).

This definition indicates that the issuing bank gives a guarantee of payment which is conditional upon the capability of the beneficiary (usually the seller), presenting specified documents to a bank usually in his country. The documents will be accompanied by a 90 days sight draft which will be accepted by the advising or confirming bank and will be payable in the seller's country 90 days after the bank has received documents presented strictly in order. Once the draft has been accepted the beneficiary is guaranteed payment.

A documentary collection is described in "Uniform Rules for Collection" (ICC Publication 322) which came into force on 1 January 1979 in the general provisions and definitions as follows:

For the purpose of such provisions, definitions and articles:

(i) "Collection" means the handling by banks, on instructions received, of documents as defined in (ii) below, in order to

 (a) obtain acceptance and/or, as the case may be, payment, or
 (b) deliver commercial documents against acceptance and/or, as the case may be, against payment, or
 (c) deliver documents on other terms and conditions.

(ii) "Documents" means financial documents and/or commercial documents:

 (a) "financial documents" means bills of exchange, promissory notes, cheques, payments receipts or other similar instruments used for obtaining the payment of money;
 (b) "commercial documents" means invoices, shipping documents, documents of title or other similar documents or any other documents whatsoever, not being financial documents.

(iii) "Clean Collection" means collection of financial documents not accompanied by commercial documents.

(iv) "Documentary Collection" means collection of

 (a) financial documents accompanied by commercial documents;
 (b) commercial documents not accompanied by financial documents.

As the collection referred to is on a sight DP basis the seller will draw up the documents themselves, obtaining the appropriate shipping or insurance documents, where necessary, present them to the remitting bank for collection with or without a sight draft drawn on the buyer. The documents will be released by the collecting bank, acting as agents's remitting bank, to the buyer or upon payment of the documents or the accompanying draft at sight i.e. immediately the documents are presented for payment.

(At least a summary of the above should have been given.)

(b) The advantages and disadvantages of each method are as follows:

Letter of Credit

Advantages

(1) The customer will have about ninety days credit and meanwhile will have been able to take over the goods and even possibly have sold them to buyers in his own country.

(2) It would be possible to call for an "Inspection Certificate" by a reputable third party organisation to examine the goods before they are shipped and this document could be presented under the credit and provide an important protection to the customer.

Disadvantages

(1) The issuing of a credit by the bank could mean that the borrowing capacity of the customer, by way of facilities, is stretched and may even have to be reduced.

(2) Once the documents are received in order, payment will be made whether the books sent are those ordered or not (this assumes that the point (2) mentioned in the advantages has been ignored).

(3) Costs and tariffs are higher for letters of credit than collections and there will be at least a UK minimum bank charge unless the seller agrees to pay the issuing bank's charges. In addition to these charges, the advising bank overseas would be likely to level their charges which may have to be borne by the customer.

Collection Sight D/P

Advantages

(1) The customer can refuse to take up documents which will mean that the books and the documents then become the responsibility of the collecting bank acting for the seller. (This does not reduce the contractual liability of the buyer.)

(2) The costs are usually less than those which apply to letters of credit and the customer could refuse to pay any charges unless it was a condition of the collection that documents must not be released until the charges were paid by Tall Tale Limited.

Disadvantages

(1) If the documents are taken up, immediate payment must be made and there is no credit period.

(2) The customer will have no opportunity to examine the goods before paying.

Answer 6.10

(a) A customer should make prior arrangements with his bank before requesting the seller to arrange to forward the wines direct to that bank. Indeed, the arrangement is governed by Uniform Rules for Collection, publication 322, issued by the International Chamber of Commerce which came into force on 1 January 1979. Article six states that goods should not be despatched direct to the address of the bank or consigned to that bank without its prior agreement. If goods are so addressed or consigned, the bank, if it so wishes, can return the goods to the remitter at the remitter's/shipper's expense. It could equally take no action and simply refuse to take up the goods so that the carrier had to arrange to hold the goods or return them to the remitter.

(b) In order to protect the interest of the seller one also may wish to consider the customer's position at the same time. The following steps should be taken:

(i) Contact the customer or the customer's agent to ascertain if the goods are required. If one is unable to contact either party one should look for instructions in the collection order.

(ii) In the circumstances described in the question, the customer appears to want the goods and he would be requested to give an undertaking, by accepting a Bill of Exchange payable at 30 days sight, that he will pay for the goods at maturity of the Bill of Exchange. The customer must be of undoubted standing and he must give an undertaking to the bank that his account can be debited on the due date. (If there is any doubt whatsoever, the bank should refuse to handle the goods on his behalf or alternatively should take the funds on a side account held specifically for the purpose of paying for the collection.)

(iii) Banks should release the documents/goods against a Trust Receipt incorporating a Certificate of Pledge in respect of this shipment and the same procedure should apply if the bank agrees to act in respect of further shipments.

(iv) It would be more appropriate to have the goods delivered in the bank's name to a Forwarding Agent who can handle them on behalf of the customer at the expense of the customer. If the consignments are of any size, the bank may agree to have the goods consigned to them care of a forwarding agent who will arrange to warehouse and insure the goods at the expense of the customer. The customer must accept his obligations to pay for the cost of warehousing and insuring the goods as well as holding the proceeds of sale for account of the bank so that the bank can honour its commitment to the sellers.

(c) The accompanying documents should be a collection order, which is often called a remittance schedule or remittance letter, and the minimum instructions which should appear in such a collection order are as follows:

(i) The full name and address of the consignee of the goods.

(ii) In this case one would expect to see documents against acceptance (D/A). If there are no instructions as to acceptance or payment, the goods and the documents could not be released until after payment has been made.

(iii) In the event of the unacceptance of the D/A Bill or non-payment whether the Bill has to be protested.

(iv) The instructions as to what to do about charges or interest and whether they can be waived if refused.

(v) If the documents and the goods are not subsequently taken up are they to be warehoused and insured against fire if possible?

(vi) How one should advise non-acceptance or acceptance, whether by cable or otherwise.

(vii) Whether one should advise non-payment by cable or otherwise.

(viii) If there is a Case of Need, the full name and address of the Case of Need and the extent of the powers.

(ix) The instructions as to how one should remit the proceeds, (whether by cable, airmail or by means of International Money Transfer etc.).

Section 7

Answers

Answer 7.1

The concept of recourse by a bank consists of the right to recover monies paid to a customer/beneficiary if the overseas buyer or issuing bank fails to make re-imbursement.

If the credit is a revocable one, then it will also be unconfirmed by the advising bank. As such it may be with recourse to the beneficiary, if the advising bank refuses to accept documents. Even an irrevocable credit need not be confirmed. This may be because the advising bank has some doubts about either the issuing bank's ability to re-imburse or the authorities in the issuing country imposing some control measures so as to restrict re-imbursement. Where an advising bank has agreed to negotiate documents in such circumstances, it will be with recourse to the beneficiary.

Answer 7.2

(a)

This is a counter-credit whereby the UK trader's bank who confirms the 1st credit also issued the 2nd credit. The Malaysian supplier will be required to deliver the goods and the documents in good time to enable the terms of the 1st credit to be met.

(b) *2nd credit. A negotiations credit*

This must be completed first. It is issued by the London bank who uses the 1st credit as security. By so doing it enables the UK trader to pay for the Malaysian tin prior to the receipt of monies under the 1st credit. As such, this is tantamount to pre-shipment finance.

The Malaysian bank has agreed to negotiate and confirm the credit: it will this be without recourse to the Malaysian supplier who receives payment when he delivers good documents to his bank.

These documents are passed to the London bank who then obtain a substitute invoice (and possibly also a substitute insurance certificate or policy) from the UK trader. The latter then receives the difference between the values of the two credits.

As the terms of the 1st credit call for the beneficiary to draw a one month bill on the London bank this pre-supposes that the bank will, on its acceptance of the draft bill, have it discounted! The resulting proceeds will (less the payment made to Malaysia) be credited to the UK trader.

The benefits to the UK trader are:
(i) He has pre-shipment finance facility
(ii) The 1st credit is without recourse
(iii) He obtains the finest interest rates (discounting)
(iv) As the buyer is given time to pay and pays in his own currency, the seller can obtain good business or increase profit margins.
(v) The name of the supplier is not revealed to the buyer.

Answer 7.3

(i) Bank overdraft or loan
(ii) Red clause credits
(iii) Back-to-back credits
(iv) Transferable credits
(v) ECGD Specific and Buyer credit guarantees

Any one of these facilities may be available to finance an exporter before he ships his goods. Their availability will depend on:

(a) the bank's willingness to grant a facility, or
(b) the appropriate credit issued overseas, or
(c) the willingness of ECGD to offer the appropriate financial guarantee.

Answer 7.4

	QUESTIONS	ANSWERS SPECIMEN A	ANSWERS SPECIMEN B
1	Who is the Drawee?	Barclays Int	Barclays California
2	Who is the Importer?	Woldal Inc	Philmen Int
3	Is Barclays International acting in a confirming or advising capacity?	Confirming	Advising
4	Who is the issuing bank?	Downtown bank	Barclays California
5	Does the credit allow for recourse to the Drawer?	No	Yes
6	Does the credit give the importer time to pay?	No	No
7	Is it a Payments, Acceptance or Negotiations Credit?	Acceptance or Payments	Negotiations
8	Could the reference to the bills of lading read "Freight Forward"?	No (CIF)	No (CIF)
9	Which Credit is more advantageous for the Importer?		*√

* Because being an Unconfirmed Negotiation Credit, incorrect documents presented to the Issuing Bank will mean no re-imbursement to the Advising Bank who can now have recourse on the Drawer (Exporter)

Answer 7.5

Documentary Letters of Credit

	QUESTIONS	ANSWERS	ARTICLE No.
1.	When instructions sent to an overseas bank are ignored is the Issuing bank liable to the Applicant?	No	20b
2.	Under what conditions is it not possible for a Transferable Credit to be allocated to more than one 2nd beneficiary?	When partial shipments are prohibited	54e
3.	What action to recover can an Advising bank take when a Revocable credit is cancelled after payment has been made against a sight draft drawn upon itself?	Recourse to the Issuing Bank	9b
4.	Must a documentary presentation always include an Insurance document?	Yes?	37b
5.	When an irrevocable credit is subject to agreed amendments and it is followed by a second credit calling on the bank to confirm on the same terms as in the first credit, is the second credit to incorporate the amendments?	No, unless so specified in the credit.	13
6.	If no last date for presentation of documents is stipulated in the credit, when will banks refuse to accept transport documents?	21 days after the issuance of the transport documents	47a
7.	Will banks accept claused transport documents?	No, unless so specified in the credit	34b

Answer 7.6

QUESTIONS		ANSWERS
If a Documentary Letter of Credit:		
1.	Does not indicate whether it is revocable or not — Is it revocable?	Article 7c. Revocable.
2.	Is confirmed; is this by way of (a) request or (b) authorisation by the Issuing Bank?	Article 10b. Either.
3.	Allows for presentation of documents including transport documents stating that goods *may* be carried on deck — will Banks refuse to accept such a presentation?	Article 28b. No, they will *not* refuse to accept, provided the transport document does not specifically state that they are *loaded* on deck.
4.	Fails to specify whether partial shipments are permitted — are they permitted?	Article 44a Yes.
5.	Is issued by *cable* to the Advising Bank, does there need to be a *mail* confirmation?	Article 12b. No, not unless the cable says "details to follow"
6.	"Deals in Documents and not Goods" — specify the Article setting this out.	Article 4.
7.	Involves the presentation of documents which includes Forwarding Agents transport documents — will the Banks accept such a presentation?	Article 25d. No, unless the credit stipulates this. However, banks can accept a freight forwarder's transport document if it is the FIATA Combined Transport Bill of Lading or if it indicates that it is issued as carrier or agent of a named carrier.
8.	Must call for *two* documents in which the description of the goods are the same — which two documents are they?	Article 41c. Invoice and the Credit itself.

Answer 7.7

(a) The letter of credit must be irrevocable and, hopefully, confirmed by a first class British bank. You as the branch manager, may even be prepared to confirm this yourself.

(b) You can offer to arrange a back-to-back letter of credit.

Disadvantages

The letter of credit cannot be regarded as adequate security for the second one because:

(i) Documents presented, paid or negotiated in Germany within the expiry of the second letter of credit may not be received in London for presentation and onward transmission to Australia under the first letter of credit. The credit could indicate that documents must be presented in the UK for payment.
(ii) Your customer may not provide "substitute" documents to be applied with the shipping documents under the first letter of credit.
(iii) The bank in Germany may avail itself of an option under Uniform Customs which will prevent those documents being available for presentation under the Australian letter of credit (Article 41b).
(iv) It may not be possible to obtain certain specified documents in Germany called for by the Australian letter of credit.

(c) Ask customer to obtain from his Australian buyers an irrevocable letter of credit, hopefully confirmed by a British bank, which is transferable and allow for part shipment from any European port. This would allow part to be transferred to the German suppliers and the bank would not need to ask for "security" from its own customers, i.e. establishment of the letter of credit will not be included in the customers "facilities".

Answer 7.8

(a)
(i) The customer's total credit liability must be ascertained as the bank will enter into a contingent liability to honour its undertaking immediately the credit is established.
(ii) Is the customer trustworthy and capable of following through this type of commercial transaction?
(iii) Ascertain the creditworthiness of the buyer in the south of England and obtain an appropriate status report.
(iv) Establish if there is a specific sales contact and what its terms are.
(v) Establish the commercial integrity of the foreign supplier by means of a bank report or through a trade organisation.

(b)
(i) When opening the letter of credit insist that one of the documents presented is an independent inspection certificate issued by an appropriate body, such as cargo superintendents.
(ii) Insist that the customer signs a letter of hypothecation incorporating a letter of pledge when signing the letter of credit application form.
(iii) Ensure that the letter of credit calls for documents which clearly demonstrate that the goods are under the control of the bank, i.e. call for a full set of Clean on Board bills of lading made out to order and blank endorsed or showing the consignee as the bank's stated agent.
(iv) The letter of credit should call for an insurance document which will be blank endorsed, i.e., be in a transferable form and should be for the full

value of the goods plus a margin of 10%. Some banks will insist that an insurance policy by a first class company is presented.

(v) Upon arrival of the documents, assuming that they are in order and the bank accepts the bill of exchange, arrange for the goods to be cleared through Customs, deposited in the bank's name with a first class warehouse and the warehouse warrants deposited with the bank. Charges for customer's account.

(vi) The bank's agent must make sure that the goods are easily identifiable and are adequately insured and that the insurance is available for the bank's protection. Charges for customer's account.

(vii) When the times comes for the goods to be released to the buyers in the south of England, provided you are totally satisfied with the customer's integrity, the goods should be released to them against a trust receipt and an undertaking to pay the proceeds of the sale directly into the bank.

(viii) To be absolutely sure, because of the difficult financial position of the customer, the warehouse-keeper may be instructed to release the goods only after payment has been received from the buyer in the south of England. The buyer will receive a delivery order in exchange for payment directly into the bank.

(ix) The funds will be placed on a side account and held until maturity of the bill of exchange accepted by the bank and under the letter of credit. Interest would normally be paid on this deposit.

Answer 7.9

The customer will be told the following:

(a) Article 10 of Uniform Customs and Practice for Documentary Credits, Publication 400 states "An irrevocable Credit constitutes a definite undertaking of the Issuing Bank, provided the terms and conditions of the Credit are complied with:

(i) to pay, or that payment will be made, if the Credit provides for payment, whether against a draft or not;

(ii) to accept drafts, if the Credit provides for acceptance by the issuing Bank or to be responsible for their acceptance and payment at maturity if the Credit provides for the acceptance of drafts drawn on the applicant for the Credit of any other drawee specified in the Credit;

(iii) to purchase/negotiate, without recourse to drawers, and/or bona fide holders, drafts drawn by the beneficiary, at sight or at a tenor, on the applicant for the Credit or on any other drawee specified in the Credit, or to provide for purchase/negotiation by another bank, if the Credit provides for purchase/negotiation."

(b) The basic documents called for under a letter of credit are:

(i) Invoices, showing the letter of credit description of the goods, the price basis, e.g. FOB, C and F or CIF etc., the shipping marks and numbers and the weight of the goods.

(ii) Insurance document, policy or certificate, not a broker's note. The documents should be in the same currency as the letter of credit for a margin of, say, 10 per cent on top of the CIF/invoice value. It must be blank endorsed or in a transferable form, it should cover the agreed risk in accordance with the commercial contract and show where claims payable.

(iii) Bills of lading (documents of title). Banks would expect to see a full set of clean on board bills of lading marked "Freight Paid" (if C and F or CIF), to be endorsed in blank enabling title to pass, etc. Bills of lading should be issued by the carrier and not a forwarding agent. They should obviously name the vessel and the point of loading and discharge.

(c) (i) The customer should be told to call for an independent inspection certificate as part of the letter of credit documents. The certificate will be issued by a reputable company such as Cargo Superintendents and would indicate the quality, the weight, the specifications etc. of the goods ordered.

(ii) If possible, the customer should arrange to open a letter of credit for an agreed percentage of the contract price, i.e. 80 per cent with the balance to be paid after inspection of the goods on arrival in the UK.

(iii) The customers should deal only with reliable sellers and should obtain a bank reference and, if possible, a trade reference before establishing credits in favour of overseas sellers.

(iv) The customer should investigate the possibility, however remote, of establishing a revocable letter of credit.

Answer 7.10

(a) (i) The basic instrument which will be used to arrange for preshipment and post-shipment finance is an irrevocable letter of credit calling for drafts at 90 days sight with a red clause attachment. The draft will be drawn on the correspondent/advising bank in the Antipodes.

(ii) Arrangements would have to be made as to who will pay the charges in setting up the letter of credit including discount charges for 90 days.

(iii) Some form of protection would be made available to Antipodes Limited if a third party inspection certificate issued by an independent body is part of the document called for under the letter of credit.

(b) (i) A Documentary credit will be subject to "Uniform Customs and Practice for Documentary Credits", Publication No. 400 which came into force on 1 October 1984.

(ii) The customer should understand the meaning of the conditional payment order, which a documentary letter of credit is, which can be described under the following terms: "An irrevocable credit constitutes a definite undertaking of the issuing bank, providing that the terms and conditions of the credit are complied with: (i) To pay, or the payment will be made, if the credit provides for payment whether against a draft or not; (ii) To accept drafts if the credit provides for acceptance by the issuing bank or to be responsible for their acceptance and payment at maturity if the credit provides for the acceptance of drafts drawn on the applicant for the credit or any other drawee specified in the credit; (iii) To purchase/negotiate, without recourse to the drawers and/or bona fide holders, drafts drawn by the beneficiary, at sight or at a tenor, on the applicant for the credit or on any other drawee specified in the credit, or to provide for purchase/negotiation by another bank, if the credit provides for purchase/negotiation (Article 10 (a))".

(iii) A third party inspection certificate which will be issued by an independent body in the Antipodes and will afford the buyer some protection.

(iv) Where red clause facilities are granted to agents, Antipodes must understand that they are having to bear a risk in that the agents will be able to obtain an advance "refundable" by the presentation of documents in accordance with the terms of the credit to the advising bank. Meanwhile, the agents will have received this cash in advance by overdraft or loan, plus or inclusive of interest depending upon the wording of the red clause which will enable them to purchase the goods and arrange for shipment. The agents, therefore, will have been given preshipment finance and the only other protection which may be called for may be to make the advances conditional in that they can be made against an undertaking by the agents to present documents of title in respect of goods, namely a warehouse warrant. Where unconditional red clause advances are made the *total* risk must be borne by Antipodes Limited.

(v) If the documents are presented in order, the advance will be technically repaid and the advising/confirming bank will, at that stage, accept the 90-day bill of exchange drawn on it and arrange to discount the bill amount paying out the proceeds immediately to the buying agent. It may well be that no cash will change hands at that stage because it will already have enjoyed the benefit of the red clause advance. Arrangements would have to be made in the original instrument, namely the letter of credit as to who would pay the discount charges.

(vi) The buying agents clearly have received an advantage in that funds have been available to them to obtain pre-shipment finance, yet at the same time will not be called upon to repay the advance where bills of exchange have been accepted by the confirming bank. Antipodes meanwhile, will not be called upon to pay for the documents relating to the underlying goods for a further 90 days. Both parties therefore have received the advantage of continuing trade although Antipodes are having to bear the risk in order to maintain the advantage of receiving 90 days credit.

Answer 7.11

1. The company having little strength in the balance sheet has not got the financial strength so that further facilities would not be granted to it.
2. Since the bank would be unable to commit itself further for this customer, the only method which would be satisfactory from the customer's point of view would be by means of an irrevocable confirmed and transferable letter of credit.
3. This credit should be established in accordance with the provision of Article 46 of "Uniform Customs and Practice", ICC Publication No. 400 (which came into force on 1 October 1984).
4. By this means, a middleman acting in accordance with the Uniform Customs can arrange to purchase, apparently on his own behalf, goods from a second beneficiary as the rules allow for the facility of the first beneficiary, in this case Counter-Trade-Limited to transfer part or all of the credit in favour of the supplier who becomes the second beneficiary.
5. The second beneficiary would have to present the documents called for in the prime credit to a bank in London (in this case it should be the bank) of Counter-Trade Limited) and at that stage Counter-Trade will have the facility to substitute their invoices for onward presentation with the rest of the documents, plus an adjustment for insurance etc., if necessary, to the buyer in France. This will enable Counter-Trade Limited to receive their commission of 25%. The supplier would then receive Counter-Trade's purchase price, but the buyer in France would pay for the gross figure. Disclosures should not take place between the parties as the banks would show Counter-Trade Limited as the opener of the second credit. Of course, disclosure can take place if the parties agree to it.

Answer 7.12

(a) The "International Practice" referred to is the new Uniform Customs and Practice for Documentary Credits, Publication No. 400, which came into force on the 1 October 1984. The main differences between this publication and the last one which was Uniform Customs and Practice for Documentary Credits, Publication No. 290, which had been in operation and accepted by the major trading nations since the 1 October 1979, lies in the basic ground rules under which Documentary Credits should be applied. Unfortunately, this latter publication had a number of deficiencies, one of which was that a number of general provisions and definitions, though applicable, were not part of the Articles of the Document and this caused confusion.

(b) The advising bank is now responsible for taking reasonable care to check the apparent authenticity of the credit it advises. This is in respect of all credits of whatever type. This means that the advising bank cannot pass on letters of credit without responsibility, although it can advise without engagement on its part. (Article 8.)

(c) Any one of the changes listed briefly below and covered by the articles mentioned would have received marks.

(i) *Articles 1 & 2:* Stand-By Letters of Credit are now to be included.
(ii) *Article 2:* Acting "on the instructions of a customer" instead of "acting at the request and in accordance with the instructions of a customer". The Issuing Bank as the *Paying Bank.*
(iii) *Article 10:* The Issuing Bank as "Paying Bank", Deferred payments, the responsibility of paying an accepted Bill of Exchange.
(iv) *Article 11:* Indication of how credits must be available i.e. by payment etc.
(v) *Article 12:* The ability to issue credits by "tele-transmission" etc.
(vi) *Article 16:* The responsibility of an Issuing Bank when refusing to take up documents to advise the Advising or Negotiating Bank without delay, stating the discrepancies.
(vii) *Article 21:* Providing the reimbursement Bank authorising it to honour claims for reimbursement with proper instructions in good time.
(viii) *Article 22:* The acceptance of reprographic systems, automated or computerised systems or carbon copies when marked as originals, if where necessary those documents appear to have been authenticated.
(ix) *Article 23:* The acceptance of documents other than transport, insurance documents or commercial invoices of specific types, as presented where the data content makes it possible to relate to the goods and/or services referred to therein.
(x) *Article 24:* Documents dated prior to the issuance of a Letter of Credit will be acceptable unless the credit stipulates otherwise and providing they conform to the terms of the credit.
(xi) *Article 25:* Presentation of Combined Transport documents or Freight Forwarder's Bills of Lading where Marine Bills of Lading are not necessary.
(xii) *Article 27:* "Receive for shipment" Bills of Lading may well be accepted.
(xiii) *Article 29:* Trans-shipment is now defined and where a Combined Transport Bill of Lading is called for, it may be acceptable even though the credit prohibits trans-shipment.

(xiv) *Article 33:* "Third Party" Consignors on Bills of Lading may be acceptable.

(xv) *Article 37:* Unless stipulated in the credit, Insurance Documents will be required for 110% of the CIF or CIP value where this is ascertainable.

(xvi) *Article 39:* Insurance Documentation and an "All-Risks" clause. Banks will accept any clause indicating "All Risks" covered.

(xvii) *Article 43:* The change of tolerances in respect of bulk shipments from 3% to 5% unless of course, the credit stipulates otherwise.

(xviii) *Article 44:* The tidying up of the meaning of Partial shipments/Partial drawings/ and the fact that as well as Bills of Lading showing shipments on the same vessel, on the same journey, being deemed as one shipment, documents evidencing despatch by other modes of transport similar to parcel post are regarded as one shipment where they are all dated on the same day.

(xix) *Article 48:* The presentation of documents on the next business day after an expiry date where the expiry of the Letter of Credit is on a day when the Banks are closed, being extended to cover the old "21 day rule".

(xx) *Article 54:* Transferable Letters of Credit and the "right" of the beneficiary to give instructions as well as the ability to substitute drafts and to call for increased insurance values in accordance with the terms of the original "prime" credit.

(xxi) *Article 55:* The assignment of "any proceeds to which the beneficiary may be or may become entitled".

Section 8

Answers

Answer 8.1

(a) The UK exporter can arrange for his goods to be leased by the overseas buyer (with his agreement). This would give the export immediate payment while allowing the buyer to spread his payments over a medium term span.
(b) An alternative method would be to obtain a forfaiting facility whereby bills of exchange or promissory notes can be forfaited (discounted) to yield an immediate payment to the exporter yet allowing the buyer to spread his payments over a number of years.
(c) Another possibility is to take out a Specific ECGD guarantee together with an ECGD bank guarantee, or, alternatively, an ECGD Buyer Credit Guarantee.

Analysis: all three offer non-recourse finance to the exporter but with leasing either there may be extended negotiations with both the leasing company and the lessee (if cross-border leasing) or the leasing company may require a substantial price discount to take on the business. An advantage of leasing is that it may give the buyer certain tax advantages which could be reflected partly in the quoted price.

Forfaiting offers the possible advantage of fixed interest rates and no currency exposure. However, it will usually entail the provision of promissory notes by the buyer. It may also be an expensive method calling for "option" and "commitment" fees.

ECGD facilities may offer the advantage of preferential interest rates and, in the case of the Buyer Credit Guarantee there is no loan arrangement between the exporter and his bank but between the overseas buyer and his bank. However, cover is not 100% and there could be considerable time delays in making a claim.

Answer 8.2

Advantages

(i) no sales ledger burden
(ii) no debt collection
(iii) improved bank finance may be possible

(iv) lower discounts to buyers
(v) no currency exposure
(vi) "open account" terms could improve sales
(vii) factor may provide market information

Factoring is more suitable for business on short-term credit terms and if the exporter is seeking to offer credit spread over a number of years he should consider alternative facilities, e.g. an ECGD specific policy together with an ECGD specific bank guarantee, or a forfaiting facility. However, none of these provide exactly the services of a factor.

Answer 8.3

The facility mentioned in the question is forfaiting and the salient points are as follows:

1. Forfaiting is an arrangement whereby exporters of capital goods can obtain medium-term finance, usually for periods between 1 and 7 years, in respect of a purchase of obligations falling due at some future date arising from delivery of goods and services relating to exports.
2. The forfaiting bank buys bills of exchange, promissory notes or other obligations arising out of international trade transactions at a discount.
3. Promissory notes are the preferred instrument of payment because it is possible for the exporter to free himself from all recourse obligations. It is possible that the forfaitist (purchasing bank) may agree to purchase promissory notes even before a contract is signed against payment of a commitment fee.
4. The purchases take place on a non-recourse basis and, therefore, the drawee or maker of the promissory note must be of undoubted standing.
5. The security will also carry the undertaking or aval of an internationally known banking name as guarantor.
6. The bill or promissory note must be unconditional and not dependent upon the export performance of his contract as the forfaitist has no right of recourse against the exporter.
7. Repayment by periodic instalments is normally a condition of granting credit. Interest is fixed at the commencement of the period and is debited immediately, thus a net figure is paid away immediately making the arrangement the equivalent of a cash sale.
8. All risks are borne by the forfaiter including the political, transfer and currency risks.
9. The currencies used are normally US dollars, Deutsche Marks and Swiss francs, namely, currencies which can be financed on a matched basis, i.e. on deposit with a forfaiter.

Advantages to the exporter

1. Relieves him of balance sheet contingent liabilities.
2. Improves liquidity. (These two advantages, viz. 1 and 2, should result in an increased credit capacity for the exporter.)
3. There is no effect on the overdraft or other credit limits granted by banks.
4. Avoids losses which can arise out of a retained risk position under Government (such as ECGD) or private insurance cover and avoids the possibility of liquidity problems, which are sometimes unavoidable during the waiting of a claim period to fall due under such schemes.
5. Fixes the interest rate and therefore reduced the risk of fluctuations.

6. Obviates the need for foreign exchange cover as it avoids the difficulties arising out of foreign exchange fluctuations.
7. Removes all administrative and collection problems and related risks.
8. If appropriate, forfaiting can provide a fast and flexible financing system, particularly where contracts are with EEC buyers and where ECGD-backed facilities are not available.

Disadvantages to the exporter

1. The costs may be relatively high as sometimes the documentation requirements are rather complicated.
2. The forfaitist will only be willing to undertake such obligations if satisfied as to the standing of, not only the buyer, but the buyer's country in settling its international indebtedness.
3. The forfait paper may only represent 60–90 per cent of the value of export, because the forfaitist might insist that between 10–20 per cent be paid as up front cash at the time that the order is placed. This, occasionally, causes difficulty due to the cash-flow problems not only of the buyer but a buyer's country.

Answer 8.4

The four methods of providing finance which have been developed in recent years outside normal bank finance are as follows.

1. *Forfaiting*

(a) Forfaiting is the purchasing of bills without recourse to the drawer where the bills have been avalised or endorsed by a first-class bank in the drawee's country. Promissory notes are sometimes issued in lieu of the bills.
(b) An exporter would obtain immediate cash and is relieved of all credit and currency risk as well as charges.
(c) Forfaiting is the equivalent of supplier credit and is available up to 7 years, usually in three major currencies notably US dollars, Deutsche Marks and Swiss francs. The forfaiter may hold the bills or promissory notes in his own portfolio or place them in a secondary market. The cost of forfaiting is more expensive than other forms of finance because of the forfaiter's risks.

2. *International leasing*

(a) Usually handled by syndicates and normally in respect of large capital items such as aircraft, ships, oil rigs, production plants etc.
(b) Export credit facilities are often combined with the lease and as far as the UK is concerned, lessors are usually members of the equipment Leasing Association.
(c) Capital allowances from the UK point of view are not as attractive as overseas, which have recently been reduced from 25 per cent to 10 per cent.
(d) Cross-border leases sometimes take place where a lessor supplies equipment in one country and leases it directly to a lessee in another. Leveraged or geared leases are not unknown where a lessor supplies only part of the capital required, the remainder is raised on the local money markets.
(e) Multi-currency packages are often involved with fluctuating interest rates which can cause difficulties for lessors when they are called upon to fund medium-term fixed rate leases.

3. *Export factoring*

(a) Arranged by a factoring company (often a subsidiary of a bank).

(b) UK seller assigns book debts to the factor and can receive up to 85 per cent advance of the invoices.
(c) The factor arranges to collect the value of the invoice and usually utilises the services of its parent bank to collect the shipping documents etc.
(d) The overseas agent factor collects payment as agent of the UK factor and will also make status/credit investigation on importers.
(e) Cost of factoring may be quite high as it is an alternative to bank finance plus ECGD cover as country, currency and credit risk are borne by factor.
(f) Factoring is best suited to companies selling raw materials, manufacturing finished consumer or light industrial products.

4. *Counter trade: Compensation trade: Linked purchases in international trade*

(a) Involves an agreed exchange of goods plus or minus some cash exchange, and is usually found where a purchaser insists on disposing of "unwanted goods".
(b) A specialist base in Vienna, London, Paris or Munich is often used to "move" the goods and Eastern European countries are often involved because they tend to insist upon some form of countertrade.
(c) Variations of countertrade are barter, where an exchange of goods without cash payment takes place or compensation deals where one contract covers the delivery of goods against a counter delivery of specified goods in payment. This may be in respect of the whole or part of the price.

Answer 8.5

COLUMN A Notes due in (no. of months).	COLUMN B Principal sum of each note. US $s	COLUMN C Balance outstanding US $s	COLUMN D Interest per annum on each balance outstanding US $s	COLUMN E Principal plus interest (B+D) US $s	COLUMN F Forfaitors straight discount percentage on notes (E) US $s	COLUMN G Net receipt by Exporter (E-F) US $s
12 months	4,050,000	81,000,000	7,695,000	11,745,000	1,174,500	10,570,500
24 months	8,100,000	76,950,000	7,310,250	15,410,250	3,082,050	12,328,200
36 months	12,150,000	68,850,000	6,540,750	18,690,750	5,607,225	13,083,525
48 months	16,200,000	56,700,000	5,386,500	21,586,500	8,634,600	12,951,900
60 months	20,250,000	40,500,000	3,847,500	24,097,500	12,048,750	12,048,750
72 months	20,250,000	20,250,000	1,923,750	22,173,750	13,304,250	8,869,500
Totals	$81,000,000	NIL	$32,703,750	$113,703,750	$43,851,375	$69,852,375

(1) Total sterling receipt of the beneficiary $= \frac{\$69,852,375}{1.4730} =$ *£47,421,843*

(2) Total dollar cost to the obligor = $113,703,750

Answer 8.6

The answer should have covered most of the following points about export factoring which:

1. Indemnifies the customer 100% against buyer default on approved sales (approval is given by local agents).
2. Provides credit control (protection and information) and a collection service in the language and according to the local customs in the appropriate market.
3. Provides a sales ledger and management information service.
4. Provides up to 80% immediate payment in multicurrency and/or sterling against export receivables and guarantees payment of the balance after an agreed period.
5. Covers the customer against exchange rate fluctuations (often by taking out forward cover by using foreign currency borrowings).
6. It is possible for the exporter to cover in full a particular currency exposure, if necessary, because the customer can take out a forward contract to cover the balance which is not "protected" by the factor, although some factors will cover the full debt amount.
7. Factoring companies act through associate/subsidiary companies or through factoring associations throughout the world and provide a comprehensive cover.
8. The service charge is between 0.7% and 2.5% of export turnover.
9. The lending is charged at the rate of between 1.5% and 3% over bank base rate or LIBOR.

Answer 8.7

(a) When a Bank is asked to guarantee a Bill of Exchange it is because the other parties to the bill want the Bank to take prime responsibility and the holder of the bill probably wishes to sell the bill without recourse to himself. This situation is usually regarded as a "forfaiting" arrangement and it usually occurs when goods are sold on long term credit i.e. over two years. The arrangement which can exist on the continent is for a Bank to endorse a bill "pour aval" and the avalised bill is regarded as being guaranteed by that Bank. Many companies ask for "off balance sheet" finance.

(b) The reason why in the United Kingdom such a method is not normally accepted is that there is no provision under the Bills of Exchange Act 1882, for avalising Bills. When a party endorses a Bill of Exchange they become liable thereon to holders in due course, but there is no suggestion that such an endorsement is a guarantee of payment. British Banks do not guarantee a Bill of Exchange by attempting to avalise it (which technically they cannot do) or by placing an endorsement on a bill because such a case has not been tested under English Law and it is doubtful what the outcome of such a case would be. Further, there is a Committee of London Clearing Banks Agreement that members of the CLCB will not attempt to avalise Bills of Exchange.

(c) (i) The best compromise solution will be to arrange for an irrevocable Letter of Credit issued in favour of the seller by the Bank, calling for drafts drawn at 90 days sight on itself.

(ii) This course would enable the seller to raise finance on the Bill of Exchange, and who would pay the discount charges would be a matter between buyer and seller.

(iii) The rate charged for discounting such a Bill would be the current rate for prime Bank Bills at 90 days sight and this will be a cheaper form of finance than ordinary trade bills.

(iv) It might be possible to arrange a Stand-By Letter of Credit as a guarantee of the customer's trade debt but this would probably be second choice from the supplier's point of view.

(v) Unusually, instead of establishing either an irrevocable Letter of Credit or a Stand-By Letter of Credit, one might agree that the buyer could draw Bills of Exchange on the Bank itself, which would be accepted by the Bank and would have the same effect as drawing under a Letter of Credit. The customer would be expected to pay the equivalent charges as and when the Bank establishes a Documentary Letter of Credit.

Answer 8.8

(a) (i) The basic instrument which will cater for all parties is a transferable Letter of Credit which is now subject to Article 54 of Uniform Customs and Practice for Documentary Credits publication No. 400 which came into force on the 1 October, 1984.

(ii) Under Article 54 the first beneficiary, in this case Woodwork Limited, would have the right to request the bank to transfer either part or all of the credit in favour of one or more other parties, namely the suppliers of the goods in Malaysia. In order to protect the customer's profit margin the amount of the terms and conditions specified in the original credit would be transferred, with the exception of:

— The amount of the credit
— Any unit prices stated therein
— The period of validity
— The latest date for presentation of documents in accordance with Article 47
— The period of shipment.

All of which may be curtailed or reduced.

In addition, the percentage for which the insurance covers must be effected, may be increased in such a way as to provide the amount of cover stipulated in the original credit.

(b) It is the change in Uniform Customers and Practice for Documentary Credits covering the insurance requirements which has particularly affected transactions such as this one.

Although the customer may have not presented documents strictly in accordance with the terms of the credit, the basic problem with CIF contracts prior to October 1984 was in connection with insurance values. With the new regulation, under Article 54, the customer can now transfer a second credit in favour of the suppliers in Malaysia, calling for an Insurance Certificate covering the shipment from Malaysia direct to West Germany for a specific sum which in effect will be the CIF value plus 10% called for in the original credit (Article 54(e)). The rest of the documents will be substituted in the normal way as they would have been under the requirements of Article 46 of Publication 290.

A further change is that the first beneficiary can now "officially" substitute his draft for that of the second beneficiary.

Section 9

Answers

Answer 9.1

(a) | | |
|---|---|
| YI = £0.0027586 – 0.0027662 | Found by dividing |
| SFI = £0.318725 – 0.319744 | the rates into 1 |
| £1 = DM3.7824 – 3.7925 | and reversing the |
| £1 = KD0.41036 – 0.41049 | equation |

(b) Bank selling: Bank buying

(i) $$\text{DK1} = \text{PE} = \frac{13.905}{195} = \text{PE}0.0713 - 0.0718 = \frac{13.925}{194}$$

Bank selling: Bank buying

$$\text{PE1} = \text{DK} = \frac{194}{13.925} = \text{DK}13.932 - 14.024 = \frac{195}{13.905}$$

(ii) First find the £1 value of Canadian dollars,

i.e. $£1 = \text{C\$}\,\frac{1}{0.5579}$ and $\frac{1}{0.5576} = \text{C\$}1.7924\text{–}1.7934$

Bank selling: Bank buying

$$\text{Then; SK1} = \text{C\$} = \frac{11.17}{1.7934} = \text{C\$}6.2284 - 6.2430 = \frac{11.19}{1.7924}$$

Bank selling: Bank buying

$$\text{C\$1} = \text{SK} = \frac{1.7924}{11.79} = \text{SK}0.1602 - 0.1606 = \frac{1.7934}{11.17}$$

(c) (i) $\$210 = £\,\frac{210}{1.3025} = £161.23$

(ii) $£157 = \$\,\frac{157}{0.7678} = \$204.48$

(d) In London sell £100,000 @ \$1.3025 = \$130,250
In Paris sell \$130,250 @ FF8.9400 = FF1,164,435.
In New York sell FF1,164,435 @ FF8.9315 = \$130,373.95
In London sell \$130,373.95 @ \$1.3035 = £100,018.37

Net profit £18.37.

Answer 9.2

(a) $\text{DM } 0.46 = \frac{1}{2.4315} \times 0.46 = \$0.1892$

$\text{Y } 34 = \frac{1}{237.10} \times 34 = \$0.1434$

$\text{FF } 0.74 = \frac{1}{6.8925} \times 0.74 = \$0.1074$

$£0.071 = \frac{1}{0.6638} \times 0.071 = \$0.1069$

+ *\$0.5400*
Total *\$1.0869* = SDR1

If \$1 = DM 2.4315 then DM 2.4315 x 1.0869 = *DM 2.6428* = SDR1

If \$1 = Y 237.10 then Y 237.10 x 1.0869 = *Y 257.70* = SDR1

If \$1 = FF 6.8925 then FF 6.8925 x 1.0869 = *FF 7.4915* = SDR1

If \$1 = £0.6638 then £0.6638 x 1.0869 = *£0.7215* = SDR1

(b) £10,000 worth of dollars @ \$1 = £0.6638 = $\left(£1 = \frac{1}{0.6638}\right) = \$1.5065$

Therefore £10,000 = (1.5065 x 10,000) = ***\$15064.78***

£10,000 worth of SDRs @ SDR1 = £0.7215 = $\left(£1 = \frac{1}{0.7215}\right) = \text{SDR}1.3860$

Therefore £10,000 = 1.3860 x 10,000 = ***SDR13860***

(c) Selling \$15064.78 for sterling. First, find cross rates for sterling/ dollars, i.e.

$£1 = \frac{\$1.3822}{1.08860} = \$1.2697$ (bank selling dollars)

$£1 = \frac{\$1.3832}{1.08850} = \$1.2707$ (bank selling dollars)

So, sell \$15064.78 @ 1.2707 = ***£11855.50***

Selling SDR 13860 for sterling @ £1 = SDR 1.3822 = $\left(\frac{13860}{1.3822}\right)$ = ***£10027.49***

Answer 9.3

1 December. Exporter sells \$400,000 3 months forward with option in the third month @ 1.3205 = £302,915.56 expected receipts.

10 February. \$300,000 received and delivered forward @ 1.3205 = £227,186.67 received from bank.

1 March. Close-out. $100,000 purchased spot @ 1.3185 = £75,843.76 cost. $100,000 is delivered forward @ 1.3205 = £75,728.89 received from bank.

Also sells $100,000 1 month option forward @ 1.3195 = £75,786.18 expected receipts.

Total receipts	=	£227,186.67	(10 February)
Less		75,843.76	(1 March)
Plus		75,728.82	(1 March)
Plus		75,786.28	(April)
	=	£302,858.01	total net receipts

Answer 9.4

1 December. Importer buys $400,000 3 months forward with option in the third month @ 1.3180 = £303,490.13 expected cost.

10 February. $300,000 paid from forward contract @ 1.3180 = £227,617.60 cost.

1 March. Close-out. Receive $100,000 from forward contract @ 1.3180 = £75,872.53 cost and sell the $100,000 spot @ 1.3195 = £75,786.28 receipt from bank.

Also buys $100,000 1 month option forward @ 1.3175 = £75,901.33 expected cost.

Total cost	=	£227,619.60	(10 February)
Less		75,786.28	(1 March)
Plus		75,872.53	(1 March)
Plus		75,901.33	(April)
	=	£303,607.18	total net cost

Answer 9.5

1 April. Customer buys $100,000 three months option forward @ 1.3462 = £74,283.17 cost.

1 July. Close-out. Customer sells $100,000 spot @ 1.3800 = £72,463.77 receipt. *Debit = £1,819.14.*

Extension

Customer buys $100,000 two months option @ 1.3800 less 0.0210 = 1.3590 = *£73,583.52 cost.*

Final total debit	=	£73,583.52
Plus		1,819.14
	=	£75,402.66

Answer 9.6

1 April. Initial payment of 10% made = DG3000. Buy DG3000 spot @ 4.26½ = £703.40 cost.

Also, buys DG10,000 one month option forward @ 4.26½ = £2,344.67 expected cost.

Also, buys DG10,000 two months option forward @ 4.26½ = £2,344.67 expected cost.

Also, buys DG10,000 three months forward with option in third month @ 4.28½ = £2,333.72 expected cost.

16 April. First machine arrives and cost of £2,344.67 is met.
28 May. Second machine arrives and cost of £2,344.67 is met.
1 July. Close-out. Customer receives DG10,000 at a cost of £2,333.72 but sells it spot @ 4.23 to receive £2,364.07 receipt.

Total costs =	£2,344.67	(16 April)
+	2,344.67	(28 May)
+	2,333.72	(1 July)
−	2,364.07	(1 July)
=	£4,658.99	

Answer 9.7

11 January. Customer sells SK500,000 three months option forward @ 11.32 = £44,169.61 expected receipts.

11 April. Close-out. Customer buys SK500,000 spot @ 11.17 = £44,762.76 cost, and delivers them forward.

Also, extends the forward contract by selling SK500,000 two months option forward @ 11.17 − 0.12 = 11.29 = £44,286.98 expected receipts.

Credit and debit entries

11 April.	Debit £44,762.76	Credit £44,169.61
3 June.		Credit £44,286.98
		net Credit = £43,693.83

Answer 9.8

1 month forward @ 1.3717
2 months forward @ 1.3612
3 months forward @ 1.3477
6 months forward @ 1.3198

He is an importer.

Answer 9.9

1 February. Customer buys $6.3 million two months forward with option in second month @ 1.3820 = £4,558,610.70 expected cost.

Also sells LIT 11000 million two months forward with option in the second month @ LIT 2362½ = £4,656,084.60 expected receipts.

19 March.	Debit £4,558,610.70
	Credit £4,656,084.60
	net credit = £ 97,473.90

Answer 9.10

1 July. Buy and Sell buy $60,000 three months option forward (option at no extra cost) @ 1.2940 = £46,367.85 expected cost.

1 August. Buy and Sell sell DM125,000 three months fixed forward @ 3.70 = £33,783.78 expected receipt.

1 September. Buy and Sell sell FF250,000 one month forward (option at no extra cost) @ 12.14 = £20,593.08 expected receipt.

Buy and Sell plc	debit	£46,367.85
	credit	33,783.78
	credit	20,593.08
	net credit	£ 8,009.01

Answer 9.11

15 March. Buy DM105,000 two months forward with option in second month @ 3.81 = £27,559.06 expected cost.

Also buys DM104,466 two months forward with option in second month @ 3.81 = £27,418.90 expected cost.

12 April. First machine shipped.

12 May. First machine paid for.

15 May. Close-out. Merchant sells DM104,466 spot @ 3.83½ = £27,240.16 receipt.

Extension

Merchant buys DM104,466 one month option forward @ 3.83½ − ½ = 3.83 = £27,275.72 expected cost.

16 May. Second machine arrives.

16 June. Second machine paid for.

Total cost of the machines

First machine	£27,559.06	debit
Second machine	27,418.90	debit
Close-out	27,240.14	credit
Extension	27,275.72	debit
Net cost	£55,013.54	

Answer 9.12

1 January. Merchant sells DF72,000 two months forward with option in second month @ 4.63½ = £15,533.98 expected receipt.

Also sells DF144,000 three months forward with option in third month @ 4.61 = £31,236.44 expected receipt.

14 January. First shipment made and paid for.

25 March. Reduced payment for second shipment received (DF72,000), and delivered forward. Balance of DF72,000 is closed-out; merchant buys DF72,000 spot @ 4.62 = £15,584.42 cost.

Merchants receipts	=	£15,533.98	(14 January)
Merchants receipts	=	15,618.22	(25 March) half payment
Merchants payment	=	15,584.42	(25 March) close-out
Merchants receipt	=	15,618.22	(25 March) balance of second contract
Net receipts		£31,186.00	

Answer 9.13

1 January. Importer buys FF29,880 one month option forward @ 11.30 = £2,644.25 expected cost. Also buys FF29,880 two months forward with option in second month @ 11.28 = £2,648.94 expected cost.

25 January. First shipment arrives and paid for.

1 March. Close-out. Importer sells FF29,880 spot @ 11.36 = £2,630.28 receipt.

Extension

Importer buys FF29,880 one months option forward @ 11.36 − .05 = 11.31 = £2,641.91 cost.

Net cost	=	£2,644.25
	+	2,648.94
	+	2,641.91
	−	2,630.28
	=	£5,304.82

Answer 9.14

1 September. Sandals Ltd buy $10,000 two months forward with option in second month @ 1.2905 = £7,748.93 expected cost. Also, buys $10,000 three months forward with option in third month @ 1.2853 £7,780.28 expected cost.

15 October. Goods received and paid for.

28 November. Goods received and paid for.

3 December. Buys $4,000 spot @ 1.3190 = £3,032.60 cost.

Total cost	=	£7,748.93
	+	7,780.28
	+	3,032.60
	=	£18,561.81

Answer 9.15

1 November. UK exporter sells $300,000 three months forward with option in third month @ 1.3350 = £224,719.10 expected receipts.

1 February. Close-out. Buys $300,000 spot @ 1.3230 = £226,757.36 cost. Extension — Exporter sells $250,000 two months forward @ 1.3240 = £188,821.75 receipt.

Total receipts	= £224,719.10	
Less	226,757.36	(Close-out)
Plus	188,821.75	(Extension)
	= £186,783.49	

Answer 9.16

At initial rates. Importer buys $200,000 three months forward with option in second and third months @ 1.3418 = £149,053.51 expected cost.

End of three months. Close-out sells $200,000 spot @ 1.3731 = £145.655.81 receipt.

New contract. Buys $250,000 two months option forward @ 1.3721 = £182,202.46 cost.

Net sterling cost	= £149,053.51
	+ 182,202.46
	− 145,655.81
	= £185,600.16

Answer 9.17

1 December 1983. Importer buys £100,000 two months option forward (option at no extra cost) @ 1.3160 = £73,529.41 expected cost.

31 January 1984. Close-out. Sell $100,000 spot @ 1.4240 = £70,224.72 receipt and deliver this sterling to his sterling (overdrawn) account.

or — hold $100,000 for one month @ 16½% per annum interest for 29 days = 100,000 x $\frac{16.5}{100} \times \frac{29}{360}$ $1,329.17 interest. Also sell one month option forward (option at no extra cost) both capital and interest of $101,329.16 @ 1.4280 = £70,958.80 receipt.

LESS interest incurred on *not* delivering £70,224.72 close-out receipt to the sterling account @ 14% per annum for 29 days =

£70,224.72 x $\frac{14}{100} \times \frac{29}{365}$ = £781.13 interest cost.

Net receipt of holding dollars	= £70,958.80
Less	781.13
	= 70,177.67
Net receipt of closing-out	= £70,224.72

so, best to close-out.

The formula expressions are:

IRD $16.5 \times \frac{29}{360} = 1.329\%$ (sell spot)

$14.0 \times \frac{29}{365} = 1.112\%$ (sell forward)

} net gain from holding dollars = 0.217%

CFC $\frac{1.4240 - 1.4280}{1.4280} \times 100 = -0.28\%$ = cost of forward cover (holding dollars)

Thus, holding dollars for one month incurs a loss of $0.280 - 0.217 = 0.063\%$

Note: This percentage result is slightly different from the result obtainable from a value calculation due to the latter's inclusion of dollar interest at forward rates.

Answer 9.18

Method (a) — borrowing the sterling equivalent

Advise customer to sell FF200,000 three months forward with option in third month @ 11.91 = £16,792.61 receipt.

Also, borrow £16,792.61 now @ 12% per annum for 91 days

$= £16,792.61 \times \frac{12}{100} \times \frac{91}{365} = £502.40$ interest cost.

Net receipts £16,792.61 – £502.40 = *£16,290.21*

Method (b) — borrow French francs

Borrow FF200,000 and sell spot @ 11.7775 = £16,981.53 receipt.

Interest equals FF200,000 $\times \frac{18}{100} \times \frac{91}{360}$ = FF9100 interest cost.

So buy, FF9100 three months forward @ 11.89 = £765.35 cost.

Net receipts £16,981.53 – £765.35 = *£16,216.18*

Answer: Best to borrow sterling (method (a)).

Formula answer

IRD $= 18 \times \frac{91}{360} = 4.55\%$

$12 \times \frac{91}{365} = 2.99\%$

} net gain from borrowing sterling = 1.56%

(sell spot) (sell forward)

CFC $= \frac{11.7775 - 11.91}{11.91} \times 100 = -1.11\%$ = net forward cost of borrowing sterling

Answer: net overall benefit from borrowing sterling = 1.56 – 1.11 = *0.45%*

Answer 9.19

Lending out £1 million @ 14% per annum for one month yields

$\frac{£1,000,000}{12} \times \frac{14}{100} = £11,666.66$ interest.

Replacing the £1m

(a) Borrow $1,326,500 @ 12% per annum for one month costs

$\frac{1,326,500}{12} \times \frac{12}{100} = \$13,265$ interest cost.

Sell $1,326,500 spot @ 1.3265 = £1m receipt.

Buy \$1,339,765 (capital + interest) one month forward @ 1.3248 = *£1,011,296 cost.*

(b) Borrow DM3,830,200 @ 5% per annum for one month costs

$$\frac{3,830,200}{12} \times \frac{5}{100} = \text{DM}15,959.17 \text{ interest cost.}$$

Sell DM3,830,200 spot @ 3.8302 = £1m receipt.

Buy DM3,846,159.10 (capital + interest) one month forward @ 3.7977 = *£1,012,760.10 cost.*

(c) Borrow DG4,315,000 @ 6% per annum for one month costs

$$\frac{4,315,000}{12} \times \frac{6}{100} = \text{DG}21,575.00 \text{ interest cost.}$$

Sell DG4,315,000 spot @ 4.315 = £1m receipt.

Buy DG4,336,575 (capital + interest) one month forward @ 4.2825 = *£1,012,626.90* interest cost.

Answer, borrow dollars at a cost of £11,296 giving a net profit over the sterling interest of *£370.66.*

Formula answers

Dollars. $IRD = \frac{14 - 12}{12} = 0.167\%$ interest gain.

(sell spot) (buy forward)

$$CFC = \frac{1.3265 - 1.3248}{1.3248} \times 100 = 0.128\% = \text{cost of forward cover.}$$

Net result = 0.167% – 0.128% = *0.039% net gain*

D.Marks $IRD = \frac{14 - 5}{12} = 0.75\%$ interest gain.

(sell spot) (buy forward)

$$CFC = \frac{3.8302 - 3.7977}{3.7977} \times 100 = 0.856\% = \text{cost of forward cover.}$$

Net result = 0.75% – 0.856% = *0.106% net cost*

D.Guilders $IRD = \frac{14 - 6}{12} = 0.667\%$ interest gain.

(sell spot) (buy forward)

$$CFC = \frac{4.315 - 4.2825}{4.2825} \times 100 = 0.759\% = \text{cost of forward cover.}$$

Net result = 0.667% – 0.759% = *–0.092% net cost.*

Answer: borrow dollars for a *0.39% net gain.*

Answer 9.20

Switching for one month

Sell £50,000 spot @ 1.4170 = \$70,850

Interest @ 9% per annum for one month $= \frac{70{,}850}{12} \times \frac{9}{100} = \$531.37$

Sell \$71,381.38 (capital + interest) one month option forward (option at no extra cost) @ 1.4190 = *£50,304.00 receipt.*

This compares with £50,000 left in sterling at 6% per annum for one month =
$\frac{50{,}000}{12} \times \frac{6}{100} = £250 =$ *£50,250.00*

There is a slight benefit from holding dollars.

$IRD = \frac{9-6}{12} = 0.25\%$ in favour of holding dollars.

(buy spot) (sell forward)

$CFC = \frac{1.4170 - 1.4190}{1.4190} \times 100 = 0.14\%$ = cost of forward cover.

Net result = 0.25% – 0.14% = 0.11% in favour of holding dollars.

Switching for 2 months

Sell £50,000 spot @ spot @ 1.4170 = \$70,850

Interest @ 9% per annum for two months $= \frac{70{,}850}{6} \times \frac{9}{100} = \$1062.75$

Sell \$71,912.76 (capital + interest) two months option forward (option at no extra cost) @ 1.4190 = *£50,678.47 receipt.*

This compares with £50,000 left on sterling at 6% per annum for two months =
$\frac{50{,}000}{6} \times \frac{6}{100} = £500 =$ *£50,500.00*

There is a gain of £178.47 from holding dollars.

$IRD = \frac{9-6}{6} = 0.5\%$ in favour of holding dollars.

(buy spot) (sell forward)

$CFC = \frac{1.4170 - 1.4190}{1.4190} \times 100 = 0.14\%$ = cost of forward cover.

Net result = 0.5% – 0.14% = 0.36% in favour of holding dollars.

Switching for 3 months

Sell £50,000 spot @ 1.4170 = \$70,850

Interest @ 9% per annum for three months $= \frac{70{,}850}{4} \times \frac{9}{12} = \$1594.13$

Sell \$72,444.13 (capital + interest) three months option forward (option at no extra cost) @ 1.4300 = *£50,660.23 receipt.*

This compares with £50,000 left in sterling at 6% per annum for three months =
$\frac{50{,}000}{4} \times \frac{6}{100} = £750 =$ *£50,750*

There is a loss from holding dollars of £89.77

$IRD = \frac{9-6}{4} = 0.75\%$ in favour of holding dollars.

(buy spot) (sell forward)

$CFC = \frac{1.4170 - 1.4300}{1.4300} \times 100 = 0.91\% =$ cost of forward cover

Net result = 0.75% − 0.91% = −0.16% against holding dollars.

Final verdict — Switch into dollars for two months

Answer 9.21

Interest on sterling lower than for dollars for all three periods. Therefore, it would only be possibly profitable to switch from dollars to sterling if there was a *negative* cost of forward cover from so doing.

In fact, a switch from dollars to sterling calling for a spot sale of dollars and a forward purchase of dollars is in all three time periods, at a *forward cost*. I.e. selling dollars spot @ 2.4180 and buying dollars forward @ 2.4170 (one month); 2.4165 (two months); and 2.4145 (three months).

Thus, there can be no possible benefit from switching dollars into sterling.

Switching sterling into dollars

Interest on £2 million

One month @ 16.375% per annum $= \frac{2m}{12} \times \frac{16.375}{100}$ = *£27,291.67*

Two months @ 16.5% per annum $= \frac{2m}{6} \times \frac{16.5}{100}$ = *£55,000.00*

Three months @ 16.625% per annum $= \frac{2m}{4} \times \frac{16.625}{100}$ = *£83,125.00*

Sell £2m spot @ 2.4170 = $4,834,000

Invest for one month @ 17% per annum $= \frac{4834000}{12} \times \frac{17}{100} = \$68,481.67$

Sell $4,902,481.67 (capital + interest) one month forward @ 2.419 = *£2,026,656.30*

Invest for two months @ 17% per annum $= \frac{4834000}{6} \times \frac{17}{100} = \$136,963.33$

Sell $4,970,963.33 (capital + interest) two months forward @ 2.4185 = *£2,055,391*

Invest for three months @ 16.9375% $= \frac{4834000}{4} \times \frac{16.9375}{100} = \$204,689.68$

Sell $5,038,689.68 (capital + interest) three months forward @ 2.4178 = *£2,083,997.60*

Hold dollars for three months to get best deal.

Formula answers

One month

$IRD = \frac{17 - 16.375}{12} = 0.052\%$ in favour of holding dollars (buy spot) (sell forward)

$$CFC = \frac{2.4170 - 2.4190}{2.4190} \text{ x } 100 = 0.083\% = \text{cost of forward cover.}$$

Result — Cost of forward cover exceeds gain on interest.
Don't switch into dollars.

Two months

$$IRD = \frac{17 - 16.5}{6} = 0.083\% \text{ in favour of holding dollars}$$

(buy spot) (sell forward)

$$CFC = \frac{2.4170 - 2.4185}{2.4185} \text{ x } 100 = 0.062\% = \text{cost of forward cover.}$$

Result — Cost of forward cover less than interest gain.
Switch into dollars.

Three months

$$IRD = \frac{16.9375 - 16.625}{4} = 0.078\% \text{ in favour of holding dollars}$$

(buy spot) (sell forward)

$$CFC = \frac{2.4170 - 2.4178}{2.4178} \text{ x } 100 = 0.033\% = \text{cost of forward cover.}$$

Result — Cost of forward cover less than interest gain.
Switch into dollars (best).

Answer 9.22

(a) *Wait for three months.* To do this would incur an unknown sterling cost. This is speculative and could result in a higher or lower cost depending on fluctuation on the lire. Not recommended.

(b) *Buy spot lire now and hold for three months, selling lire interest forward*

Buy LIT 1000m @ 2305 = £433,839.40 cost
Hold for three months @ 20.75% per annum

$$= \frac{1000\text{m}}{4} \text{ x } \frac{20.75}{100} = \text{LIT } 51.875\text{m interest}$$

Sell interest three months option forward (option at no extra cost) @ 2354.5 = £22,032.20 receipt.

Deduct the loss of interest on £433,839.40 @ 13.9375% per annum for three months

$$= \frac{433839.40}{4} \text{ x } \frac{13.9375}{100} = £15{,}116.59 \text{ interest cost.}$$

Summary:	Cost of spot lire	=	£433,839.40
	Add sterling interest cost	=	15,116.59
	Less lire interest	=	22,032.20
	Net cost	=	£426,923.79

⋆ (But see alternative below.)

(c) *Buy forward lire*

Buy LIT 1000m three months forward @ 2349.5 = *£425,622.40 cost*

Thus, (c) is cheaper than (b).

**Alternative to (b)*

An alternative to (b) is to buy only the *Net Present Value* of LIT 1000m.

$$\text{i.e.}\quad \frac{LIT\ 1000m}{\left(1+\frac{5.1875}{100}\right)} = \text{LIT } 950.6833\text{m}$$

So, buy LIT 950.6833m spot @ 2305 = £412,443.95 cost.
(Interest accrued of LIT 49.3167m will make up the LIT 1000m)

Add sterling interest on £412,443.95 @ 13.9375% per annum for three months

$$= \frac{412443.95}{4} \times \frac{13{,}9375}{100} = £14{,}371.09 \text{ cost.}$$

Total cost = £412,443.95 + £14,371.09 = *£426,815.04*

Although this is cheaper than buying LIT 1000m (b) it is still more expensive than (c).

$$\textit{Formula}\quad IRD = \frac{20.75 - 13.9375}{4} = 1.703\% \text{ in favour of holding lire}$$

(buy spot) (buy forward)

$$CFC = \frac{2305 - 2349.5}{2349.5} \times 100 = 1.894\% = \textit{negative} \text{ cost of forward cover (i.e. gain).}$$

Thus, method (c) gives a CFC gain *greater* than the loss of not holding lire.

Answer 9.23

Lire value of goods shipped

£10,000 @ LIT 2102 sold three months option forward (option at no extra cost)
= LIT 21.02m

Lire trading and interest profits accrued by UK parent

The Milan subsidiary receives	LIT 30m
and incurs costs of	LIT 21.02m
but accrues interest on LIT 30m @ 23% per annum for two months	
$= \frac{30m}{6} \times \frac{23}{100} =$	*LIT 1.15m*
Net receipt =	*LIT 10.13m*

One half of this is attributable to the UK parent = *LIT 5.065m*

Answer 9.24

Invoice value of goods = LIT 21.02m

(a) *Remit as planned* = sell forward three months to yield £10,000 (@ 2102)

(b) *Or hold for one month*

Buy LIT 21.02m spot @ 2056 for cost of £10,223.70 and deliver the lire as per the forward contract. Close-out loss = £223.70

Hold LIT 21.02m on deposit for one month @ 22.5% per annum

$= \frac{21.02m}{12} \times \frac{22.5}{100}$ =LIT 394,125 interest received.

Sell LIT 21,414,125 (capital and interest) one month forward @ 2067.75 = £10,356.24 receipt

Less interest forgone on sterling of £10,000 @ 16.6% per annum for one month

$= \frac{10{,}000}{12} \times \frac{16.5}{100}$ = £137.50

Summary:	Sale of forward lire	=	£10,356.24
	less close-out loss	=	223.70
	less interest forgone	=	137.50
	Net receipt	=	£ 9,995.04

Result: do *not* hold LIT 21.02m for one more month.

Formula

$IRD = \frac{22.5 - 16.5}{12}$ = 0.5% in favour of holding lire

(buy spot) (sell forward)

$CFC = \frac{2056 - 2067.75}{2067.75} \times 100$ = 0.568% = cost of forward cover (holding lire)

Thus, there is a net *loss* of 0.5 – 0.568 = 0.068% in holding lire for another one month.

Interest and trading profits = LIT 5.065m

(a) *Remit as planned* = sell spot @ 2057 = *£2,462.30 receipt*

(b) *or hold for one month* sell LIT 5.065m one month forward @ 2067.75.
Interest on LIT 5.065m for one month @ 22.5% per annum
$= \frac{5.065m}{12} \times \frac{22.5}{100}$ = LIT 94968.70

Total = LIT 5,159,968.7 @ 2067.76 = £2,495.45 receipts less loss of sterling interest on £2,462.30 (being sterling receipt of sale of spot LIT 5.065m) @ 16.5% per annum for one month =

$\frac{2462.30}{12} \times \frac{16.5}{100}$ = £33.86 interest cost

Summary:	Receipt from forward sale	=	£2,495.45
	less interest foregone	=	£ 33.86
	Net receipt	=	£2,461.59

Net receipt from remitting as planned = £2,462.30

Thus, remit as planned.

Formula

$IRD = \frac{22.5 - 16.5}{12}$ = 0.5% in favour of holding lire (sell spot) (sell forward)

$$CFC = \frac{2057 - 2067.75}{2067.75} \text{ x } 100 = 0.52\% = \text{cost of forward cover (holding lire).}$$

Thus, there is a net loss of 0.5 – 0.52 = 0.02% from holding lire for one more month.

Answer 9.25

1 September. Receive $300,000 less payment of $200,000 = $100,000 net receipt. Use this to buy FF600,000 spot @ 8.2050 = $73,126.14 cost. This leaves balance of $26,873.86 which is sold spot @ 1.4635 = *£18,362.73 net receipt.*

Also buy $200,000 one month forward @ 1.4633 (to make dollar payment on 1 October) = *£136,677.37 net cost.*

Also, buy FF600,000 three months forward @ 8.2670 (to make franc payment on 1 December) = *$72,577.71 cost.* Use the $400,000 receipt on 1 December for this and sell the balance of $327,422.29 three months forward @ 1.4660 = *£223,343.99 receipt.*

Also, sell net $50,000 receipt on 1 March six months forward @ 1.4682 = *£34,055.31 receipt.*

Summary:	1 September	receipt	£18,362.73
	1 October	payment	136,677.37
	1 December	receipt	223,343.99
	1 March	receipt	34,055.31
		Net receipt	£139,084.66

Answer 9.26

To ensure that the short-term investment is both profitable and non-speculative, the investor would have to consider a covered interest arbitrage deal. This would require information about short-term interest rates in the UK and overseas as well as spot and forward currency rates against sterling. It is usual that when interest rates abroad are higher than in the UK (for similar instruments) the currency concerned is at a forward discount against sterling. Thus, a gain in interest rates is offset by a loss on forward cover. This can be put into a formula:

$$\frac{r^o - r^d}{t} = \textit{the interest rate differential} \text{ (IRD)}$$

and $\frac{S - F}{F}$ x 100 = *the cost of forward cover* (CFC)

As long as the IRD is greater than the CFC a profit will be made.

Answer 9.27

(a) Buy the currency six months forward with options in the last three months. This will ensure that he has a pre-determined sterling cost and that he can call on the bank to deliver the currency at any time between the fourth to the sixth month.

(b) Buy the currency spot (at the outset) and hold until required. The advantage of this could be that the forward rate is at a premium and therefore more of it can be purchased per £1 spot than for forward delivery. However, the disadvantage could be that the interest gained on the currency deposit is more than offset by the interest incurred on the reduced sterling balance (or increased sterling overdraft). Thus, the importer would need to consider the interest rate differentials and spot and forward exchange rates.

(c) If the importer is also an exporter he may be able to match his future currency receipts and payments. Any time differences can be dealt with by appropriate forward transactions.

(d) Wait until payment date to purchase the currency. This is speculative and renders the importer open to a possible currency loss or gain. However, if the currency of payment is in a weak position and all professional advice is that its weakness is likely to persist for some time it might be advisable to wait for at least some time before either buying it spot or forward.

Answer 9.28

This situation is, in principle, the same as a covered interest arbitrage one; namely that the importer must take into account the following data:

(a) the size of the discount expressed as a percentage
(b) the interest cost of paying now
(c) the spot rate for the purchase of currency now
(d) the forward rate for the purchase of currency in the future.

If the forward rate is at a premium (that is the domestic currency can buy fewer units of foreign exchange forward than spot) then there is an obvious advantage in buying spot and paying now to receive the price discount.

However, if the forward rate is at a discount, then buying spot will incur a higher domestic currency cost than buying forward, and this will only be profitable if this cost is more than offset by the price discount.

Answer 9.29

Supply of forward currencies and demand for forward currencies will determine rates in the forward markets.

As in the spot markets there are transactors wishing to sell and to buy for forward delivery. These factors together with the resulting positions taken up by the dealing banks (in effect, bank supply and demand) will formulate rates.

These transactors can be distinguished as follows:

(a) *Hedgers* — traders, investors, etc, who wish to cover against the currency risk by selling forward expected receipts and buying forward expected payments. Thus, a deterioriating balance of payments will tend to make the latter group's purchases greater than the former group's sales. The result will tend to be that the domestic currency will command fewer units of foreign exchange forward.

(b) *Speculators* — "Passive" speculation (where an open position is not covered) or "active" speculation where a transactor deliberately opts for an uncovered position by buying a currency he doesn't require or selling a currency he doesn't possess. In both cases there will be an impact on supply and demand forward. In the former case, a lack of supply or demand and in the latter case, an increase in supply or demand.

(c) *Interest arbitrageurs.* These transactors, seeking to profit from interest rate differences around the world will enter the forward markets to buy or sell in order to cover a spot transaction. Failure to do so will mean that they become speculators and will be included in section (b). In effect, by covering forward, they are hedging, and so really form a sub-set of section (a).

(d) *Central Banks.* Central banks can, from time to time, enter the forward markets to achieve aims not so easily available (perhaps) by other means.

For example, if they feel that their currency is over-valued in the spot market, but prefer not to enter the spot market for fear of increasing domestic money supply, they can, instead, sell the currency for forward delivery. This will tend to reduce any forward discount or increase any forward premium (other things being equal). Covered interest arbitrageurs who had been buying the currency spot and selling it forward will now find that it buys less forward than before. This will reduce their profitability and reduce their activities. As a result, there will be a decline to buy the currency spot, and, other things being equal, the spot rate should fall (depreciate).

In this way a currency depreciation can be obtained without any intervention in the spot market or any change in interest rates. However, when the forward contract matures there will be a need to supply the domestic currency or roll-over the forward deal. In any case circumstances may, by then, have altered.

Answer 9.30

(a) *Traders*

(i) *Covered interest arbitrage*

Here the trader importer who has to make a currency payment in the future but has the option of making payment immediately with a price discount, or, who is considering either borrowing the currency now for immediate payment with a price discount, or lastly, buying the currency now and holding until required. In all these cases, the trader will become a covered interest arbitrageur if he takes the interest rates and price discounts into account together with the exchange rates at both spot and forward delivery.

A trader exporter who is to receive a currency payment in the future but who offers a price discount for immediate payment, or who is considering borrowing the currency now to sell spot, must also take both interest rates and price discounts into consideration together with spot and forward rates.

(ii) *Speculation*

A trader importer who fails to buy currency forward or who fails to purchase the currency now and hold until required is, other things being equal, a "passive" speculator because he will not know his domestic currency cost of buying the foreign exchange until he eventually makes the purchase.

A trader exporter who fails to sell currency forward or who fails to borrow the currency now to sell spot is also a "passive" speculator because he will not know the domestic currency value of his currency receipts until they are delivered.

(b) *Investors*

(i) *Covered interest arbitrage*

Investors (and dis-investors) who cover their investment positions by making an opposite transaction in the forward markets, are arbitrageurs because they are protecting the value of their investments. That is, the purchase of a (say) dollar asset will require a spot purchase of dollars. An offsetting forward sale of dollars (capital plus interest) will ensure that the investor is aware of the domestic currency receipts of his investment as and when it matures.

(ii) *Speculation*

Failure to cover forward will mean that the investor is unable to calculate the domestic currency value of his currency investment. He becomes a "passive" speculator.

Answer 9.31

Up to October 1979 anyone who had contracted to buy or sell currency for forward delivery but who did not require the currency when delivered for the purpose for which it had been bought, or who did not possess the currency which had been sold forward, would, by the provision of the then regulations have to be closed-out.

That is, a purchaser of currency forward who did not require it, had to sell it spot; the seller of currency forward who did not receive it, had to buy spot. In both cases the initial forward contract which had provided cover (hedging) is unwound, and a currency exposure is opened up.

Since October 1979, it is no longer a requirement that a close-out be entered into. Now, an alternative is:

(a) for the forward purchaser to take delivery and hold in a currency account or use the currency to purchase an overseas asset, and
(b) for the forward seller to borrow the currency and deliver the proceeds forward as agreed.

In other words, the lending and borrowing of currency to meet forward liabilities is now possible. Whether or not they (or a close-out) are to be employed depends on the principles underlying the concept of covered interest arbitrage.

These are:

(i) interest rate differentials between the domestic and overseas rates
(ii) differences between spot and forward exchange rates.

For example: Where a currency has been purchased forward but is not required for the purposes which it had been bought, then it may be preferable to take delivery of the currency and hold in a currency account. This would be profitable, if the interest yield from the currency deposit is in excess of the interest cost of not delivering the domestic currency to the domestic currency account, provided the cost of selling the foreign currency forward does not offset this excess interest. If it does, then a close-out is to be preferred.

Answer 9.32

Covered interest arbitrageurs will tend to influence interest rates by raising them in the domestic market (when they are relatively low) and reducing them in overseas markets (when they are relatively high). This is because, in the process of borrowing relatively cheap domestic money in order to sell spot for the higher gains available abroad, the home demand for borrowed funds rises, while overseas, the supply of loanable funds rises. Thus, other things being equal, interest rates at home should rise and overseas should fall.

As far as forward exchange rates are concerned, the effect of the sale of the domestic (borrowed) currency spot and its purchase forward, will tend to cause the spot rate to depreciate and the forward rate to appreciate. That is, the gap between spot and forward will widen. Any existing discount forward will become larger until the twin effects of diminishing interest rate differentials and increasing forward discount will eliminate further covered arbitrage.

However, these are not the only factors that will impinge on forward rates. In addition, there will be the effects of traders who will be hedging forward and speculators who will be taking open forward positions. Also central banks may be taking forward positions to influence exchange rates. All of these other factors may entirely offset (or accentuate) the impact of the arbitrageur.

Answer 9.33

Short-term interest rates tend to be different for different currencies. Amongst other things this can be due to different policies followed by central authority around the world. As a result, arbitrageurs will tend to take advantage of these differentials and move short-term capital to the higher interest rate centres. In so doing, they will have to exchange their low interest rate currencies for the higher interest rate currencies and this will tend to affect the spot rates for currencies.

Other things being equal, a spot sale of a currency will cause it to depreciate and a spot purchase to appreciate. In order not to take a currency position, the arbitrageur will tend to make an offsetting forward contract. That is, a sale of currency spot is offset by a purchase forward, and vice versa. Such tactics ensure that the original currency is returned to at a pre-determined exchange rate.

Now, the result of the above outline is to open the gap between spot and forward rates until the percentage difference is equal to the percentage difference in interest rates. At such a point further arbitrage is unprofitable because the gain in interest is lost in the forward cover. This is the interest parity theory.

It fails to apply in practice because of a number of additional factors; namely:

(a) *transaction costs*

Charges made by the banks, and the costs that the banks themselves incur, will tend to reduce the profitability of arbitrage even if the differentials exist.

(b) *exchange restrictions*

Some central authorities prohibit or limit the extent of arbitrage or add to its costs by one method or another.

(c) *inequality of comparable assets*

The theory implies that short-term assets of the same maturity are equal in status. This is not necessarily so. Thus, an investment overseas may be viewed as a more risky one than for a similar investment at home. I.e. the problem of default.

(d) *inelastic supply of funds*

Investors may not be will to tie up funds in this way if there are alternative (and more profitable) uses to which they could be put domestically. E.g. bank loans to customers.

(e) *speculation*

Where investors (and others) take a view on a currency and are prepared to hold an open position, then the interest differential will not necessarily be offset by the spot/forward differential simply because of lack of forward cover.

Answer 9.34

(1) What is the commercial business of your customer?

Answer CARRIERS

(2) Complete the following table concerning their use of other companies' property:

Type of property	1 roll on/roll off vessel	1 tug and landing barge with derrick	1 general cargo vessel
Country of Origin	USA	HOLLAND	SINGAPORE
Period of use (show dates)	1/6 – 1/7	1/6 – 1/7	1/6 – 1/12
Non-£ cost	$100,000	DM300,000	$500,000
Date of payment	1/6	1/6 DM150,000 1/9 DM150,000	1/7 $250,000 1/12 $250,000

(3) Complete the following table concerning their receipts and payments, showing dates and values:

	Date	*Dollar value*	*Date*	*DM value*
Receipts due on	1/6 1/9 1/12	$200,000 $500,000 $200,000		
Payments due on	1/6 1/7 1/12	$100,000 $250,000 $250,000	1/6 1/9	DM150,000 DM150,000

(4) Specify the spot and forward exchange contracts called for in order to avoid the exchange risks and calculate the net sterling receipts. Do this in date order.

Answer 1/6 Net $ receipts = $100,000
Net DM cost = DM150,000
So, buy DM150,000 spot @ 2.4096 = $62,251 cost leaves $37,749 left; so, sell spot @ 1.618 = £23,330.66 receipt.

1/7 Must pay £250,000 so buy this on 1/6 one month forward @ 1.6079 = £155,482.30 cost.

1/9 Must receive $500,000 and pay DM150,000. So buy DM150,000 three months forward @ 2.3196 = $64,666.32 cost. This leaves $435,333.68 net receipts. So sell three months forward @ 1.6134 = £269,823.77 receipt.

1/12 Net payment of $50,000. So, buy six months forward @ 1.6034 = £31,183.73 net cost.

(5) Complete the following table.

Date of Forward Contract	*Date of Contract Maturity*	*Contract Currency Value*	*Customer Buying or Selling*	*Exchange rate. Show whether $s or DMs*	*Sterling receipts or payments*
1/6	1/6	DM150,000	Buy	DM2.4096	—
1/6	1/6	$37,749	Sell	$1.6180	+£ 23,330.66
1/6	1/7	$250,000	Buy	$1.6079	−£155,482.30
1/6	1/9	DM150,000	Buy	DM2.3196	—
1/6	1/9	$435,333.68	Sell	$1.6134	+£269,823.77
1/6	1/12	$50,000	Buy	$1.6034	−£ 31,183.73

Net £ receipts £106,488.40

Answer 9.35

(a) *Acceptance Credit*

An arrangement whereby a bank agrees to accept bills drawn upon it by its customer against the security of a trade bill due to mature either slightly before or on the same date as the bank's own acceptance.

The bill accepted by the bank is discounted to provide the drawer with immediate funds, and the bank will use the proceeds received from the trade bill to meet its own acceptance at maturity. In the even of non-payment of the trade bill, the bank will have recourse to its customer.

The bank acceptance will qualify for a finer rate than the trade bill (which might not be discountable on the market); the arrangement often provides a means of obtaining cheaper finance, even though the bank would charge at least an acceptance fee.

(b) *Problem*

Which is better, finance in currency or in sterling, i.e. which provides greater profit?

Facts Amount to be paid initially is — US $255,000
Amount to be received three months later — US $290,000

Currency finance

Rate 12% per annum

Amount borrowed	US $255,000
Interest for three months at 12% per annum	US $ 7,650
	US $262,650
Amount to be received at end of three months	US $290,000
Therefore profit	= US $ 27,350

Profit can be anticipated and therefore sold three months forward on 6 August

Rate $2.3555 − 3.47c = 2.3208
US $27,350 @ 2.3208 = £11,784.73

Sterling support:

Purpose is to produce sufficient sterling to purchase the dollars due to associated company.

Means

Term bill for US $255,000 accepted by bank.
Converted into sterling at spot rate.
As dollars have to be bought, use buying rate.

Therefore US $255,000 @ 2.3545 (Amount required to purchase dollars due)	= £108,303.25
Discount for three months @ 15½% $= \frac{108,303.25}{100} \times \frac{31}{2} \times \frac{1}{4}$ (Debited to current account).	= £ 4,196.75
Overdraft on discount amount for three months @ 18% $= \frac{4,196.75}{100} \times \frac{18}{4}$	= £ 188.85
Acceptance commission for three months @ 1% per annum $= \frac{108,303.25}{100x4}$	= £ 270.75
	£112,959.60 (a)
US $290,000 sold forward on 6 August @ 2.3208 (see above)	= £124,956.91 (b)
PROFIT: (b) less (a)	= £ 11,997.31

Sterling produces greater profit, therefore better.

Answer 9.36

CREDIT (A)

Arrange F/C on estimated profit of 2,000 tons @ $50 i.e. US $100.00 @ 2.4215	£41,296.72
Actual profit (2000 – 1990) = 10 tons @ $50 less i.e.US $500 bought by M. & Co. at Spot to meet shortfall F/C @ 2.3330 *less*	214.32
Amount received	£41,082.40

CREDIT (B)

	DR	CR
Arrange F/C on estimated profit of 1,000 tons @ $40		
i.e. US $40.00 @ 2.4215		£16,518.69
Spot purchase to meet forward @ 2.3330	17,145.31	
2.3202 (a)		£17,239.89 (a)
New F/C 1,000 tons @ $40 @ 2.3212 (b)		£17,232.47 (b)
Actual profit (1,020 less 1,000) = 20 tons @ $40 more $800		
Sold by M. & Co. at Spot $800 @ 2.3410		341.73
		£34,100.31 (a)
	17,145.31	£34,092.89 (b)
		17,145.31
Amount received		£16,955.00 (a)
		£16,947.58 (b)
		£41,082.40
Total profit		£58,037.40 (a)
		£58,029.98 (b)

(a) Extension
(b) New contract

Answer 9.37

(a) Dollars lent by bank and total sterling raised immediately:

US $100,000.00 @ 1.9150	= £52,219.32
deduct interest charges @ 17⅞%	
= $4468.75 @ 1.905	= £ 2,345.80
	£49,873.52

(b) Amount advanced under Bills and Notes Schemes and the amount repaid by the customers

Rate applied	1.9150	
plus	.0254	
	1.9404	
US $100,000 @ 1.9404		= £51,535.77
Interest charged = £51,535.77 @ 12⅝%		= £ 1,626.60
Customer's net proceeds		= £51,535.77
less interest charged		= £ 1,626.60
Net proceeds under (b)		£49,909.17
Difference between (a) and (b)		= £49,909.77 (b)
less (a)		£49,873.53
(b) more profitable than (a) by		= £ 35.65

Answer 9.38

(a) The immediate task is to cover forward transactions and where possible to "offset" payments against receipts.

1 and 4

On 15 July arrange for the bank to buy US$150,000 and retain US$100,000 on an interest bearing currency account up to 30 September. On this date remit to Alnite's bankers. Interest balance (less transfer charges) to be bought from the customer for sterling. (Possible to arrange retention of enough dollars to produce a net figure of US$100,000 on 30 September.) Alternative: to arrange two formal contracts; bank buys $250,000 on 15 July (option to end of July) and sells US$100,000 value 30 September fixed.

2 and 5

If a market is available for Australian dollars, the bank can now arrange to sell A$20,000 value 15 November fixed and remit A$75,000 that date, the balance of A$55,000 coming from payment due end of October. If not, forward cover is available to handle effectively the transaction at the end of October. If necessary, hold the A$55,000 until payment is due on 15 November when the bank will sell a further A$20,000 spot to the customer.

3 and 6

At the end of June, when the Deutsche Marks are received, arrange a cross-rate deal to meet the payment of Swiss Francs 50,000 which will have to be sent to Hamburg during July.

(b) (i) Investigate the use of currency accounts for future use. Where surpluses are likely to occur credit interest may be arranged to "compensate" the customer for leaving credit balances until payments are due either in the same currency or by using cross rates.

(ii) If the customer is in a net borrowing situation use might be made of currency overdrafts, repayable against currency receivables.

This, of course, would be applicable if the interest rates are favourable in currency compared with sterling interest rates.

(iii) Forward exchange contracts may be desirable in some cases.
(iv) In connection with (ii) and (iii), arrange suitable "limits" for further transactions so obviating the need to "agree" each future transaction as and when it arises.

Answer 9.39

It is noted that the question indicates that payment is secure and that one has to ignore commercial risks, charges, interest etc. One has also to assume that the vessels sail on the day the contracts were awarded, namely 1 June.

(a) Since the company is sterling based they will have to bear an exchange risk because they are entering into a series of contracts where they will receive US dollars and have to pay away US dollars and Deutsche Marks in settlement of their company's own commitments. There is a possibility therefore that exchange rate fluctuations may take place from the time that the contract is signed through to the final sale of surplus dollars for sterling.

(b) To minimise the exchange risk, the company should establish a US dollar account immediately so that payment in can match payments out as far as is possible. They will also have to arrange forward contracts so that dollars are sold for Deutsche Marks thus providing the appropriate funds to settle payments due to the Dutch owner. The company will have to understand that they are entering into a firm commitment with the bank to purchase dollars against Deutsche Marks and for a technical description one could advise them what the standard forward contract definition is, namely, "an immediately firm and binding contract between the customer and the bank for the purchase or sale of a specified quantity of the stated foreign currency, at a rate of exchange fixed at the time of making the contract for performance by delivery and payment at a future agreed time or between two agreed future dates. The contract is binding and performance must take place although it is possible to arrange an 'option' contract where the company has the option of taking delivery or delivering the appropriate foreign currency between two specified future dates".

(c) Two forward contracts need to be established. First, the price of Deutsche Marks to be delivered on 1 September to the Dutch owners is as follows:

(i) DM150,000 are to be paid to the Dutch owners on 1 September. The price will be worked out as follows:

Spot rate	2.4096
Less three months premium	0.0900
Outright forward rate	2.3196
(DM150,000 at 2.3196 = US$64,666.32)	

The second forward contract is the sale of surplus dollars which will take place at the end of the contract period, namely 1 December.

(ii) The bank will buy the balance of US dollars on 1 December and these can be established immediately on 1 June as follows:

Spot price for bank buying US dollars 1 June	1.6180
Less 6 months premium	0.0061
	1.6119

As payment of the Deutsche Marks to the Dutch owners takes places on 1 June, the date on which the contract was signed and the sailing took place, the US dollar/ Deutsche Mark cross rate of 2.4096 is used (spot). On that date the first dollar payment is made and the first dollar receipt is credited to the account. The rest of the payments followed in chronological order until a final sum was available of US$173,082.68 credit. The balance had already been calculated on 1 June when a forward contact as indicated above, was taken out so that the total sterling proceeds is as follows:

US dollar account Ancient Mariners Limited

	Debit $	Credit $	Balance $
1 June		200,000	200,000CR
(a) Payment re roll-on, roll-off vessel)	100,000		100,000CR
(b) Payment to Dutch owners of DM150,000 @ 2.4096 as in (ii) (Spot rate) =	62,251		37,749CR
1 July			
Payment to Singapore owners US$250,000 as in (iii) =	250,000		212,251DR
1 September			
Proceeds under (iv) from main contractors		500,000	287,749CR
Payment to Dutch owners under (ii) of DM150,000 @ 2.3196 =	64,66.32		223,082.68CR
1 December			
Receipt from main contractors		200,000	423,082.68CR
Final payment to Singapore vessel owners of US$250,000	250,000		173,082.68CR

The balance is to be sold on 1 December at the Forward Contract price mentioned under (b) above, namely 1.6119.

The final sterling figure to be credited to the company's sterling account is calculated as follows:

US$173,082.68 @ 1.6119 = £107,378.05 Sterling Credit.

Answer 9.40

(a) US$100,000 lent by bank converted immediately at spot rate of 2.4360	= £41,050.90
US$1,250 interest charged on repayment of loan, i.e. at 2.42	= £ 516.53

	Net yield to customer		£40,534.37
	Advance repaid in US$ when bill of exchange paid.		
(b)	Amount advanced under bills and notes guarantee US$100,000 @ 2.4325 (midway between 2.4290 and 2.4360)	= £41,109.97	
	Advance repaid by conversion of US$100,000 @ $2.4360 less forward premium of 1.80c = $2.4180	= £41,356.49	
	Gain	£ 246.52	
	Customer receives	£41,109.97	
	Plus gain	£ 246.52	
		£41,356.49	
	Less interest at 7½ per cent per annum for three months on £41,109.97	£ 770.81	
	Net yield to customer		£40,585.68
	Course (b) is more profitable by		£ 51.31

Answer 9.41

On 25 May the bank will arrange two forward option contracts to purchase Japanese Yen from the customer during July and August as follows:

July shipments	Spot 434.50	Estimated	
less 1 months' premium	2.00	Japanese Yen	
	432.50	21,500,000 @ 432.50 =	£49,710.98
10 August	Spot 434.50	Estimated	
less 2 months' premium	3.10	Japanese Yen	
	431.40	21,500,000 @ 431.40 =	£49,837.74

Shipments effected as follows:

15 July

490 x Yen 43,000 = $\frac{21,070,000 \times 95}{100}$ = Yen 20,016,500 @ 432.50 = £46,280.92

less close-out
Yen 1,483,500 @ 429.00 = £3,458.04

Balance F/Contract
Yen 1,483,500 @ 432.50 = £3,430.06 — 27.98

£46,252.94

10 August

526.316 x Yen 43,000 = $\frac{22,631,588 \times 95}{100}$

= Yen 21,500,008 @ 431.40 = £49,837.76

There is no close-out under the forward contract

31 October		
Balance of Yen 43,500 received at the current spot rate of 434.40	=	100.25
Total customer proceeds	=	£96,190.95

Answer 9.42

(a) As the bank will in effect be buying the currency from the customer in three months' time, they will arrange to buy the currency using the three months rate as follows:

Bank buys

1 April spot	1.7775	
Plus three months' forward margin	.0245	
	1.8020	
Value of forward contract US$250,000 @ 1.8020 =		£138,734.74

15 May
As shipment is US$760,000 exactly one-third of this will make up the first beneficiary's claim on the bank.
This amounts to US$253,333.33.

The proceeds are made up as follows:

As per forward contract US$250,000 @ 1.8020	= £138,734.74
Plus balance of US$3,333.33 at current spot rate of 1.8000	= £ 1,851.85
Total proceeds	£140,586.59

(b)
- (i) International Rules are the 1974 Revision of Uniform Customs and Practice for Documentary Credits – Publication 290 which came into force on 1 April 1975 (superseded by No. 400 in 1984).
- (ii) Transferable letters of credit are covered by Article 46.
- (iii) The first beneficiary has the right to give instructions to the bank called upon to effect payment, acceptance or negotiation to make the credit available in whole or in part to one or more third parties (second beneficiaries).
- (iv) The bank shall be under no obligation to effect such a transfer.
- (v) The bank charges must also be paid by the first beneficiary, (unless otherwise specified in the credit).
- (vi) To be transferable the letter of credit must be so designated.
- (vii) The letter of credit can be transferred only once. (NB There can be more than one second beneficiary but those second beneficiaries cannot transfer any part made available to them to another beneficiary.)
- (viii) A letter of credit can only be transferred on the terms and conditions specified in the original letter of credit, with the exception of the amount of the credit, any unit prices stated therein, and the period of validity or period of shipment, any or all of which may be curtailed.
- (ix) The first beneficiary has the right to substitute his own invoices for those of the second beneficiary for amounts not in excess of the original amount stipulated in the credit, and for the original unit prices and upon substitution of invoices the first beneficiary can draw under the credit for

the difference, if any, between his invoices and the second beneficiary's invoices.

(x) If the first beneficiary fails to supply his invoices upon demand to the paying, accepting or negotiating bank, then that bank has the right to forward to the issuing bank the second beneficiary's documents received under the credit, including the second beneficiary's invoices without any further responsibility to the first beneficiary.

Answer 9.43

(a) There are two methods by which the customer can protect himself from exchange risk:

(i) Establish a forward contract with his UK bankers arranging to sell forward immediately for delivery on 30 June, 100,000 US dollars. (This means the custmer will continue to borrow sterling on overdraft.)

(ii) Arrange to borrow US dollars immediately at the going US dollar LIBOR rate plus 1½% margin. The funds borrowed will be sold immediately at the current spot rate (the bank's buying rate) to provide the company with working capital. The borrowing in US dollars will be repaid upon receipt of the proceeds of the bill on 30 June.

(b) (i) Contractual Relationship — by entering into a forward contract the customer takes on an obligation which must be fulfilled as in any other legal contract. A definition of a forward contract is as follows: "An immediately firm and binding contract between a bank and its customer for the purchase, or sale, of a specified quantity of a stated foreign currency at a rate of exchange fixed at the time that the forward contract is made, for performance by delivery of and payment for, the stated foreign currency on, or between, two specific dates in the future."

An option contract is a firm contract but the customer has the option of completing the contract between two future dates. However, he must complete the terms of the contract because it is a binding contract on both parties. The only option is the date of delivery and not of the due performance of the contract itself.

(ii) When entering into a borrowing relationship the customer again enters into a firm legal contract undertaking to repay to the bank the amount of the sum borrowed, in the currency borrowed, on demand or on an agreed date. Interest can be paid separately by the customer or can be added to the debt.

(c) (i) If the customer takes out a forward contract the rate applied will be as follows:

	$
Bank's current spot buying rate	1.5260
Plus 3 months' discount	.0012
Outright forward rate (fixed) =	1.5272

The proceeds of this method are US$100,000 @ 1.5272 =	£65.479.31
Less interest charges $\frac{£65,479.31 \text{ x } 3 \text{ x } 11.5}{12 \text{ x } 100}$	£ 1,882.53
Total proceeds =	£63,596.78

(ii) If the customer borrows US dollars @ LIBOR 10.25% + 1.5% = (= 11.75%) the proceeds will be as follows:

Dollars lent by the bank to the customer and sold by him (bought by the bank) immediately at the current spot rate of

1.5260 = 100,000 ÷ 1.5260 = £63,530.80

Less interest charged at 11.75% =

$\frac{65530.80 \text{ x } 3 \text{ x } 11.75}{12 \text{ x } 100}$	£1,924.97
Total proceeds . . .	£63,605.83
Difference between (i) and (ii) =	£9.05

(d) Without entering into a specific sterling calculation it is possible to use a formula which will include the interest differential, plus or minus the cost or advantage of forward cover. A simple calculation without recourse to sterling is therefore possible using the following formula:

$$\frac{\text{Discount or premium x 360 x 100}}{\text{Outright forward rate x number of days involved}}$$

Therefore, using the calculations in (c)(i) the percentage one would calculate would be as follows:

$$\frac{.0012 \text{ x } 360 \text{ x } 100}{1.5272 \text{ x } 90} = 0.3143\%$$

(If one used the current spot rate figure of 1.5260 as opposed to the outright forward rate in this calculation the answer would be 0.3145% per annum.)

This is the cost to the customer of covering forward since the forward dollar is at a discount. One must therefore add this cost to the cost of sterling borrowing as under:

	11.5
Plus	0.3143
	11.8143% (total cost of borrowing sterling).

If one compares this to the US dollar borrowing (of 11.75%) the sterling is more expensive by 0.0643% per annum.

Answer 9.44

(a) As Tiger Moth is sterling based there will be an exchange risk because it is entering into two contracts, one involving the payment of chartering fees and the expected receipts for running an airline. These contracts are in dollars and the company will enter into an exchange risk the moment contracts are exchanged between the parties.

(b) In order to minimise the exchange risk the company should open a currency account in US dollars so that expected receipts can match some of the payments which fall due. The customer should arrange to take out a forward contract immediately so that the expected net surplus receipts can be protected in sterling terms. The company should be told that when it enters into a forward exchange contract it is entering into an immediately firm and binding contract between the bank and the customer for the purchase or sale of a specified quantity of a stated foreign currency at a rate of exchange fixed at the time of making the contract for performance by delivery and payment at an agreed future time or between two agreed future dates. The contract is binding and performance must take place.

(c) The customer will be expected to establish a US dollar account and the proceeds are shown below.

Further, the company would expect the bank to establish a forward contract on the 1 June so that the bank buys the expected surplus US dollars on the 1 June next year. The forward contract is based on the following rates.

Spot	1.3210	
Plus 12 months discount	0.0105	
Outright forward rate	1.3315	(US$600,000 @ 1.3315 = £450,619.60)

The actual currency account will be shown as follows:

	Debit	*Credit*	*Balance*
1 June to charterer	US$300,000		US$300,000 DR
1 September from the contractor		US$500,000	US$200,000 CR
1 December to charterer from	US$300,000		
contractor		US$500,000	US$400,000 CR
1 June (next year) To the charterer	US$300,000		
from contractor (only ½ expected receipt)		US$250,000	US$350,000 CR

As the customer only receives US$250,000 on the 1 June next year, as opposed to the expected proceeds of US$500,000 they will not be able to deliver to the bank the balance of $600,000 which is expected. On the 1 June next year the bank will close out this forward contract by purchasing from the customer $600,000 and selling to the customer at spot, a shortfall balance of $250,000.

These figures are shown below:

1 June (next year) forward contract	US$600,000 @ 1.3315 = £450,619.60
Close out shortfall balance	US$250,000 @ 1.4610 = £171,115.67
Net credit to customer's account	£279,503.93

Answer 9.45

(a) (i) The company has an adverse cash flow situation in that it will be paying away funds for the engines to the Scandinavian supplier at least 90 days before it is paid for the vessels.

(ii) A shortfall in cash will be in Deutsche Marks and the value of the Deutsche Marks in sterling terms will not be known unless the customer purchases forward or alternatively is able to "balance out" Deutsche Marks receipts from the alternative sources mentioned in the question.

(iii) The exchange risk applies from the date of signing the contract.

(b) (i) The company should investigate the possibility of obtaining stage payments to overcome the adverse cash flow. It should be pointed out to the customer that advance payment/stage payment guarantees might be necessary if the buyer agrees to this course of action, which will be treated as normal banking facilities.

(ii) The company should try to utilise the Deutsche Mark income it has from the Federal Republic of Germany to cover its foreign exchange commitment.

(iii) The company may be able to establish an Interest Bearing Deutsche Mark Account to assist the company to hold available Deutsche Marks, obtaining interest benefit yet at the same time protecting its exchange risk vis-à-vis the purchase of the Scandinavian engines.

(iv) The company may be having to borrow money from the Bank to finance the operation and if it has no Deutsche Marks at the present time it should investigate the interest rate for borrowing Deutsche Marks as opposed to sterling. Exchange risk may be covered by income received from the Federal Republic of Germany. It would be appropriate to borrow Deutsche Marks if sufficient Deutsche Mark income is forthcoming and Deutsche Mark interest rates are lower than sterling rates.

(v) If, for some reason, borrowing Deutsche Marks is not a practical proposition, namely for interest rate purposes or because the Bank and the customer do not wish to enter into firm liabilities, contingent liabilities on a reduced scale might be acceptable with matching forward exchange positions thus covering the foreign exchange risk for the company.

Section 10

Answers

Answer 10.1

(a) *Expected receipts in Krone if all goes well*

April 1st. The 3 months option forward rate is 9.08. So, exporter uses this rate to formulate his Krone charges which are 9.08 x £100,000 = *SK 908,000* = net receipt in Krone.

(b) *Swedish importer fails to pay by January 1st*

(i) The UK exporter is closed-out on July 1st. He must buy SK 908,000 spot @ 9.04 = £100,442.47 cost and deliver the Krone to his forward contract.

(ii) The risk incurred is "buyer's failure to pay within 6 months of due date for goods which have been accepted". Claim on ECGD will be 6 months after due date — namely January 1st.

(iii) 90% of loss plus close-out losses.

(c) *Exporter's net losses in sterling*

1 April	*£ debits*	*£ credits*
Insurance costs	400.00	
Bill guarantee	150.00	
Bank charges	40.00	
Bank facility		100,000.00
1 July		
Interest @ 12⅝% per annum for 3 months	3,156.25	
Close-out loss	442.47	
(Bank cannot recover from ECGD until 1 January so advance to exporter is rolled-over for 6 months).		

1 January

Exporter claims 90% of loss from ECGD		90,000.00
Exporter claims close-out loss		442.47
Overdraft redeemed	100,000.00	
Interest @ 16% per annum for 6 months	8,000.00	
Balances	£112,188.72	£190,442.47

Net receipt = £78,253.75; Net receipt expected = £96,253.75
Net loss = £18,000

Answer 10.2

The termination of *confirmed* credits means that while it may be possible for the exporter to continue financing his exports through credits opened abroad, he must face the possibility that under certain circumstances the bank either may refuse to make payment to him until they have themselves received reimbursement from the issuing bank, or, alternatively, they may make payment available but subject to recourse.

The exporter should also understand that the ending of confirmation is an indication that his (or the confirming) bank, may feel that the situation in the buyer's country is riskier than before with the possible result that payment could be delayed or suspended indefinitely.

The ECGD could provide the exporter with an alternative form of cover to ensure without recourse finance through their:

(i) Comprehensive Insurance Policy, and
(ii) Bills and Notes Guarantee (or the equivalent)

However, to qualify the exporter must:

(a) be covered for all or a wide spread of his overseas markets;
(b) not make credit available for more than 6 months (although Extended periods are possible);
(c) be covered for at least one year;
(d) be covered either from the date of despatch of the goods or the date of the contract;
(e) pay the appropriate premiums to ECGD.

On the basis of the Comprehensive Insurance Policy, the exporter can take out a Bills and Notes Guarantee enabling him to obtain bank finance at 5/8% over bank base rate without recourse, provided he fulfils his export contract properly.

Essentially, this form of ECGD cover substitutes for a confirmed letter of credit except that the cost of premiums to ECGD for most of the export turnover may prove expensive and also that ECGD indemnifies for only up to 95% of losses and sometimes much less.

Answer 10.3

(a) No. As the credit is unconfirmed and negotiable, the negotiating bank reserves the right to recourse on the exporter in the event that they themselves do not receive reimbursement from the overseas issuing bank.

(b) Yes. The exporter is covered by one of ECGD's "market" risks, namely, "general moratorium on external debt decreed by the government of the buyer's country".

(c) Yes, as there appears to be no reason to believe that the exporter has failed either to comply with his export contract or with the terms of the ECGD Policy.

(d) ECGD is prepared to meet proper claims in these circumstances four months after the due date of payment. They will indemnify 95% of the exporter's loss, namely, 95% of the sterling value of FF500,000 (see value in Section (e)). As due date is 1 September, the claim is to be met on 1 January.

(e)

Exporter's receipts and payments.	*Debits*	*Credits*
1 June. Documents negotiated = FF500,000 sold 3 months option forward (option at no extra cost) @ 11.11 = £45,004.50.		£45,004.50
1 September. Close-out. Exporter buys FF500,000 spot @ 10.97 = £45,578.85	£45,578.85	
Bank interest @ 18% per annum for 3 months	£ 2,025.20	
Bank overdraft		£45,004.50
1 January. Claim on ECGD @ 95% of £45,004.50		£42,754.28
Bank overdraft closed	£45,004.50	
Bank interest @ 18% per annum for 4 months	£ 2,700.27	
1 February. FF500,000 arrives and is sold spot @ 10.99		£45,495.91
ECGD is reimbursed	£42,754.28	
Balances	£138,063.10	£178,259.19
Net receipts =		£40,196.09

Answer 10.4

The UK exporter appears to be qualified to take advantage of the bank's own credit insurance scheme.

(a) (i) *Cost to the exporter of the bank's own scheme*

Sell FF120,000 2 months option forward @ 11.68¼ = £10,271.77 expected receipts.

Bank pays 90% of £10,271.77 on presentation of documents and the draft bill of exchange = *£9,244.59*

Less interest for 80 days @ 15½% per annum =

$$\frac{£92,44.59}{100} \times \frac{15\frac{1}{2}}{365} \times 80 = £314.06$$

Less bank charges @ 1% = *£102.71*

Summary.	Payment on presentation of documents	£9,244.59
	Less interest	314.06
	Less charges	102.71
	Total Net	£8,827.82

On final payment by the buyer the exporter receives the 10% balance = £1027.18.

Total receipts = £8,827.82 + £1,027.18 = £9,855.00
Total cost = £10,271.77 − £9,855.00 = £ 416.77

(ii) *Cost of direct ECGD cover*

ECGD premiums @ 70p per £100 on £10,271.77	= £ 71.90
Interest @ 14⅝% on £10,271.77 for 2 months	= £329.26
Total costs	= £401.16

(b) Direct ECGD cover has the following advantages:

(i) Seemingly cheaper costs but would require premium payments for all or most of the exporter's turnover. Bank cover does not require this.
(ii) Full payment of bill made on day of presentation of documents. With the bank scheme only 90% is available.
(iii) Where the buyer fails to accept the bills of exchange, under the ECGD direct scheme, the exporter can claim 90% of his losses if the cause of the default is insolvency. Otherwise, if it is a matter of the buyer refusing to take up the goods, then the exporter can only claim 90% of 80% of the loss. If the full £10,271.77 is lost then the claim is for 90% of

$$\frac{£10{,}271.77}{100} \times 80 = £7{,}395.67$$

This, however, is a superior position relative to the bank scheme, where failure to accept the bill of exchange entails recourse by the bank of the exporter for ***£9,244.59.***

Summary. The bank scheme is cheaper but is less comprehensive in its cover. May be suitable for a one-off, export transaction, where the rest of the exporter's business does not warrant ECGD cover.

Answer 10.5

Medium-term Supplier Credit

(1) ECGD provides guarantee to bank for 100% of the finance provided, plus interest.
(2) Exporter must have ECGD basic credit insurance cover — either comprehensive or specific.
(3) Exporter pays premium to ECGD for basic credit insurance and bank guarantee.
(4) Exporter signs recourse agreement with ECGD under which ECGD can claim from exporter any amounts paid to bank in excess of exporter's basic insurance cover — the excess is usually 10%.
(5) Bank provides finance to exporter against bills of exchange promissory notes accepted/issued by buyer securing amounts payable over credit period.
(6) Usually for 80% to 85% of contract price and credit period two to five years.
(7) Without recourse from bank to exporter after bills/notes have been validly accepted/issued.
(8) Usually provided in sterling, but foreign currency finance (e.g. US dollars) is available for larger contracts.
(9) Interest rates are fixed for the whole period of the contract and range from 7½% p.a. to 8¾% p.a. depending on the buyer's country and the length of credit.

These preferential fixed rates are not available for exports to other EEC countries. *Note:* These rates are subject to periodic changes.

(10) Interest make-up: banks receive an interest make-up from ECGD for all finance at preferential fixed rates, whenever these are lower than agreed rates.

Answer 10.6

Support can be provided by ECGD.

The customer must first hold a comprehensive short-term guarantee. For an additional premium, ECGD may then be prepared to issue to his bankers:

— Comprehensive bank guarantee (bills or notes) — for 45 day bills.
— Comprehensive bank guarantee (open account) — for invoice 30 days net.

A facility letter is sent by the bank to the customer setting out the terms on which advances are made.

The customer enters into recourse agreement with the ECGD in relation to any payment made under guarantee to the bank.

Advances are made by the bank at a preferential interest rate, currently 5/8% over base rate.

In the case of bills or notes —

After shipment the buyer forwards the documents with a bill of exchange to his bank for collection together with the form of warranty as required by ECGD.

Until the bill is accepted, advance by the bank is with recourse to the customer, after which it is without recourse.

ECGD will pay 100% of any sums overdue on an accepted bill which is three months overdue; or one month after demand for repayment from the exporter in respect of an unaccepted bill.

In the case of an open account —

Advances made against:

- Copy invoice
- Evidence of shipment
- Standard warranty
- Promissory note by exporter undertaking to pay amount of loan usually on last day of month in which payment is due from overseas buyer.

Claim made by the one month after demand for payment of promissory note from exporter.

Answer 10.7

(a) ECGD Buyer Credit guarantees available to banks making loans in respect of capital goods contracts worth £1m or more or equivalent in foreign currency.

(b) Loan is made by bank or syndicate of banks to overseas buyer or overseas borrower acting on its behalf. Buyer normally required to pay 15% – 20% to exporter by delivery from non-ECGD guarantee sources.

(c) Balance of 80% – 85% paid to exporter by UK bank(s) from loan which is guaranteed by ECGD 100% as to principal and interest. Four main legal agreements are necessary:

(i) Supply contract between UK exporter and overseas buyer.
(ii) Loan agreement between lending bank(s) and overseas borrower.
(iii) Guarantee agreement between ECGD and lending bank(s).
(iv) Premium agreement between ECGD and exporter.

(d) ECGD's guarantee does not relieve exporter, lender or borrower of the commercial responsibilities to each other.
(e) Loans can be in sterling or approved foreign currency, usually US dollars.

Answer 10.8

(a) CIF Charleston must include the cost of goods, the insurance and freight charges up to the named port of destination, i.e. Charleston.

120 Days Sight Draft D/A means that the draft is payable 120 days after it has been signed or accepted by the buyer in the United States. Documents will be released to the buyer against this acknowledgement of the debt, and control of the goods will therefore be lost virtually as soon as the documents arrive in the United States. The documents will include invoices, insurance documents and a document of movement, usually a bill of lading.

(b) The credit risks are:

(i) Non-acceptance by the buyer, leaving the seller with the consignment of goods many miles away which will have to be warehoused and insured. A new buyer may have to be found or it is possible that the goods may have to be re-shipped to the United Kingdom with all the attendant charges. The worst possible thing is that the goods may have to be abandoned in the United States, meaning a total loss.
(ii) Non-payment at maturity, control of goods being lost when the documents were handed over. The customer may therefore have to take action in a US Court in order to try to obtain recompense from the purchaser.

(c) ECGD Comprehensive Guarantee will give up to 90% cover in respect of the Credit risk.

(d) (i) The bank can arrange to purchase the dollars forward by way of a forward option contract for the customer.
(ii) if appropriate, i.e. US dollar interest rates are lower than sterling rates, the customer may be able to borrow dollars against a bill of exchange (by overdraft, an advance or a discount on the bill), selling the dollar spot for sterling for working capital purposes. The dollar loan will be repaid from the proceeds of the bill of exchange at maturity.
(iii) Ensure that the ECGD policy bears a foreign exchange cover endorsement.

Answer 10.9

(a) *ECGD Bank Guarantee Scheme*

If ECGD is agreeable — which depends upon the company's balance sheets and trading position — they may issue in favour of the bank, a direct guarantee. The appropriate guarantee in this instance would be the bills and notes scheme which would allow the bank to lend without recourse to the customer immediately after acceptance of the appropriate bill of exchange. Finance is often cheaper than overdraft being at 5/8 of 1% over base rate, although the cost of the additional bank guarantee together with bank collection charges must be taken into consideration.

(b) *Confirming Houses*

Confirming Houses act as agents for the buyers and place orders on behalf of their principals. They take on responsibility for the debt and in respect of a sight bill immediate payment is effected as soon as they take the goods over for shipment. In the event of credit being allowed the bill will be accepted by the Confirming House who would normally command fine trade bill rates in the discount market. Selling through a Confirming House is equivalent of a domestic sale.

(c) *Export House/Export Agents/Export Managers*

These organisations act in a similar manner to the Confirming House, except they are acting as agents for the exporters. This means that the contractual relationship with the overseas buyer is maintained as far as the seller is concerned. Export Houses do, however, give credit to the overseas buyer and as such are responsible for effecting payment to the seller. If a sight bill is involved, immediate payment will obviously be effected whereas if acceptance is involved the name of the Export House will obviously rank higher than that of the ordinary overseas buyer.

(d) *Export Merchants*

These organisations are often confused with Export Houses or Confirming Houses but, in effect, buy goods in their own right from suppliers and arrange to ship and sell them to their own buyers abroad. In effect this is equivalent of a domestic market sale.

(e) *Factoring Companies*

(i) Some factoring companies will arrange to handle the sales ledger of the company arranging to collect the debts on their own behalf. Payment of the invoice amount is guaranteed at maturity without recourse to the exporter.
(ii) In cases of approved buyers and countries the factoring company may agree to advance a substantial proportion of the invoice value immediately the goods are shipped to the importer. The balance will be paid upon settlement of the invoice by the buyers but the original advance will be made without recourse to the seller.

Both systems relieve the supplier of the sales accounting and debt collection services and also bad debts are not incurred. If foreign currency is involved the factoring house will arrange to take out forward cover thus obviating any exchange risk.

(f) *International Credit Unions*

These are organisations and associations of finance houses in the buyers' and sellers' countries. Finance is arranged through the medium of the Credit Union for the importer to have time to pay for the goods. These Unions consist of a number of European finance houses or banks which introduce an instalment credit basis to their foreign partners on a reciprocal arrangement. The importer, having received credit, can arrange to pay the exporter without too much difficulty. The exporter does receive payment without recourse to himself.

Answer 10.10

(a) (i) Tender bonds — issued in support of tenders thus reassuring overseas buyers that the tenderer is competent and capable of fulfilling the contract terms.
(ii) Performance bonds — undertakings given by banks that the sellers or contractors can satisfactorily perform their contract obligations.

(iii) Advance payment bonds — is a special type of performance bond which enables buyers to be sure that payments made in advance will not be lost due to the contractor's or supplier's default in performing the terms of the contract.

(iv) Progress/retention and maintenance payment bonds — similar considerations as applies to advance payment bonds.

(v) Standby letters of credit — can be established in lieu of (i), (ii) and (iii) above and may be called for by companies established in the USA. The credits can be conditional or unconditional and fulfil a similar role to bonds. Two advantages do exist from a banking point of view in that:

- the letter of credit will bear an expiry date.
- it will not be subject to local law but will be issued in accordance with "Uniform Customs and Practice for Documentary Credits" (Publication 400).

(b) (i) ECGD gives support to commercial banks issuing bonds expressed under (i) above provided the value of the contract exceeds £¼m in value.

(ii) When requiring ECGD to issue a bond in support of a tender performance or advance payment guarantee, for an additional premium, the contractual supplier can obtain cover for unfair calling of that bond.

(iii) In 1977, ECGD started to issue bonds in respect of the foreign exchange risk which applies when a contractor or supplier is tendering for a large contract which has to be expressed in foreign currency. ECGD, after the first 3%, will cover up to 25% depreciation of value of currency between the time that the tender is submitted and the contract is awarded. Any gains, however, are for ECGD's account!

Answer 10.11

(i) The exporter must have ECGD basic credit insurance cover — either comprehensive or specific.

(ii) ECGD provides a guarantee to the bank for 100% of the finance provided, plus interest.

(iii) The exporter pays the premium to ECGD for the basic credit insurance and the bank guarantee.

(iv) The exporter signs a recourse agreement with ECGD under which ECGD can claim from the exporter any amounts paid to the lending bank in excess of the exporter's basic insurance cover — the excess is usually 10%.

(v) The bank provides finance to the exporter against bills of exchange or promissory notes accepted/issued by the buyer securing the amounts payable over the credit period.

(vi) The amount lent is usually for 80% to 85% of the contract price and the credit period is usually between two and five years in duration.

(vii) Lending is without recourse from the bank to the exporter after bills/notes have been validly accepted/issued.

(viii) Loans are usually provided in sterling, but foreign currency finance (e.g. US dollars) is available for the larger contracts.

(ix) The preferential interest rates are fixed for the whole period of the contract and at the time of writing range from 10% to 12.5% for two to five years and 10% to 12.40% minimum for credit periods in excess of five years depending on the buyer's country. These preferential fixed rates are not available for exports to other EEC countries.

(x) Interest make-up: the banks receive an interest make-up from ECGD for all finance at preferential fixed rates, whenever these are lower than agreed rates, by HM Government which are now five-eighths of one per cent.

Answer 10.12

(i) Suggest customer takes out ECGD cover.
(ii) Unsecured loan/overdraft in sterling.
(iii) Unsecured loan/overdraft in currency — depending upon the currency of the sale contract.
(iv) With recourse advances against collections taking the collections as collateral security (take a Letter of Hypothecation/Certificate of Pledge).
(v) Negotiation/purchase of bills or cheques with recourse to the customer, where the bills of exchange/cheques are drawn on overseas buyers/banks, and are payable abroad.
(vi) Discount of acceptances where a bill has been drawn on a London bank under a documentary acceptance letter of credit. Such bills carry little risk and can therefore be discounted at the finest rate.
(vii) Advances in sterling against documents or bills of exchange using the ECGD basic policy as a collateral/secondary security where the policy can be assigned to the bank.
(viii) Advances against bank guarantee schemes either under the ECGD Bills and Notes Schemes or the Open Account Scheme.
(ix) By merchant banking operation utilising the facility of an acceptance credit. This is where accommodation bills are drawn on the bank which lends its name so that bills can be discounted on the London market at cheaper rates than overdraft. The term should be arranged to ensure that the proceeds of the collections, etc. are received in time to settle the bills prior to maturity of the accommodation paper.
(x) Using the bank's factoring company/associated company to arrange the collection of invoice debts and, where appropriate, to make advances not only in sterling but also foreign currencies, against those invoices at the normal rate, ranging between 75 and 90% of the value of the invoices.

Answer 10.13

(a) (i) Using the protection of the ECGD Guarantee (Policy) itself and assuming the company is a good credit risk, finance can be made available against assignment to the bank of the ECGD guarantee (policy) as under:

(a) Any proceeds due under the exporter's guarantee (whole assignment).
(b) Proceeds of claims relating to a particular market or buyer(s).
(c) Proceeds of claims relating to individual bills.
(d) In all cases (especially under (b) and (c)) the bank should insist that the bills are collected through its own offices.

(ii) The bank's repayment is by the receipt of the assignment of monies due to the bank. This is dependent upon the customer (the policy-holder) having fulfilled all the conditions of the policy and is therefore able to make a valid claim. A bank can never be in a position to ensure that this is so, and therfore such security cannot be regarded as 100 per cent cover.

(iii) The ECGD comprehensive guarantee (policy) is limited to the payment of claims made under it, ranging between 90 per cent or up to perhaps 95 per cent of the value of the invoices. In these circumstances, the bank will usually advance up to 90 per cent of the bill/invoice value only.

(b) (i) The customer must apply to ECGD for a comprehensive bankers guarantee (bills and notes).

(ii) Direct guarantee is given to the bank to cover advances made by it to the exporter subject to the terms and conditions of the warranty (completed by the exporter in respect of each bill presented).

(iii) The bank gets full cover despite the failure on the part of the customer (policyholder) or a dispute between the parties.

(iv) The customer obtains 100 per cent advance at a rate of (currently) ⅝ of 1 per cent over base rate. The customer must, however, pay for the cost of the bank guarantee.

Answer 10.14

Banks assist by giving the following bonds:

(1) Tender bonds.
(2) Performance bonds.
(3) Advance payment bonds.
(4) Retention moneys, progress bonds, maintenance bonds.

ECGD give assistance by indemnifying banks or contractors in certain circumstances.

(i) Tender to contract bonds — usually called tender to contract cover.

(ii) Performance, advance payment, progress payment and retention bonds — in respect of contracts worth £250,000 or more on cash or near cash terms which will be insured by ECGD against normal pre-credit and credit risks. ECGD does not provide the bonds but provides an Indemnity to a bank willing to issue a bond.

(iii) Unfair calling of bonds — ECGD can offer insurance to exporters against unfair calling of bonds raised without direct ECGD support.

(iv) Cost escalation cover — This cover is available in respect of contracts worth £1m or more but is not available where contracts are arranged with countries in the European Economic Community. (Since withdrawn).

(v) Project participation and insolvency cover — where British members of a consortium contract overseas are involved in respect of major export contracts of £20m or more, 90% of the loss arising from the unavoidable cost, expenses or damage due to the insolvency of a sub-contractor or fellow consortium member can be covered by this facility.

(vi) Joint and several cover — This is an extension of the projects participation insolvency cover and is available in respect of minimum contract values of £50m or more. The contracts must be judged by ECGD to be of exceptional national interest. Payments are made when a nominated sub-contractor defaults which necessitates the termination of a sub-contract and has to be replaced by another sub-contractor.

NB: Cost escalation cover was withdrawn by the Government with effect from December 1983 because of the nationally low rate of inflation.

Answer 10.15

This was not a popular question yet the majority of those who attempted it obtained good marks. The average mark fell because a number of candidates waffled their way through in what must have been the certain knowledge that whatever question they attempted in Section C would produce a fail paper. The question was fairly straightforward in that it was seeking to ascertain if the candidates appreciated that the ECGD Bankers Guarantee (Bills and Notes Scheme) was appropriate. Despite the fact that candidates were asked to show a package which is available to *all* banks, a number quoted the Smaller Exporters Scheme at present operated by Barclays, Midland and the Royal Bank of Scotland.

We also had various explanations of the meaning of ECGD which turned out to be in the words of some candidates "Exchange Control Guarantee Department", and "European Credits Guarantee Department"! A number of candidates felt this must be a "Bonding" question and a number felt that factoring was the answer.

The following points should have been considered and set out by candidates to obtain marks:

It is noted that the company has an ECGD Shorter Term Guarantee and the following notes are made in connection with schemes which are available from *all* banks:

(i) The bank must be fully secured.
(ii) Support can be provided by ECGD.
(iii) For an additional premium, ECGD may, and should in these circumstances, provide the bank with a Direct Comprehensive Bank Guarantee (Bills and Notes) re the 30 days Sight D/A Bills.
(iv) A facility letter is sent to the bank stating the terms under which advances may be made.
(v) The customer enters into a Recourse Agreement with ECGD covering any payments which ECGD may have to make under the Bank Guarantee.
(vi) Bank makes advances of 100% of the value of the Bill.
(vii) Advances are made at a preferential rate which is currently ⅝ of 1% over the current Base Rate.
(viii) Bills of Exchange must be collected through the bank and must be accompanied by appropriate shipping documents.
(ix) The customer submits a Warranty in the form required by ECGD indicating that all their stipulations have been observed.
(x) Bank holds recourse to the customer until the Bills of Exchange are accepted, then lending is without recourse to the customer.
(xi) ECGD pays the Bank 100% of the bill amount if unpaid.
Note: Where sight or unaccepted bills are involved the bank's first claim is upon the customer and if he does not pay within one month of the claim, ECGD will pay the bank 100% of the value. Where the bills have been accepted the bank does not claim from the customer and ECGD will pay the bank the amount of the advance six months after the due date of that unpaid bill.
(xii) In the event of non-payment of an unaccepted bill, ECGD pay to the bank one month after the demand for repayment from the exporter.
(xiii) ECGD in all cases provides cover/insurance to the exporter under the Comprehensive Shorter Term Guarantee to the extent of between 90–95% of the value of the invoice.

Section 11
Answers

Answer 11.1

The Euro-currency system is a world-wide system of largely inter-bank deposits of currency denominated in units other than the local one, i.e. dollars in the UK. They are deposited for fixed periods of time (eg three months) and are on-lent to banks, central banks, companies and individuals.

The special role of London (which is the most important centre for the market):

(a) To accept deposits (largely in dollars) to the credit of overseas banks and lending them out to other overseas banks.

(b) To take on the maturity risk, i.e. to accept deposits on short maturities — up to one year, and to on-lend for longer maturity periods — beyond one year. While an interest "turn" can be made from this situation, it carries the risk that it may be called upon to repay deposits when they fall due when assets are tied-up. This is, of course, the basic banking problem and must be met by the same principles as apply to domestic business, namely prudent lending policies.

In addition, banks face the problem that in this market there is no official lender of last resort to which banks can turn for support in the event that there are large defaults by their borrowers. However, it may be that in the event of such circumstances the Federal Reserve may stand ready to support parent banks whose overseas branches face liquidity problems.

Answer 11.2

(a) When (say) a UK customer wishes to remit sterling to the credit of an overseas resident's account, the following bank transactions are effected:

(i) UK bank debits the sterling account of the UK customer and credits the sterling account of either the overseas resident's bank (if there is one) or a correspondent's account. This is the VOSTRO account.

(ii) Notification of the sterling credit (together with a request to credit the local currency account of the overseas resident) is sent to the appropriate overseas bank.

(iii) The overseas bank will debit its sterling record VOSTRO account and credit the overseas recipient's local currency account with the spot rate equivalent (unless he has a sterling account).

As a result of these transactions, the overseas bank has an increase in its sterling assets but also an increase in its local currency liabilities. It may wish to restore the position by selling sterling in the market.

(b) A UK customer wishes to remit (say) D.marks to a West German recipient. The following transactions take place:

(i) The UK bank debits the UK customer's sterling account (unless he has a D.mark account) and credits the record NOSTRO account with the spot rate equivalent.

(ii) The UK bank sends instructions to the overseas bank to debit its D.mark NOSTRO account and to credit the overseas recipient's account.

In this case, the UK bank has reduced sterling liabilities and also reduced D.mark assets. It may wish to enter the market and buy D.marks.

(c) A UK customer wishes to remit (say) US dollars to a West German recipient. The following transactions take place:

(i) The UK bank will debit its customer's sterling account and credit the record NOSTRO account of a third (US) bank with the spot rate equivalent.

(ii) Instructions are sent by the UK bank to the US bank asking them to debit their dollar NOSTRO account and to credit the dollar NOSTRO account of the West German bank.

(iii) Notification is sent by the UK bank to the West German bank that its dollar account has been credited and that it should credit the West German recipient's account. This it does by applying the spot rate.

The effect on the UK bank is to reduce their dollar assets and sterling liabilities; the West German bank has increased its dollars assets and D.mark liabilities. The UK bank may want to buy spot dollars and the German bank to sell spot dollars.

Answer 11.3

(a) *Sterling*

Cheques remitted to international branch, where they are sent:

(1) to the bank abroad on whom they are drawn;

or

(2) in bulk to the bank's overseas agent (for whom they are usually holding a sterling account) in the country or centre on which they are drawn.

In (1) the bank abroad will be asked to remit proceeds (under advice) which, provided the cheque is paid, they will do through whatever system they use for making sterling payments in the UK.

In (2) the bank abroad will arrange for presentation of the cheque in its own country. If paid, it will eventually authorise the remitting bank to debit sterling account in its books.

(3) the remitting bank then credits the customer's account as contra.

Dollars

Similar procedure to above, but in the case of (1) the remitting bank would request the bank abroad to remit funds to a correspondent bank in USA where it had an account.

(1) The remitting bank would request the collecting bank to credit its dollar account in their books.
(2) US$ are then sold and sterling account credited.

(b) (i) *Sterling*

Suggest that buyers in Europe forward payment by bankers draft on UK, mail transfer or SWIFT.

(ii) *Dollars*

Where possible request buyers to obtain bankers drafts or International Money Orders. In future, arrange for all items, including individual or company cheques, to be negotiated rather than collected, i.e. the bank purchases with recourse, and the sterling account is credited straight away.

Whilst the customer under this system does not receive confirmation of actual payment of individual items, after a lapse of a specified time, he will be reasonably safe in assuming this is the position, if the cheque has not been returned. If the cheque is unpaid, the customer will have to buy the dollars and could thereby sustain exchange loss, although, equally of course, he might make a profit.

Answer 11.4

Banks provide:

(1) Foreign exchange markets.

These are markets where foreign currencies can be bought and sold either on spot or forward basis. Additionally, UK banks are prepared to borrow (or accept on deposit) and lend (or place on deposit) major foreign currencies. Travel facilities may also be included under this heading.

(2) Worldwide network for the transfer of funds and collecting proceeds.

This is effected either through branch networks or correspondent relationships whereby accounts are held in the books of each other.

Means by which transfers are arranged include the following:

issuing of drafts; mail transfers; telegraphic transfers; SWIFT; collections related to financial and commercial documents.

(3) Economic and credit information.

Through their intelligence departments they can give information on market conditions relating to:

general political and economic conditions in particular countries or areas;
potential for sale of specific commodities;
names and creditworthiness of potential customers.

(4) Facilities and funds for financing imports and exports.

Facilities — documentary and acceptance credits
— guarantees

Financing — ECGD backed loans, short and medium terms
— produce loans
— discounting and making advances against bills with or without documents

Answer 11.5

(a) This means that the issuing bank, on being advised that documents in order have been negotiated, will issue instructions by cable or telex, or urgent SWIFT to its US (New York) correspondent to make payment to a US (New York) bank for the account of the negotiating bank at the latter's request.

Such messages will include a test key or authenticator for verification purposes.

(b) Telex messages will be sent:

(i) to the issuing bank requesting them to arrange for the UK bank's account with its New York agents to be credited with the sum of $1,094,500 in respect of their documentary credit.
(ii) to the UK bank's correspondent bank to pay $995,000 to the New York correspondent bank of the negotiating bank in India for the latter's account.

The balance of US$99,500 will be used by the UK bank to take up part of the forward contract, whereby the customer's sterling account is credited.

(c) From the point of view of a UK bank, its nostro accounts are those currency accounts which are maintained in its name in the books of banks overseas.

From the point of view of a UK bank, its vostro accounts are those sterling accounts in the names of overseas banks that are maintained with it.

In this case these entires will be passed over a nostro account of the UK bank.

The entires will appear as follows:

in New York bank's books a/c of UK Bank
DR. 995,000 CR. US$1094,500

in UK bank's books a/c with New York Bank
DR. 1094,500 CR. 995,000

Answer 11.6

Travellers' Cheques

"Cheques" issued in various fixed denominations and a variety of currencies drawn on banks or well-known companies whose names are known as providers of this facility.

They can be purchased from banks and agencies.

On receipt the purchaser signs his own name on the cheque in a space provided. When wishing to use the cheque for obtaining funds or payment for goods, the cheque is signed again in the presence of the person accepting it.

Collection of the amount due to the payee is arranged by presentation through normal banking channels.

Credit Cards

Cards issued by bank card systems e.g. Barclaycard and Access who are themselves members of international bank card systems. They can be used in the normal way for purchase of goods and serives abroad, subject to the holders' credit card limit, and also cash advances can be obtained subject usually to a daily limit.

The holder signs the voucher at the time of purchase or obtaining the advance, against which the recipient obtains payment from the card system, and the amount is debited to the holders' account in the latter's books.

Statements are submitted monthly to holders, but repayment may be spread over a period.

Debit Cards (Travel and Entertainment Cards)

Similar to the above but the initial and yearly subscriptions have to be paid by the holder. They are usually available for an unlimited amount, but no credit is allowed and full payment is due on receipt of the statement. Examples are American Express, Diners Club, Carte Bleue.

Eurocheque Card

Permits personal cheques to be cashed when backed by cheque card of a member bank.

Under the Uniform Eurocheque Scheme, where special cheques are issued, these are also available for purchase of goods and services.

Proceeds are collected through normal banking channels, although as regards the special eurocheques, separate clearing systems in the country of encashment have been established.

Note Since May 1983 the Eurocheque scheme has been supplanted by the Eurocheque encashment card.

Answer 11.7

(a) Issue the customer with a draft in the name of the nephew for the equivalent of £20 in Swiss francs drawn on a correspondent bank in Zurich.

Buy Swiss francs and debit the customer with the sterling equivalent.

Where arrangements required it, issue advice to the Swiss bank of the details of the draft.

The customer then sends the draft to the forwarding address.

(b) The customer may either:

(i) enter into forward contract for payment of $110,250 in three months' time and place sterling funds on deposit; or
(ii) buy dollars at spot and place on deposit to meet the commitment in three months' time.

(c) Issue delivery order against an undertaking by the customer to make payment in accordance with instructions from abroad when received. It might be prudent to debit the customer with at least the amount of the pro-forma invoice and hold on suspense account pending receipt of instructions.

(d) Suggest that when the bill is accepted, the par aval endorsement of the drawee's bank must be added. By this means the bank guarantees payment at maturity.

Answer 11.8

(a) Is the product "exportable"? Information concerning the type of market available, i.e. the type of product now being bought, is available from banks and the British Overseas Trade Board.
(b) Is the country liable to allow payment? What are the local exchange control regulations, if any? Can the country pay its debts?
(c) The creditworthiness of the potential buyers. Use the banks and British overseas Trade Board to obtain general status reports.
(d) Seek help from the bank (international/overseas branch) about methods of payment, terms of payment, etc. Again the British Overseas Trade Board, Export Club, local Chamber of Commerce, or the Small Business Club may help in this matter, in that they may have members exporting to that country who are willing to assist.
(e) Investigate cover for credit risks by making an approach to ECGD.
(f) Visit the potential buyer; letters of introduction by banks, etc.
(g) Obtain a specific status report covering the actual terms discussed with the buyer.
(h) If necessary, seek the help of a good forwarding agent/export packer. Ask the bank, Chamber of Commerce or Business Clubs for the names of reliable companies.
(i) Use the banks to obtain payment, i.e. by means of documentary collections, letter of credit, etc.
(j) Investigate ECGD facilities concerning help for bank finance (the type will depend upon the business being entered into).
(k) Use "official" bodies to obtain cheap subsidised foreign visits to check out new markets, i.e. trade missions sponsored by the BOTB, Trade Association Missions, etc.
(l) Approach the BOTB to ascertain if the Market Entry Guarantee Scheme (MEGS) is available.
(m) The Department of Industry (under the Government "new" loans guarantee scheme) may assist in the provision of necessary capital in a start-out situation for those companies who would not otherwise have been able to raise finance for such a project.

Answer 11.9

1. The daughter requires immediate funds; father and mother will pay:

(a) Remit funds by telex or SWIFT to correspondent bank near place where daughter is staying. Payment to be made against personal application and positive identification. If possible quote daughter's passport number.
(b) Remit funds out in drachma.

Account procedures

(i) Debit customer's account with £ sterling equivalent, and credit the bank's nostro account with the Greek bank.
(ii) Advise Greek bank by telex/SWIFT, instructing them to debit UK bank's account with payment and place daughter in funds.
(iii) Give full details of Greek bank and branch to the parents so the daughter can be advised by them where she can apply for money.

2.

(a) (i) Just before customers leave for their holiday, sell small supply of Spanish peseta notes (exchange risk fixed immediately).
(ii) Sell supply of Spanish peseta travellers cheques (exchange risk fixed immediately).
(iii) Customers can take a supply of sterling travellers cheques (they can bear the exchange risk when these are exchanged in the Canary Islands).
(iv) Advise customers to take Bankers Card (Euro-Cheque Card) and their credit card for emergency.
(v) If Mr. and Mrs. White are staying in the Canary Islands for some time, arrangements can be made to remit funds out to an agreed named correspondent bank for payment to them against personal application and positive identification.

(b) (i) There is no UK exchange control reason why the Whites should not buy a property in the Canary Islands and they should be given advice to ensure that remittance of funds complies with the Spanish Exchange Control Regulations.
(ii) Arrange a letter of introduction addressed to a correspondent bank asking them to arrange appointments with estate agents, lawyers, etc. so that proper legal advice can be given to the Whites.
(iii) The Whites could be told that if they do decide to buy a property a local bank account for "servicing" the property will be arranged on their behalf, using the same correspondent bank to whom the letter of introduction has been addressed.

Answer 11.10

Funds will be available, either locally in Holland or through the Euro-currency market raised in other centres.

1. *Short Term*

Currency borrowing in either Dutch Guilders or Euro-currency can be raised in the United Kingdom from UK banks.

(i) Overdraft facilities in foreign currency, rates based upon the average Euro-currency LIBOR, plus a margin.
(ii) Shorter term loans in Euro-currency on a fixed basis; terms again would be based upon Euro-currency LIBOR plus a margin.
(iii) Overdraft facilities arranged at a Dutch bank either in Guilders or in a Euro-currency secured by a guarantee from the United Kingdom bank.

2. *Medium Term: Euro-currency loans*

For terms in excess of one year and up to five years. Facilities can be arranged in Euro-currency as follows:

(i) *Fixed rate loans*
Rates will be the appropriate LIBOR plus a margin. Fixed for the entire period agreed, with the total loan repayable on the final date (Bullet). Difficult to arrange as market conditions usually preclude "fixtures" of more than one to two years.
(ii) *Roll-over syndicated loans*
For a period of two to five years or more where large sums of currency are

concerned. A Euro-currency loan can be arranged either direct through a UK bank or, if appropriate, through a syndicate of banks where large scale sums are involved. Although the loan would be fixed for a long period of time and for a substantial sum of money, the interest rates charged would be linked to LIBOR rate plus a margin and would be subject to change at each roll-over date. Roll-over may be at three, six or twelve month periods, where the bank effectively relends the funds for each relative period at the rate of interest prevailing at the time of roll-over. In order to obtain the benefit of a syndicated roll-over loan, customers have to be a first class name.

3. *Long Term*

(a) Foreign Securities: issued in a traditional manner.

(i) Underwritten by a national syndicate.
(ii) Securities would normally be sold principally in the country of the syndicate.

(b) Eurobonds: usually for substantial sums of money.

(i) Raised and issued by international syndicates and underwritten by international banks or financial institutions, for first class "names".
(ii) Usually sold on international capital markets and one would expect them to be sold in a country other than that of the currency of the bond.
(iii) One advantage of raising funds this way is that there is no withholding tax and usually a secondary market is available.
(iv) It is usually possible to raise longer term funds by bond issues than by Euroloans.
(v) Bond issues may be either at "fixed" or "floating" rates of interest.

Answer 11.11

(a) Customer instructs bank on the appropriate form to debit his sterling account with the sterling equivalent of US$50,000. This is done by completing the appropriate draft, mail transfer, T/T (including SWIFT) form.

(b) (i) *Draft*

Bank draws a draft for US$50,000 on its correspondent in the USA and hands the draft back to the customer to despatch it to the payee in Genoa. (Some banks send an advice of drawing to the New York correspondent, drawee bank.)

Bank debits the customer's sterling account with the sterling equivalent of US$50,000 (bank sells dollars to customer at current spot selling rate) and credits the Mirror/nostro account held with the New York bank.

Upon presentation the US bank will debit the UK banks nostro Account (*vostro* from the US banks point) and pays the dollars to the remitting bank by crediting the remitting bank dollars in accordance with its schedule. The remitting bank will be acting on behalf of the Italian payee.

Alternatively, an unusual but possible method would be for the UK bank to draw a draft expressed in US dollars on an Italian correspondent, arranging for its US correspondent to debit its dollar account and credit the dollar account of the Italian bank upon presentation of the draft.

In either case the payee will have to arrange for a bank in Italy to either negotiate or pay the US dollar draft when presented.

(ii) *Mail Transfer/Payment Order*

The bank debits the customer's account with the sterling equivalent of US$50,000 (in effect sells the customer US dollars at spot), and either sends the payment order direct to a correspondent in Genoa requesting that bank to advise and pay the beneficiary dollars or, alternatively, sends a payment order to its USA correspondent requesting that bank to make payment in dollars to Genoa.

In both case, the US correspondent bank will debit the *nostro* Account of the UK bank and credit the *nostro* account of the Italian Bank, the appropriate reimbursement instructions having been sent to the US correspondent.

Beneficiary will recive dollars in Genoa and will have to accept the rate of exchange given to him by the Italian bank when converting the dollars into lire, unless the payee has authority to hold a US dollar hold account.

(iii) *Telegraphic Transfers*

This would be handled on the same basis as the mail transfer except the instructions would be sent to both banks by telex or cable. This would necessitate the instructions being authenticated by a bank test key.

(iv) *SWIFT*

Payment methods as per mail transfer or telegraphic transfer except that they are routed via SWIFT. Test keys are involved but payment instructions are not sent over by mail or by telex, but via the SWIFT system, which in effect is a method by which the payment instructions can be received by the banks abroad through a computerised system which incorporates a printer at the receiving banks' end.

Answer 11.12

(a) (i) First, establish a bank account for him with a correspondent bank in Stavanger.
(ii) The remittance of funds on a standing order basis by mail or telegraphic transfer to be credited to the customer's account with the nominated bank in Stavanger. Funds can be remitted in Norwegian Kroner or in Sterling.
(iii) The use of the cheque-card under the Eurochque Scheme.
(v) Cheque encashment facility with nominated bank.

(b) Advantages and Disadvantages

(i) The customer can arrange to have a chequebook issued locally which will enable him to use cheques as if he were a Norwegian national. However, it may well be that the Norwegian bank may not be willing to issue an appropriate Norwegian bankers card.
(ii) There may be possible delays in a remittance by mail or through difficulties in administration in Norway. However, the exchange risk can be fixed in the United Kingdom if the funds are sent out in Norwegian Kroner.
(iii) Insofar as the Eurocheque Scheme is concerned the customer will need to carry his cheque-card as well as the sterling chequebook, although encashment facilities will be available at any participant bank. They, however, limit use to the amount mentioned in the general encashment regulations.
(iv) The need to carry his sterling chequebook as well as means of identification. In addition to that the cheque cashing facility is only available through a nominated bank in Stavanger.

One further disadvantage is that in connection with methods (a)(ii) and (iv) the amounts will be received in Norwegian Kroner locally and the rates will have to be fixed by the Norwegian bank when arranging encashment of the cheques.

Answer 11.13

It is important to ascertain from Mr. Bowler something of his itinerary, bearing in mind that the West Indies is made up of a group of islands. It is important to remember that a number of currencies may be involved. In addition to that Mr. Bowler is likely to be staying in each centre for no longer than approximately a week and therefore, if one can ascertain his itinerary well in advance, the facilities mentioned under numbers (iv) and (v) below might be appropriate as "back-up" to the arrangements mentioned under points (i) to (ii). Candidates should now remember that "Worldwide Travellers Letters of Credit" are no longer available from the majority of Western banks. This method therefore should not be regarded as being an appropriate method neither should the use of the bank draft. The methods available to Mr. Bowler in order of preference are as follows:

(i) Foreign currency notes in West Indian dollars or US dollars (Exchange rate fixed immediately).

(ii) A quantity of foreign currency travellers cheques expressed in US dollars available for encashment quite freely throughout the West Indies (e.g. American Express Company; exchange rate fixed immediately).

(iii) Credit Card/Charge Card/Cheque Card which will enable Mr. Bowler to obtain facilities at hotels, stores and banks throughout the West Indies. (Unless the credit card allows for drawings in foreign currency, the exchange rate will be fixed at the time that the claims are received from the credit card company or the cheque is presented at the bank's counters.)

(iv) If Mr. Bowler can specify and name the areas where he will be staying and the duration of his stay, it would be possible to establish an open credit/encashment facility, thus enabling him to cash his own cheques at specified banking points.

(v) The customer may arrange for funds to be remitted out in foreign currency to specified banks which will be available for collection by him against personal application, and positive identification at specific named points at agreed periods throughout his tour.

Answer 11.14

The recommendations would be as follows:

(a) (i) Issue a small supply of Hong Kong dollar notes.
(ii) Issue a supply of travellers cheques in the appropriate currency namely Hong Kong dollars/US dollars/sterling.
(iii) Suggest that each representative should take their bankers', charge or credit card with them.

(b) (i) Establish with a Hong Kong subsidiary/correspondent bank a local Hong Kong account for each representative requesting that Hong Kong bank to arrange for a local cheque book to be issued if required (there is a possibility that the customer may be called upon to give references through the bank).
(ii) Remit out to the Hong Kong bank part of the representatives' salary in sterling or in Hong Kong dollars. If sent out in Hong Kong dollars the exchange rate will be fixed and borne by the company whereas if funds are

sent in sterling the representative would bear the exchange risk. If the company arranges to remit out in Hong Kong dollars, they may consider the purchase of Hong Kong dollars forward by means of a firm contract (or a series of F/Cs) in order to fix the exchange rate.

(iii) Arrange for the representatives to meet the taxation/trust department to discuss tax matters during their stay in Hong Kong.

(c) Establish a drawing facility with the Hong Kong subsidiary/correspondent bank enabling a senior representative(s) to

(i) draw either sterling up to the agreed amount in any one week/month or
(ii) Hong Kong dollars up to an agreed amount in any one week/month etc. It may be necessary to arrange for the establishment of a local Hong Kong dollars account for use by the senior representatives, as strict control must take place so that the representative cannot misuse the account.

The remarks in connection with exchange risks mentioned under (b) also apply. If the Hong Kong subsidiary/correspondent pays out Hong Kong dollars which can be credited to an account in Hong Kong the UK company will have to pay interest at the Hong Kong rate for the time that the Hong Kong bank is out of its funds. The company will in effect bear the exchange risk whatever method is used.

(d) It may be possible to arrange for a company credit card to be issued to the representatives if the company is satisfied that there will be no misuse of these cards.

Answer 11.15

(i) The Government has made finance available through the Market Entry Guarantees Scheme (MEGS).
(ii) Operated by the Department of Trade through the auspices of the British Overseas Trade Board (BOTB).
(iii) Eligibility

(a) Exporters of manufactured goods or services in new markets or where sales have been made but major increases in sales are now planned.
(b) Firms must provide evidence that they are able to carry out the venture and that their aim is to obtain substantial increases in export sales in the period of the venture proposed.

(iv) Eligible Costs

(a) *Overseas office accommodation:* rental, property and contents insurance; maintenance; services; local property taxes; office equipment; office consumable supplies; purchase and running costs, or rental, of cars.
(b) *Staff costs:* salaries; recruitment and relocation costs in respect of overseas based administration; sales and warehouse staff.
(c) *Training:* training in the selling and servicing of the venture product(s)/service(s) of overseas based staff only.
(d) *Travelling Expenses:* travel and subsistence costs for the overseas based staff; and of home based staff visiting the market direct in connection with the venture.
(e) *Sales promotion:* advertising, publicity, sales literature specific to the venture markets; production demonstration costs.
(f) *Overseas warehousing:* costs of storage facilities, including showrooms under similar headings of those for overseas accommodation.

(g) *Commercial and legal costs:* legal costs in setting up the overseas operation; external audit costs; costs/fees for patents; trade marks; licences; testing and approving of venture product(s) to local standards.

(v) Limits

50 per cent of the eligible costs, i.e. minimum funding of £20,000 maximum £150,000 meaning the total eligible funding will relate to a minimal eligible cost of £40,000 with a maximum £300,000.

(vi) Costs

(a) A 3 per cent flat charge is levied by the BOTB based upon the amount of the funding.
(b) A charge of 2½ per cent over the UK banks weighted average base rates is made on the amount of the funding. This is to take care of interest charges at commercial rates. The levy on sales plus the interest is payable for the agreed period or until the departments funding plus interest has been repaid, whichever is the sooner. If the venture is unsuccessful, the firm is relieved of any shortfall in repayment of the departments funding that remains due at the end of the agreed period.

(vii) Application must be made to the British Overseas Trade Board for consideration by them of any proposals under this scheme, as soon as market research has been completed and before any additional costs are incurred in the chosen market area.

Answer 11.16

(a) (i) CIF UK Airport

Cost, Insurance and Freight UK Airport. This means that all charges up to delivery at the UK airport have been paid for by the seller. The price is the cost of the goods, the insurance charges together with the freight charges up to the UK airport. The seller is responsible for booking space on an aircraft and advising the airline, the flight number, the date of appropriate shipment to the buyer or the buyer's agent. The buyer is responsible for arranging to clear the goods through customs at the UK airport (this is usually done by the airline, all charges against the goods).

(ii) FOB Oslo Airport

This means "Free on Board the aircraft at Oslo". The seller is responsible for getting the goods up to the aircraft in Oslo and for covering the insurance and freight charges up to the point. The price therefore includes the cost of the goods, the insurance and carriage charges up to the aircraft. The buyer is responsible for booking the aircraft (and advising the details etc. to the seller) as well as arranging his own insurance and for paying the freight charges into the UK.

(b) (i) SWIFT — Society for Worldwide Interbank Financial Telecommunications.

Payment will be made in Deutsche Marks and remitted by the SWIFT system to the named bank in Germany 10 days after the date of despatch to the UK Airport. The UK bank will arrange to sell Deutsche Marks to the buyer, namely Bright Sparks Limited.

The Deutsche Marks will be remitted out to the German bank using the computerised "telex" system. In effect the British bank will arrange for either the named bank or one of its correspondent banks in Germany through the SWIFT system to debit its account in Deutsche Marks and pay the funds over to the sellers.

(ii) TT — Telegraphic Transfer.

The British bank will arrange to remit by telex/cable to the named bank in Oslo. The British bank will arrange to credit the sterling account held with itself by the named Norwegian bank, or alternatively will place the funds at the disposal of the named Norwegian bank in sterling, in accordance with that bank's wishes. It will telex the payment details to the Norwegian bank indicating that it has either credited its sterling account or is holding the funds at its disposal, and asking for instructions. At the same time the Norwegian bank will be asked to pay the sterling to the sellers in Norway. This means that, in this particular case, the Norwegian bank will arrange, if appropriate, to purchase the sterling from the seller in Norway and pay to him Norwegian Kroner in settlement.

Answer 11.17

The alternative methods which are available are telegraphic transfers, express international money transfers, mail transfers/international money transfers. The difference between a TT and a EIMT is simply that the TT is sent by telex or by cable to the paying bank, whereas the EIMT is despatched by means of an urgent SWIFT message. Similarly, an MT would be despatched by mail or airmail whereas an IMT would be despatched by ordinary SWIFT. SWIFT stands for The Society for Worldwide Interbank Financial Telecommunications and this system is operated by a number of banks using the services of switching computers so that instructions can be passed from the instructing country to the receiving country speedily and without the intervention of a telex line, a cable company or relying on normal mails. As the speed of settlement appears to be the essence of the complaint by By-Overseas Limited, it is suggested that they or their sellers should decide if either one of them will pay for a transfer to be sent by urgent SWIFT or by TT.

The methods of settlement would be as follows:

Sterling

The customer will instruct the bank, on the bank's standard form, to pay a beneficiary in another country. The instructions can indicate a nominated bank and where appropriate a bank account of the beneficiary. Otherwise the remitting bank will normally be asked to "advise and pay" beneficiary. The customer would undertake to accept a debit to its account with or without charges, in accordance with the arrangements made by the beneficiary. The UK bank, in the instance quoted, will debit the customers with the appropriate sterling with or without charges, and arrange immediately to credit the Sterling account held with it by its correspondent, the paying bank. This means that the Vostro account of the overseas bank would be credited in sterling. Where the UK bank has no relationship with the paying bank, a third party bank will be asked to pay the funds to the third party bank passing on the appropriate instructions. Alternatively, where no relationship exists between the two banks, it is possible to credit a sterling account held by the paying bank with a third bank in London and in the instructions, when asking the paying bank to forward the funds to the beneficiary, indicate where cover has been placed.

Currency

When a currency, other than the currency of the remitter, is involved, similar instructions must be taken as for sterling. However, instead of indicating that a sterling (Vostro) account has been credited in the United Kingdom, the instructing bank would either have to advise the paying bank that foreign currency is being placed by way of cover, or give an instruction to that bank to debit its own (the instructing bank's) currency account held with the bank (Nostro). Charges may be deducted according to the agreement between the parties. The customer would normally accept a debit to its sterling account for the sterling equivalent of the currency involved. (This means the bank sells currency at the current spot rate, unless a forward contract is involved, debiting the customer with the sterling equivalent). The memorandum/mirror account of the remitting bank will be credited with the appropriate currency. Upon receiving instructions, the bank overseas will arrange to pay the beneficiary, either by means of a cheque or by credit to an account and will immediately debit the instructing bank in currency. If the remitter has a currency account with the instructing bank, that instructing bank will of course debit the currency account as opposed to the sterling account with the sterling equivalent of the currency involved.

Risks (where currency is involved as opposed to sterling)

The real risk is foreign exchange exposure and this can be overcome only if the importer takes out forward cover or has the use of a currency account.

Answer 11.18

(a) (i) The system to be adopted will be as follows:
The Bank takes the customer's written instructions together with the authority to debit his account. If he has a US dollar account this will be debited with the appropriate sum or more likely, the Bank will arrange to sell to him dollars for sterling. In this event, the sterling equivalent of the appropriate dollars will be debited to his sterling account at the bank's current selling rate for dollars.

Funds can be remitted to the United States in US dollars by Mail or Telegraphic Transfer or by International Money Transfer or Express International Money Transfer. The latter two systems are the equivalent of the MT and TT except they are sent via the SWIFT system (Society for Worldwide Inter-Bank Financial Telecommunications) which uses a computerised system to switch funds from one country to another.

(ii) The accounting procedures will be as follows:
Debit the customer's US dollar or sterling account with the sterling equivalent of those dollars, credit the Nostro "Mirror" account held with a chosen correspondent. Upon receipt of the instructions, the correspondent will debit the Nostro account (Vostro in its eyes) and credit the beneficiary under advice.

If the beneficiary does not bank at a bank which is a correspondent bank, arrangements will have to be made to pay the funds away through a third party bank, that third party bank having an account relationship with the paying bank.

(b) The provision of suitable funds in priority order should be as follows:
(i) Foreign currency notes in US dollars (exchange rate fixed immediately).
(ii) A quantity of currency travellers cheques expressed in US dollars available for encashment quite fully throughout the United States e.g. American Express or similar other company (exchange rate fixed immediately).

(iii) The customer should carry a credit card/charge card which would enable him to obtain facilities at hotels, stores and banks throughout the United States (unless the credit card allows for drawings in foreign currency, the exchange rates would be fixed when the claim is received by the British bank).

(iv) The customer should be made aware of the bank's emergency cash procedures in the case of need.

(v) If A. Rose is to be away for some considerable time, perhaps the bank may consider as a safeguard, giving him a Letter of Introduction to a number of correspondents in those centres where the visits are to take place.

Section 12

Answers

Answer 12.1

Invoicing in currency (buyer's currency)

Advantages

(i) Encourages sales as the buyer has no need to enter the foreign exchange market.
(ii) If the currency appreciates a capital gain is made.
(iii) If the currency is at a forward premium (i.e. the domestic unit buys fewer units of currency forward than at spot) then the forward sale of the currency receipt will give a larger domestic currency value than at spot.
(iv) Where the interest rate for the currency is lower than for the domestic unit, exporters may borrow it and sell for spot domestic money rather than selling forward.
(v) Where a currency account is held the exporter can put his receipts to that account. If he also makes payments in the same currency, he may be able to match receipts and payments without incurring the currency risk.

Disadvantages

(i) May entail a loss through sales in the forward market (currency at a forward discount).
(ii) A currency depreciation may leave the recipient with losses if no forward cover is taken out.
(iii) Interest cost of borrowing the currency may be high.

Being Invoiced in Currency (sellers currency)

Advantages

(i) May allow buyer to induce the seller to reduce his commercial price.
(ii) If the currency depreciates, a capital gain is made.
(iii) If the currency is at a forward discount then the forward purchase of the currency will cost less domestic currency that at the spot rate.

(iv) If the interest rate for the currency is low, then borrowing it to meet a debt could be cheaper than borrowing the domestic currency equivalent.
(v) A currency account can be used to match payments and receipts.

Disadvantages

(i) May entail an extra cost through purchases in the forward market (currency at a forward premium).
(ii) A currency appreciation may leave the payer with extra costs if no forward cover is taken out.
(iii) Interest costs of borrowing the currency may be high.

Note: if a third currency unit is used then the above advantages and disadvantages could apply to both recipient and payer at the same time.

Answer 12.2

(i) *UK Exporter Invoices in Sterling*

UK exporter's expected receipts = *£10m*

UK exporter's actual receipts = *£10m*

German importer's expected payments

£10m @ $\frac{2.6245}{0.61005}$ = DM4.3021 = *DM43,021,000*

German importer's actual payments

£10m @ $\frac{2.7955}{0.73433}$ = DM3,80687 = *DM38,068,700*

(ii) *UK Exporter Invoices in D. Marks*

UK exporter's expected receipts

£10m @ $\frac{2.6245}{0.61005}$ = DM43,021,000 = *£10m*

UK exporter's actual receipts

DM43,021,000 @ $\frac{2.7955}{0.73433}$ = DM3.80687 = *£11,300,884*

German importer's expected payments

DM43,021,000 = *DM43,021,000*

German importer's actual payments

DM43,021,000 = *DM43,021,00*

(iii) *UK Exporter Invoices in US Dollars*

UK exporter's expected receipts

£10m @ $\frac{1.22834}{0.61005}$ = \$2.0135 = \$20,135,000 = *£10m*

UK exporter's actual receipts

\$20,135,000 @ $\frac{1.05670}{0.73433}$ = \$1.4390 = *£13,992,355*

German importer's expected payments

$\$20{,}135{,}000\ @\ \frac{2.6245}{1.22834} = \text{DM}2.1366$ $= \textit{DM43,020,441}$

German importer's actual payments

$\$20{,}135{,}000\ @\ \frac{2.7955}{1.05670} = \text{DM}2.6455$ $= \textit{DM53,267,142}$

(iv) *UK Exporter Invoices in D. Marks Equivalent of SDRs*

UK exporter's expected receipts = the D. Mark value of the current SDR worth of

£10m where $£1 = \frac{1}{0.61005} = \text{SDR}1.63921 = \text{SDR}16{,}392{,}100.$

At SDR1 = DM2.6245, this is worth DM43,021,066.

At $£1 = \frac{\text{DM}2.6245}{0.61005} = \text{DM}4.3021 = £10\text{m}$

UK exporter's actual receipts = SDR16,392,100
@ SDR1 = DM2.7955 = DM45,824,115

@ $£1 = \frac{\text{DM}2.7955}{0.73433} = \text{DM}3.80687 = £12{,}037{,}215$

German importer's expected payments = SDR16,392,100

@ SDR1 = DM2.6245 = DM43,021,066

German importer's actual payments = SDR16,392,100

@ SDR1 = DM2.7955 = DM45,824,115

Analysis

(i) German payments less than expected due to the appreciation of the D. mark against sterling.

(ii) UK receipts more than expected due to the depreciation of sterling against the D. mark.

(iii) UK receipts more than expected due to the depreciation of sterling against the dollar.
German payments more than expected due to the depreciation of the D. mark against the dollar.

(iv) UK receipts more than expected due to the depreciation of sterling against the SDR.
German payments more than expected due to the depreciation of D. marks against the SDR.

Answer 12.3

Since the advent of floating rates of exchange in the early 1970s there have been violent movements in exchange rates especially for the US dollar which, at first depreciated and then appreciated strongly against other major currencies.

Even within currency blocs like the European Monetary System (EMS) the wide margins applied to Italian lire and the periodic re-alignment of central rates has added to the degree of uncertainty and sterling's exclusion from the currency aspect of the EMS has underlined the uncertainties.

Traders, investors and others who expect to make or receive payment in foreign exchange have been, therefore, more open to risk than ever, of receipts falling below expectations or payments rising above expectation.

One way to reduce this problem is to hold a basket of currencies so that likely depreciations are offset by likely appreciations to give a degree of constancy to deposit values expressed in local currency. An SDR-denominated bank deposit is one such basket, consisting as it does, of the five major currencies in the weights laid down by the IMF.

Problems

(i) As SDR units are not available to the private sector such deposits must be paid for in the major national currencies and withdrawals made also in such currencies.

(ii) There are no international clearing arrangements in SDRs, so transactions are effected in a currency (or currencies) equivalent. This tends to limit the usefulness of SDR denominated accounts.

Answer 12.4

(i) *EMS*

Stands for European Monetary System, the objective of which is to develop European economic and monetary union and to stabilize exchange rates between currencies in the EEC.

Present participating countries are West Germany, France, Italy, Netherlands, Belgium (including Luxembourg) Denmark and Eire (1981).

For each currency a central rate is fixed in ECU (European Currency Units).

Unit is based on a basket of national currencies (all participating countries plus UK). Amounts based originally on importance of each country in EEC trade.

Bilateral exchange rates are established on the basis of the central rate.

Around these rates, margins of fluctuation must not exceed 2¼% or, in the case of Italy, 6%.

Intervention points are fixed, whereupon central banks are obliged to intervene to keep exchange rates within agreed limit.

Participating states placed part of their gold and dollar reserve in Central Fund and received a supply of ECUs to regulate central bank intervention.

Short-term swops are available between central banks to enable countries with limited reserves to support their currency.

(ii) *Floating Rate*

Rate resulting from the free operation of market forces. In practice sterling is not allowed to float entirely freely. The Bank of England does intervene from time to time in an endeavour to exercise some control over sterling exchange rates.

Answer 12.5

In order to limit exchange rate movements between members of the European Community in farm produce, a system of "green" or special exchange rates applies to such goods. This is to effect one of their important principles, namely, the protection of farm revenues.

When one member's currency appreciates against the others, the cost of its imports from the rest falls and, other things being equal, there will tend to be an increase in demand for the products (including food) of other members. However, food producers in the country of the appreciation will therefore tend to suffer a decline in demand for their products with a resulting fall in their incomes.

To mitigate this effect, Monetary Compensation Amounts (MCAs) are payable to these producers being the difference between the new exchange rates and agreed (but lower) "green" rates of exchange.

In effect, farm produce is partially protected from currency fluctuations because such movements are not allowed to have the full impact on trade in such goods.

Answer 12.6

First, we must find the D. mark value of each of the basket currency amounts at market rates.

I.e. French francs	$\frac{1}{3.07253} \times 1.15$	= D. marks 0.3743
Sterling	$\frac{1}{0.26330} \times 0.08850$	= D. marks 0.3361
Guilders	$\frac{1}{1.12950} \times 0.286$	= D. marks 0.3230
Lire	$\frac{1}{615.17} \times 109.00$	= D. marks 0.1772
B. francs	$\frac{1}{20.257} \times 3.660$	= D. marks 0.1807
D. Krone	$\frac{1}{3.6561} \times 0.217$	= D. marks 0.0593
Irish punts	$\frac{1}{0.3253} \times 0.00759$	= D. marks 0.0233
L. francs	$\frac{1}{20.257} \times 0.1400$	= D. marks 0.0069
Plus the D. mark		= D. marks 0.8280
	Total ECUI	= D. marks 2.3088

Answer 12.7

Commercial banks play a major role in international capital movements by their recycling of surplus funds to countries in external financial difficulty. In such transactions, banks have to employ a number of guidelines basic with prudent bank activity. These guidelines relate to the risks faced by the banks in their lending, relative to the income so derived by way of interest received.

However, when lending to governments or official bodies banks can be in the difficult position of not being able to press for those changes in its borrowers' policies that it may see as essential if outstanding loans are to be adequately serviced or new loans made.

By contrast, the International Monetary Fund (IMF) has, as its basic philosophy the principle that members can only draw on their credit tranches if they are seen to accept what the IMF may regard as essential policy changes.

Whilst there are no direct links between the IMF and commercial banks, it is evident that adherence by a member government to IMF requirements will tend to assist that member in gaining a more sympathetic response from the banks in connection with (say) a re-negotiation or roll-over of existing debt. Although no direct use of IMF facilities are available to the banks, the use of such facilities accompanied by the IMF approved policy measures has an obviously important bearing on banks' lending policies.

Answer 12.8

When members of the IMF wish to obtain currencies from it they do so by way of a "purchase". That is, they buy the currency or currencies with units of their own money. Similarly, when a repayment (or repurchase) is made, it is effected by returning the appropriate currencies to the IMF in return for their own currency.

Although the terms given to these operations are "purchase" and "repurchase" respectively, as a result of the requirement for these transactions to be offset, sooner or later, by a reverse operation, in effect the purchase is really a loan and a repurchase is really a repayment of a debt.

Thus, a member who makes a purchase becomes a debtor but only if it takes the member into its credit tranches. A member who makes a repurchase is repaying a debt and therefore reducing or eliminating a debtor position. In practice, to make it clear to all members what their IMF positions are, the Fund uses the concept of the 75% rule. This figure relates to the initial (and neutral) position of IMF members on first joining. It comprises the 75% of the member's quotes payable in the member's own currency. Any purchases of foreign exchange adds to the IMF's holdings of that member's currency and any repurchases reduces it. Thus, a debtor is defined as any member whose currency the IMF is holding above 75% of that member's quota and a creditor is any member whose currency the IMF is holding below 75% of that member's quota.

Answer 12.9

Table 12.9

Total Quotas = SDR 61059.8m

IMF Drawings

Member	USA	UK	W. GERMANY	"OTHER"	INDIA	"OTHER"
Currency	Convertible	Convertible	Convertible	Convertible	Inconvertible	Inconvertible
Quota	SDR 12607.5m	SDR 4387.5m	SDR 3234.0m	SDR 20,000m	SDR 1717.5m	SDR 19113.3m
(a) Reserve currency sub. = of which:	SDR 3151.9m DMs.40% £s.10%	SDR 1096.9m $s 100%	SDR 808.5m $s 100%	SDR 5000m $s 100%	SDR 429.4m $s 100%	SDR 4778.3m $s 100%
(b) Dom currency sub. =	SDR 9455.6m	SDR 3290m	SDR 2425.5m	SDR 15000m	SDR 1288.1m	SDR 14335.0m
(c) Total IMF Holdings in =	US $s SDR 21568.7m	£s = SDR 3605.79m	DMS = SDR 3686.26m	"Other" Convertible = SDR 16575.95m	Rupees = SDR 1288.1m	"Other" Inconvertible = SDR 14335.0m
(d) Above as a % of country quota	171.08%	82.18%	114%	82.88%	75%	75%
(e) India and other inconvertible currency members draw as shown in their section					India draws: Convertible currencies to bring IMF holdings of Rupees to 200% of India's quota US $s 60% DMs 10% "Others" 30%	"Others" draw: Convertible currency drawings to bring "others" currencies held by IMF to 200% of "other" quotas US $ 65% DMs 10% £s 5% "Others" 20%
(f) Total IMF holdings of the respective currencies as a % of the quotas =	US $s SDR 37.68%	£s SDR 54.96%	DMs SDR 33.47%	"Other" Convertible SDR 55.77%	Rupees 200%	"Other" Inconvertible 200%
(g) USA now draws up to her Reserve Tranche level in "other" Convertible currencies						
(h) Total IMF holdings of the respective currencies as a % of the quotas =	US $s SDR 100%	£s SDR 54.96%	DMs SDR 33.47%	"Other" Convertible SDR 16.48%	Rupees SDR 200%	"Other" Inconvertible SDR 200%

Answer 12.10

International Monetary Fund (IMF)

Uses member's subscriptions to supply members with medium-term capital for the purpose of restoring external financial balance under an agreed package of fiscal, financial and monetary policies. In recent years the IMF has enlarged its operations to include the Compensatory Financing Facility to offset falls in export earnings; a Buffer Stock Facility to fund the stabilization of prices of approved primary goods; and other additional facilities designed to increase developing countries access to IMF funds.

The World Bank

A sister organization to the IMF has the special function of supplying long-term development finance to members at below market interest rates. The supply of capital comes largely from bonds floated on members private capital market.

The International Development Agency (IDA)

This is an offshoot of the World Bank and uses the subscription of the developed members to provide very long-term development capital at zero rates of interest to the least developed members.

The Euro-markets

The banks and other financial institutions who go to make up this market attract deposits from surplus capital countries (including the issue of bonds). Loans are made ranging right through the maturity spectrum largely to the self-financing development ventures or to private companies and governments for non-project finance. All transactions are at market rates of interest.

There is an unofficial link between all these bodies in the sense that the Euro-banks keep an eye on the IMF to see to what degree prospective borrowers are deemed to be acting in a financially sound manner.

The World Bank also requires prospective borrowers to keep within existing IMF guidelines (if any), and in any case, their funds together with the funds of IDA, are designed to be for long-term development purposes rather than for balance of payments purposes.

Finally, sometimes the World Bank and the commercial banks operate on a co-financing basis; each prepared to participate in a part of a given project. The private banks usually taking the capital equipment segment and the World Bank the civil works segment.

Answer 12.11

A balance of payments deficit implies that a country's total external expenditure is greater than its external receipts for a given period of time — usually one year. The deficit can originate in any part of the balance of payments account, e.g. capital account or current account.

The concept of the price elasticities of demand usually relates to items in the current account — exports and imports, presumes that given the "correct" set of elasticities, a depreciation of the country's currency can expand export receipts faster than import payments (or reduce import payments).

The basic requirement is that the combined sum of the price elasticities of demand for the country's export *and* its imports must be greater than unity (1), and in most cases substantially greater than unity.

There are, however, a number of qualifying problems, i.e.

(i) *Time Lag*

There is usually some time before a depreciation has an impact on export and import volume. In the meantime a deficit situation could worsen.

(ii) *Supply Elasticity*

It may be that the domestic supply situation is bedevilled by bottlenecks and increased overseas demand cannot be met. The result could be a general price rise generating inflation with consequent adverse effects on the balance of payments by making exports dearer and imports relatively cheaper than domestic substitutes.

(iii) If money supply is permitted to expand it may be possible for consumers of imports to meet higher import prices and/or export capital. This would have a second-round effect on the currency causing it to depreciate further. If condition (ii) applies this could add to the inflationary effect.

(iv) Other countries could take steps to nullify the depreciation either by depreciating their own currencies and/or restrictive measures to limit their own imports.

Answer 12.12

(i) A European Currency Unit (ECU) is based upon a basket of all the currencies of the European Community, other than the Drachma. It includes Sterling, even though the United Kingdom has remained outside the European Monetary System.

The weight of each currency in the basket is allocated on the basis of EMS central rates, so that it shifts when the central rates are adjusted (as they were in March 1983). Its current value stands at approximately 58 pence. The present basket is made up as follows and the figures show the value of each currency included in an ECU as well as the approximate percentage of that currency. Each currency unit must vary according to its rise and fall in value compared to the other currencies in the basket.

Deutsche Marks	34%	Dutch Florins	11%	Luxembourg Franc	½%
French Franc	18%	Italian Lire	8%	Danish Kroner	3%
Pounds Sterling	15½%	Belgian Franc	9%	Irish Punt	1%

The ECU has a powerful attraction for citizens of countries with weak currencies. These include those currencies which have been devalued in the past, or are likely to be devalued in the future e.g. Belgium, France and Italy. By denominating deals in ECUs, buyers are increasingly availing themselves of the protection offered by an ECU against the down-grading of their own national currencies. This is because the spread of the basket over a number of stronger currencies means that the dramatic changes which occasionally occur between two currencies are spread out over all the currencies in the basket. This also means that those countries with strong currencies do not have any great incentive for going into the ECU investment. (In the Federal Republic of Germany, ECU issues are not authorised.)

(ii) Currency Certificate of Deposits are

(a) a negotiable bearer instrument issued by a bank certifying that a stated sum has been deposited with that bank;

(b) documents of title showing the interest paid on the deposit on the basis of a 360 day year and the date of repayment over the instrument. Interest is paid annually on the anniversary of the date of issue and at maturity;

(c) issued for periods up to five years by banks to increase their deposits in the appropriate currency of the certificate;

(d) the purchaser (depositor) secures a freely negotiable instrument which can be used as security for other borrowings;

(e) UK banks issue certificates of deposit (CDs) in US dollars and more recently in Deutsche Marks and ECUs at rates slightly below that of the ordinary fixed term deposit. (There is a limited secondary market for certificates denominated in US dollars.)

(iii) Eurobonds are:

(a) issued in European capital markets and are denominated in a currency (or currencies including ECUs) other than that of the currency of the issuer;

(b) issued on behalf of government agencies, financial institutions, large corporations and multinational companies;

(c) their use is for obtaining funds for long-term capital borrowing i.e. five years and upwards and the interest which applies to the bonds may be fixed or variable;

(d) the issues of such bonds are normally placed i.e. an issuing consortium of banks arranges for purchasers to take up the offer;

(e) there is a secondary market for subsequent sales and purchases.

www.ingramcontent.com/pod-product-compliance
Ingram Content Group UK Ltd.
Pitfield, Milton Keynes, MK11 3LW, UK
UKHW050037081026
476416UK00006B/489
* 9 7 8 0 8 6 0 1 0 5 8 6 2 *